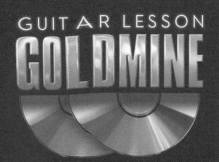

GUITAR LESSON GOLDMINE

100

COUNTRY LESSONS

BY CHAD JOHNSON & TROY NELSON

ISBN 978-1-4234-9881-0

HAL•LEONARD®
CORPORATION

7777 W. BLUEMOUND RD. P.O. BOX 13819 MILWAUKEE, WI 53213

In Australia Contact:
Hal Leonard Australia Pty. Ltd.
4 Lentara Court
Cheltenham, Victoria, 3192 Australia
Email: ausadmin@halleonard.com.au

Visit Hal Leonard Online at
www.halleonard.com

CONTENTS

Lessons 1–50 by Troy Nelson

Lessons 51–100 by Chad Johnson

LESSON #1: G MAJOR OPEN-CHORD LICKS

Bluegrass may be considered a subgenre of country music, but it has had a profound influence on contemporary country guitar, particularly lead playing. Due to the acoustic nature of the music, bluegrass guitar solos are predominantly played in open position, where notes are more easily articulated. Although not a problem on electrics, open-position playing lends a distinct country sound to solos, due in large part to the incorporation of open strings.

"Open-chord" playing is relatively simple—rather than relying on a specific scale or mode, licks are formed around open-position chord voicings, using the shapes as a roadmap to navigate from chord to chord. While the notes are typically derived from a combination of the major pentatonic and blues scales, it's the chord shapes that actually guide the solo.

G Major Chord and Scale Shapes

In country, a few chords/keys are used more frequently than others—specifically, G, C, D, A, and E major. Consequently, in this lesson we're going to focus on open-chord licks in the key of G major, all of which are based on a common open-position G chord shape.

OPEN-POSITION G MAJOR CHORD

○ = fretted root
◎ = open-string root

OPEN-POSITION G MAJOR PENTATONIC SCALE

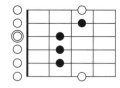

OPEN-POSITION G BLUES SCALE

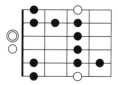

Examples

LICK 1

This first example is a simple ascending lick that moves from the sixth-string root note to the open G string—another root. The notes are borrowed from the G major pentatonic scale (G–A–B–D–E), with the minor 3rd (B♭) thrown in to lend some chromaticism (see string 5) to the festivities. (Note: These pitches [G–A–B♭–B–D–E] are sometimes referred to as the G country composite scale.)

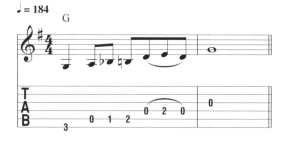

LICK 2

The first measure of the next lick is a duplication of the first bar of Lick 1. In measure 2, however, the phrase reverses course and makes its way back down the major pentatonic/blues hybrid scale to the sixth-string root note. Notice the variation in phrasing and note order during the lick's descent.

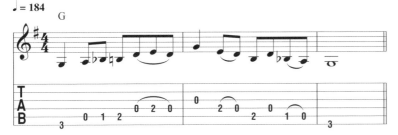

LICK 3

This example is a lot of fun to play and works well as a climactic phrase on which to end a song or solo. It's a "banjo roll"-inspired lick that combines two-note legato passages with open strings before concluding on a half-step bend to the root (G) on the sixth string. For assistance, pick-hand fingerings are provided between the notation and tab staves (P = pick, 2 = middle finger, and 3 = ring finger).

LICK 4

This next lick is a (mostly) descending phrase that works its way from the open G string to the 3rd-fret G note on string 6. Similar to Licks 1 and 2, this figure contains chromaticism. This time, however, the chromatic line (A–Bb–B) is located on strings 2–3. An F# note, the major 7th, also makes its first appearance, creating tension when played in sequence with the open G string due to these notes being just a half step (one fret) apart.

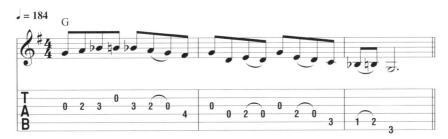

LICK 5

This phrase works well over a dominant (G7) harmony due to the emphasis of the b7th (F) on string 1. Overall, the notes are derived from the G blues (G–Bb–C–Db–D–F) and the G major pentatonic (G–A–B–D–E) scales, which is similar to the previous four licks.

When playing any one of these five licks, be sure to use the shape of the open-position G chord as your guide. In fact, when practicing these lines, give the open G chord a full strum before and after the phrases to reinforce the harmony. Each of these licks can be played over both G major and G dominant chords.

In country music, no key or chord is more ubiquitous than C major. Not only is it often used as the tonic (I) chord, it also serves as the IV chord in G major and the V chord in F major, two other common keys in country music. And since the I, IV, and V chords are the foundation of country progressions (as well as most popular music forms), you begin to understand the popularity of C major.

C Major Chord and Scale Shapes

The basic open-position C major chord provides the foundation for countless open-position licks in country guitar solos. With notes derived from both the C major pentatonic (C–D–E–G–A) and C blues scales (C–E♭–F–G♭–G–B♭) scales, the chord voicing acts as a guide as your hand moves through the open-chord licks. The root notes of the voicing (strings 2 and 5) anchor the lines as scale and chord tones fill in the gaps.

OPEN-POSITION C MAJOR CHORD

OPEN-POSITION C MAJOR PENTATONIC SCALE

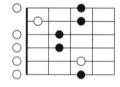

OPEN-POSITION C BLUES SCALE

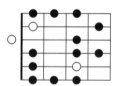

Examples

LICK 1

This first phrase is an ascending lick that moves from the fifth-string root note to the second-string root. The notes are borrowed from the C major pentatonic scale, with the blues scale's minor 3rd (E♭) lending chromaticism to the line (see string 4). (Note: These pitches [C–D–E♭–E–G–A] are sometimes referred to as the C country composite scale.)

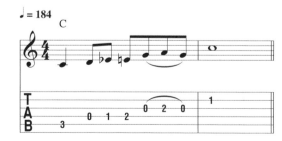

LICK 2

The first measure of the next lick is a duplication of the first bar of Lick 1. In measure 2, however, the phrase reverses course and makes its way back down the major pentatonic/blues hybrid scale to the fifth-string root note. Notice the variation in phrasing and note order during the lick's descent.

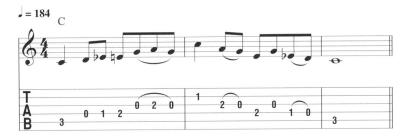

LICK 3

This lick's distinguishing characteristics are the chromaticism (D–E♭–E) on strings 1–2 and the triplet pull-offs on strings 3–4 (measure 2). Although most of the phrase's notes are derived from the C major pentatonic and C blues scales, the A♭ in measure 2—which is used to chromatically connect the A (6th) and G (5th) tones—is not found in either scale, yet doesn't sound out of place due to the lick's fast tempo and the note's short duration.

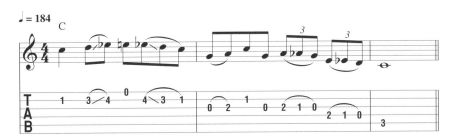

LICK 4

This lick is a variation of Lick 3. It commences on the first-string G note (the 5th) and, like the previous lick, incorporates some chromaticism while working its way down the C major pentatonic/C blues hybrid scale. Notice that the lick moves past the fifth-string root note, to the sixth string, before moving back up to the root for resolution.

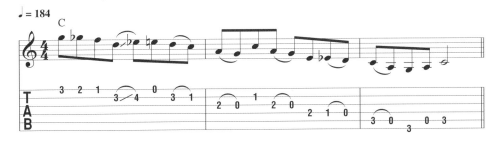

LICK 5

Due to multiple iterations of B♭ notes (the ♭7th), this lick works well over a C dominant (C7) harmony. Like Lick 4, this figure descends all the way down to string 6 before resolving to the root note on string 5. One of this lick's interesting characteristics is the inclusion of the major 7th (B) in measure 2, which allows for a short, half-step walk-up to the root note in measure 3.

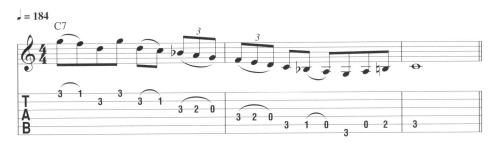

When encountered with a C major or C dominant chord while soloing, give any one of these five licks a try, as they work well over either chord quality. Plus, the open strings will lend your lead lines some requisite country twang. And remember—use the open C major chord shape as a guide for your fret-hand fingers.

LESSON #3: D MAJOR OPEN-CHORD LICKS

Nothing imparts a "country sound" to a guitar solo like open strings. The incorporation of open strings into country solos is a practice borrowed from acoustic bluegrass players, who regularly string together a steady stream of up-tempo 8th notes that are equal parts fretted notes and open strings, mostly played in open position. Consequently, many country and bluegrass songs are written in key centers whose tonic notes match one of the guitar's open strings (E, A, D, G, or, to a lesser degree, B).

D Major Chord and Scale Shapes

In this lesson, we'll focus on creating guitar licks that are based on the basic open-position D major chord shape. Like the approach used by bluegrass players, the shape will serve as a landmark as you navigate the licks. Although the notes are derived from the D major pentatonic (D–E–F♯–A–B) and D blues (D–F–G–A♭–A–C) scales, the chord shape is used to guide and anchor your fret hand. As you will see, the flow of the licks closely follows the contour of the chord voicing.

OPEN-POSITION D MAJOR CHORD

OPEN-POSITION D MAJOR PENTATONIC SCALE

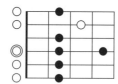

OPEN-POSITION D BLUES SCALE

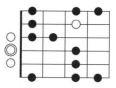

Examples

LICK 1

This first lick is a simple, ascending phrase that moves from the open fourth-string root to the root at fret 3 of the second string. Notice the short chromatic (E–F–F♯) line on string 4, which follows the opening root note. Except for the F note (the ♭3rd), which is derived from the D blues scale, the entire phrase is rooted in the D major pentatonic scale.

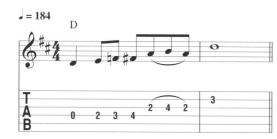

LICK 2

Measure 1 of the next lick is identical to the first measure of Lick 1. In measure 2, however, the phrase shifts course and descends the D major pentatonic/D blues hybrid scale, returning to the open D string for resolution.

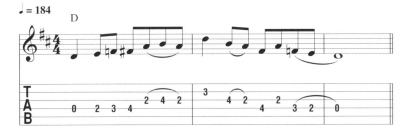

LICK 3

This lick begins by framing the D chord's 3rd, F#. Framing is the act of playing, in succession, notes that are above and below the note that is being targeted, or vice versa. In this case, G and F notes "frame" the F# note. The entire lick is derived from the D major pentatonic/D blues hybrid scale and concludes on the open D string.

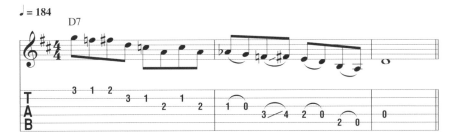

LICK 4

Framing is utilized in this lick as well. This time, however, it occurs on string 6 and incorporates legato technique (i.e., a pull-off and hammer-on). In fact, legato technique is used liberally in this example. Be sure to execute the triplet figures in time, giving the three notes equal duration within the beat.

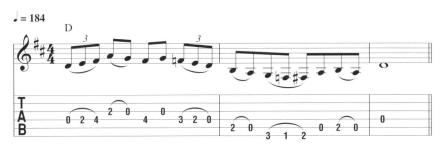

LICK 5

Like Lick 4, legato technique is prevalent in this example. In measure 1, hammered triplet figures give way to a whole-step oblique bend, whereby a fretted note on a higher string is played while the bend is being held. After the bend and release, the lick descends to the open D string via a smooth legato sequence.

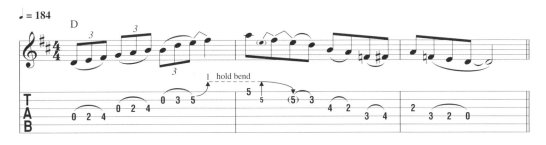

These licks work nicely over both major and dominant (D7) harmonies. As with any "open-chord lick," use the open-position chord shape as a guide as you navigate your way through each of the licks. Being cognizant of the chord's shape will help you locate the lick's most important notes—the chord tones! After all, non-chord tones are essentially "filler"—it's the chord tones that outline the chord changes and give your lead lines a sense of cohesion and melodic heft.

LESSON #4: A MAJOR OPEN-CHORD LICKS

A major is a favorite key center of not only rock and blues players, but also country musicians. For prime examples, look no further than Nashville session ace Brent Mason's tour de force, "Hot Wired," or Merle Haggard's country standard "Workin' Man Blues." Consequently, it's imperative that any aspiring country picker have a firm grasp of how to navigate an A major or A dominant chord in solo settings.

A Major Chord and Scale Shapes

Much of country lead guitar playing is influenced by the fluid flatpicking of bluegrass players whose solos predominantly are rooted in open position and based on basic open-position chord shapes, with A major being one such example. This lesson consists of five open-chord licks that are derived from the A major pentatonic (A–B–C#–E–F#) and A blues (A–C–D–Eb–E–G) scales, with the open A major chord acting as a fret-hand anchor and roadmap to help you navigate and visualize the phrases.

OPEN-POSITION A MAJOR CHORD

OPEN-POSITION A MAJOR PENTATONIC SCALE

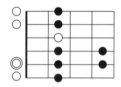

OPEN-POSITION A BLUES SCALE

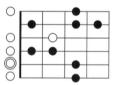

Examples

LICK 1

Here is a short lick that ascends strings 5–3, moving from the open A string to the root note on fret 2 of the third string. The phrase is mostly rooted in the A major pentatonic scale, with the minor 3rd (C) thrown in to lend the line a bit of chromaticism (see string 5).

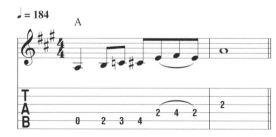

LICK 2

After a measure that is a duplication of Lick 1's first bar, the next phrase reverses course and works its way down to the open A string to resolve the line. Notice how the lick incorporates both the minor 3rd (C) from the A blues scale and the major 3rd (C♯) from the A major pentatonic scale.

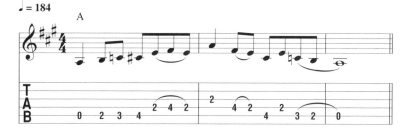

LICK 3

This example is a (mostly) descending phrase that derives most of its notes from the A blues scale, with the one exception being the major 3rd (C♯), which is borrowed from the A major pentatonic scale.

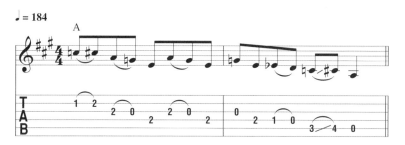

LICK 4

Due to multiple iterations of the ♭7th (G), this lick works especially well over A7 chords (although it can be used over A major chords, as well). After a triplet- and legato-based ascent of strings 4 and 3, the lick repeats an A–G–F♯ pull-off motif along the middle string pair before descending the hybrid A major pentatonic/A blues hybrid scale to the open A string.

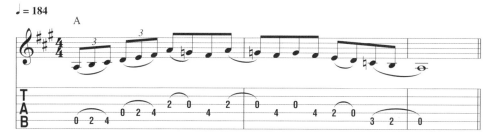

LICK 5

After a quick G–F♯–E pull-off on string 1, the lick "frames" the major 3rd (C♯) on string 2 with D and C notes, which are located one half step to each side of the C♯ note. Notice how closely the lick follows the contour of the A major chord voicing. Before the lick resolves to the open A string, the phrase moves down to the sixth string for an F♯–E pull-off.

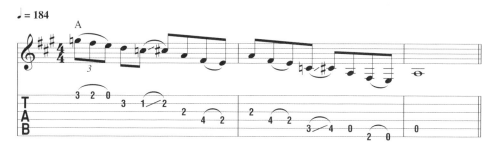

These open-chord licks can be a great starting point for learning to solo in the key of A major or can supplement an existing arsenal of licks. They are equally effective in electric or acoustic settings, especially when combined with phrases that are played higher up the neck.

LESSON #5: E MAJOR OPEN-CHORD LICKS

Due to the guitar's pair of open E strings (first and sixth), no key center is better suited for open-position soloing than E major. As such, E major is a popular key for countless country, bluegrass, rock, and blues tunes. In addition to its popularity as a tonic (I) chord, E major also serves as the V chord in the key of A major, another ubiquitous key center. Consequently, it's imperative for guitar players of any stripe to have a firm understanding of the E major key center, as well as how to attack an E major (or dominant) chord when improvising a solo.

E Major Chord and Scale Shapes

In this lesson, a basic open-position E major chord serves as a navigational aide, or "landmark," for five open-chord licks. These phrases were inspired by the open-position flatpicking of bluegrass players who have influenced countless contemporary country guitarists. While the E major chord anchors the licks, the E major pentatonic (E–F#–G#–B–C#) and E blues (E–G–A–Bb–B–D) scales provide the tones.

OPEN-POSITION E MAJOR CHORD

OPEN-POSITION E MAJOR PENTATONIC SCALE

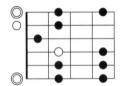

OPEN-POSITION E BLUES SCALE

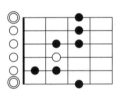

Examples

LICK 1

This first lick is a short E major pentatonic lick that moves from the open low-E string to the E note at fret 2 of the fourth string. Notice that, on string 5, both the major 3rd (G#) and minor 3rd (G) tones have been included—a common technique of country, blues, and jazz players. The minor 3rd, derived from the E blues scale, is the only tone that is not part of the major pentatonic scale.

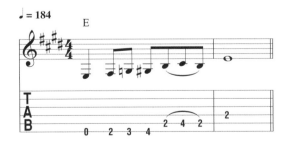

LICK 2

After duplicating the first measure of Lick 1, the next phrase makes its way back down the E major pentatonic scale. Again, both the major 3rd and minor 3rd are present, lending a minor-against-major sound to the lick that is so common in country, blues, and jazz.

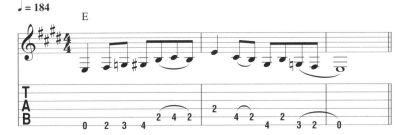

LICK 3

This descending lick is a composite of the E major pentatonic and E blues scales, as nearly every note from each scale is present (the only omitted note is F♯, from the E major pentatonic scale). To perform the lick, assign one finger per fret starting with your index finger at fret 1, and stay in position throughout.

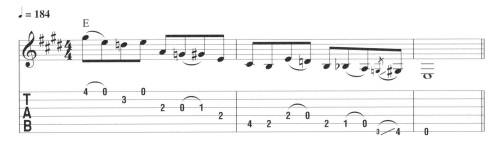

LICK 4

After a couple of triplet-based hammer-ons, this lick creates tension by juxtaposing the major 6th (C♯) and minor 7th (D) scale tones along strings 4–5. The tension is released via a quick, legato descent of the E major pentatonic/E blues hybrid scale to the open low-E string.

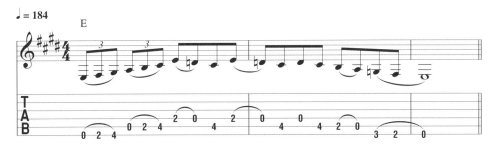

LICK 5

This lick is a lot of fun to perform. Played exclusively with pull-offs and a triplet rhythm, the phrase incorporates every open string into a minor-against-major tonality that can be played over E major or E dominant (E7) chords.

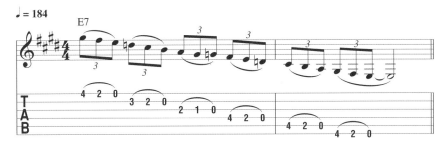

Once you have these five licks under your fingers, try pairing them with phrases that you know in other keys. For example, if you're soloing over a I–IV progression in the key of E major (E–A), practice transitioning from one of these E major licks to a lick in A major. Then, you can resolve your line by returning to another E major lick or by landing on an E note.

THE ROOT/5TH ("BOOM-CHICK") RHYTHM TECHNIQUE

Without a doubt, the most popular approach to rhythm guitar in country music is the "boom-chick" technique. This rhythm style involves playing a bass note (the "boom") on beats 1 and 3 of each measure, followed by a partial chord strum (the "chick") on beats 2 and 4. The bass notes most often consist of the root and 5th of the chord and mimic the cut-time rhythm that is played by the bassist. Meanwhile, the chords reinforce the song's harmony via chord partials that are strummed on the guitar's highest three or four strings. To keep finger movement to a minimum while executing the bass lines, common open-chord or barre-chord shapes are typically used.

In this lesson, we'll take a look at five common boom-chick rhythms, with each increasing in complexity. The first four examples utilize a common C–G7–C (I–V7–I) progression; the last example is an A–D–E7–A (I–IV–V7–I) progression that is played fingerstyle.

The Chords

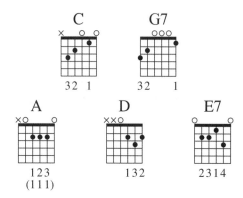

The Rhythms

RHYTHM 1

This first rhythm is pretty straightforward. In measures 1, 2, and 4, the C and G (root and 5th) bass notes are plucked on beats 1 and 3, and the C major chord partials are strummed on beats 2 and 4. To execute the bass notes, alternate your ring finger between the fifth and sixth strings, leaving your other fingers in position for the C chord. In measure 3, simply pluck the G7 chord's sixth and fourth strings for the root-5th (G–D) bass line.

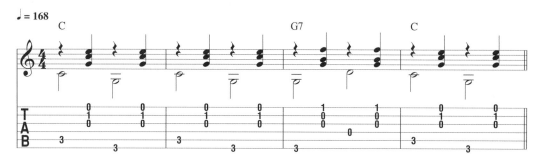

RHYTHM 2

This example advances the rhythm from the previous figure, replacing the quarter-note chord partials with 8th notes. Play the bass notes with downstrokes, followed by a down-up combination for the 8th-note strums.

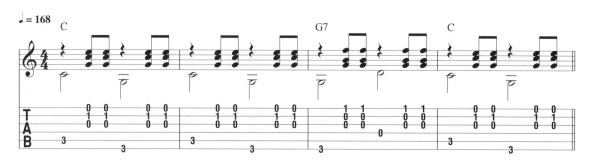

RHYTHM 3

In measures 2 and 3 of this example, the strict root-5th bass line is briefly replaced with a hammer-on sequence that moves from each chord's 2nd to its 3rd (D to E for the C chord; A to B for the G7 chord). Play each chord's hammer-on with your middle finger.

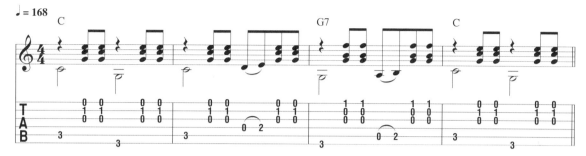

RHYTHM 4

In this example, the complexity of the bass line is ratcheted up a notch. After a three-note, scale-wise walking bass line leads into the first measure, the standard root-5th bass movement is used over the C chord. At the midpoint of measure 2, however, the bass line walks back down to the 5th of the C major scale, G, which happens to be the root of the new chord, G7. Here, the bass line reestablishes the root-5th movement; however, rather than strumming chord partials on beat 4, the bass line climbs from D to E along string 4 before returning to the root-5th movement for the final C chord.

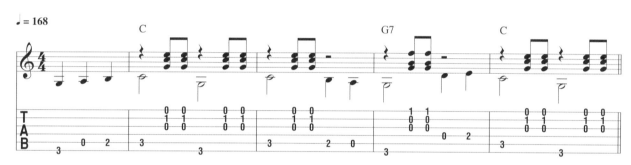

RHYTHM 5

This example deviates from the root-5th bass lines of the previous four exercises in favor of a fingerstyle figure that makes use of open-position A, D, and E7 chords. The picking pattern that is used here is a variation of "Travis picking"—a pattern made famous by country guitarist Merle Travis. Instead of a half-note bass line like the previous examples, this root-5th pattern is played in steady quarter notes. Notice that, for the A and D chords, the root-5th movement on beats 1 and 3 is offset with upper-octave 5ths on beats 2 and 4 (E notes for the A chord; A notes for the D chord). Similarly for the E7 chord, higher-octave roots (E notes on the fourth string) offset the root-5th movement on beats 1 and 3. While the thumb alternates between the lower three strings to play a steady, quarter-note bass line, the middle and index fingers pluck chord tones on the higher strings.

Once you have these short examples under your fingers, apply them to other chord progressions that you know, whether from a country song or otherwise. Although open chords and barre chords work best with this technique, practically any chord can be given the boom-chick treatment. If you have trouble locating the 5th, let your ears be your guide. What's important is discovering a pattern that sounds good to you—not being theoretically correct.

LESSON #7: THE EXTENDED MAJOR PENTATONIC SCALE

While learning major and minor scales and their associated modes in several positions on the fretboard certainly is important, being able to move horizontally/laterally along the neck to play in lower or higher registers and add dynamics and melodic interest to your lead lines is just as important. This type of movement can be used to connect melodic ideas from a common key center or to connect ideas from divergent keys. Since musical ideas are often played in disparate fretboard locations, one needs a melodic device to "connect the dots." Instead of lifting your fret hand off the neck to jump from one position to another, sometimes covering several frets, horizontal scales can make position shifts more efficient and seamless. Enter the extended major pentatonic scale.

The Horizontal Scale Pattern

Due to the preponderance of major-key songs in country music, no scale is used more extensively in guitar solos than the major pentatonic. Fortunately, this five-note scale works well as a horizontal pattern. In addition to its symmetrical, easy-to-use pattern, the extended major pentatonic scale covers a lot of fretboard territory. For example, when played across all six strings, the extended G major pentatonic scale (G–A–B–D–E) spans ten frets!

In this lesson, the extended G major pentatonic scale provides the melodic material for five G major licks that demonstrate both the pattern's range and its effectiveness as a note source for country-style lead lines.

EXTENDED G MAJOR PENTATONIC SCALE

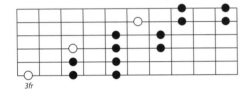

3fr

Examples

LICK 1

This first lick incorporates a slide and hammer-on to cover the first octave (five notes) of the scale, moving from third position to fifth position. At measure 2, an oblique bend is used to emphasize the 3rd and 5th (B and D) of the G chord before the phrase resolves to the fourth-string root note.

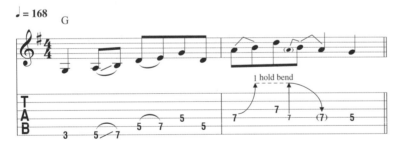

LICK 2

This pivot-note lick is played in the upper regions of the extended G major pentatonic scale. The term "pivot" comes from the fact that one stationary, or pivot, note is played multiple times while other notes move above or below the pivot note. In this case, a B note (second string, 12th fret) acts as a pivot while D and E notes alternate on string 1. At measure 2, the lick shifts down to seventh position for resolution to a second-string root (G) note.

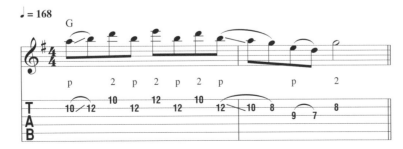

LICK 3

In measure 1, a first-inversion G major triad (B–D–G) connects a fourth-string legato figure and a second-string oblique bend. Use the ring and pinky fingers of your fret hand for the bend. Also, notice the E pivot note (third string, 9th fret) at the end of the phrase, which alternates with A and G notes on string 2. Pivot notes are a popular country guitar device.

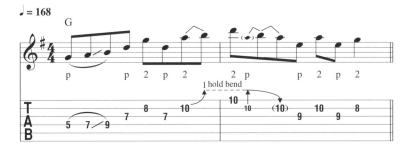

LICK 4

This lick exemplifies the use of the extended major pentatonic scale to play a melodic motif in multiple octaves without having to alter your fingering or stray from the scale pattern. After an oblique-bend motif is established on strings 1–2, the melodic idea is restated an octave lower, on strings 3–4, without venturing outside of the extended G major pentatonic scale.

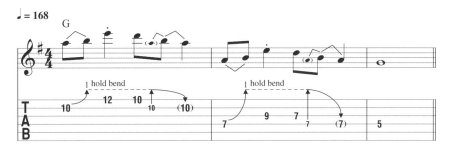

LICK 5

In our final lick, a rhythmic motif is repeated as it descends the G major pentatonic scale. At measure 2, a triplet-base legato figure shifts the fret hand down to fret 3, positioning your ring finger for the sixth-string whole-step bends. For added strength, reinforce the bends with your middle and index fingers.

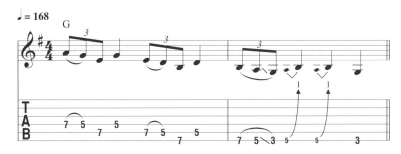

As you can see, the extended major pentatonic scale works well as a stand-alone melodic device for creating licks, as well as a means by which to traverse the neck. Once you have the G major licks under your fingers, transpose them to other keys and practice using the scale to connect musical ideas from different locations of the neck.

THE EXTENDED MINOR PENTATONIC SCALE

Like its major counterpart, the extended minor pentatonic scale is a useful melodic tool for connecting musical ideas that are located in disparate positions on the neck, spanning large chunks of the fretboard to arrive at higher or lower registers. This helps to create a change in dynamics and sonic interest, restating melodic motifs in multiple octaves without having to alter fingerings or venture outside of the scale pattern.

One Pattern, Two Scales: Relative Minor and Major

The beauty of the extended minor pentatonic scale is that, like the scale's popular "box" patterns, once you learn the scale's relative major, all that changes are the target notes (i.e., scale tones)—the notes of both scales are exactly the same. For example, the target notes of the G major pentatonic scale (G–A–B–D–E), the relative major of E minor pentatonic, are the tones that comprise the G major chord: G, B, and D. However, the target notes of the E minor pentatonic scale (E–G–A–B–D) are the notes of the E minor chord: E, G, and B. All that you need to do to convert the extended G major pentatonic scale into the extended E minor pentatonic scale is start on the former's fifth scale degree, E, which is now the root of the new scale.

This lesson serves two purposes: 1) to get you familiar with the extended minor pentatonic scale and, 2) to get you acclimated to soloing over the common I–vi progression (in a major key, the vi chord is the relative minor). First, here's the extended E minor pentatonic scale.

EXTENDED E MINOR PENTATONIC SCALE

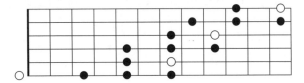

Examples

The following five licks utilize the extended E minor pentatonic scale to navigate a I–vi–I chord progression in the key of G major (G–Em–G). (Note: You can think of the licks either as being wholly derived from the E minor pentatonic scale or as alternating between the G major pentatonic and the E minor pentatonic scales, depending on what chord you are soloing over at the time. Remember, the two scales contain identical notes.)

LICK 1

After a whole-step pre-bend to the G chord's 3rd (B), this lick makes its way from third position to fifth position, switching from emphasizing G major notes to emphasizing E minor notes for the Em chord change via several iterations of the root note, E (fifth string, fret 7). In measure 3, the lick continues up the scale, concluding on a G/D double stop.

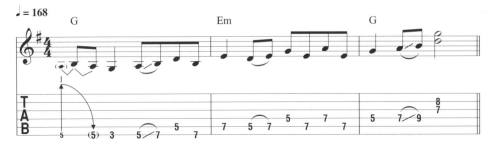

LICK 2

The next lick is entirely based on a recurring pre-bend motif. Played in the upper region of the G major/E minor pentatonic scale, the motif is slightly altered in measure 2 to briefly pause on E, the root of Em, instead of G, the root of the G major chord. Use your pinky to fret all of the first-string notes and your ring finger for the pre-bends.

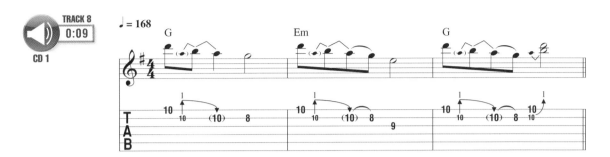

LICK 3

This legato passage is a bit tricky, so take it slowly at first. After some back-and-forth shifting in measure 1, a whole-step bend and release leads to a pull-off to the open low-E string, which signals the new chord, Em. In measure 2, the lick continues up the scale, ultimately landing on the G note at fret 5 of the fourth string, which serves as both the 3rd of Em and the root of G.

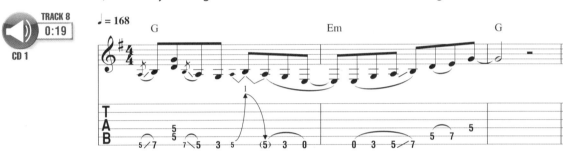

LICK 4

This lick is constructed entirely of fourth-string slides and double stops that are played on strings 2–3. While the slides remain constant, the double stops are slightly altered to emphasize the chord changes (a G/D double stop is played over the G chord and a G/E double stop is deployed for Em).

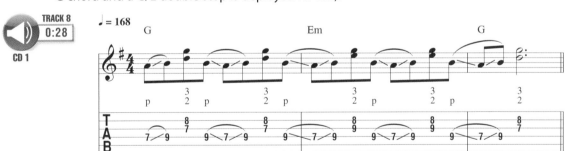

LICK 5

At first glance, this lick may not look like it is wholly derived from the extended E minor pentatonic scale, but it is. In measure 1, a B (the 3rd of G) pivot note offsets pitches that are played on string 2. In measure 2, an E (the root of Em) pivot note offsets pitches on string 2, followed by a first-string whole-step bend and release that resolves to a second-string root note (G).

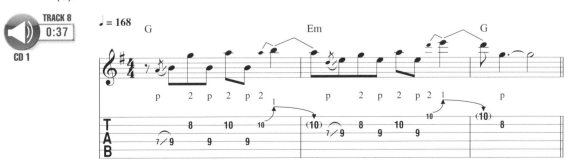

LESSON #9: MAJOR ARPEGGIOS

Although most often associated with rock and classical music, major arpeggios frequently find their way into country, typically in very creative ways. In fact, there's video evidence of Chet Atkins sweep-picking five-string arpeggios way back in 1975! Was it a harbinger of rock's neoclassical shred movement of the eighties? Maybe not, but major arpeggios certainly play an important role in country music.

In this lesson, we'll take a look at five common approaches to major arpeggios that are used by country guitarists—everything from banjo rolls to pedal steel bends to rapid-fire pull-offs. Let's get started.

LICK 1

This lick is a banjo-roll approach to a I–IV–V–I progression in the key of A major (A–D–E–A). Based solely on major-triad arpeggios, this type of banjo roll is also referred to as a "forward roll" due to the forward motion of the pick hand. The entire phrase is performed with hybrid picking; specifically, a sequence of your pick (P), middle finger (2), and ring finger (3). On beat 3 of the first measure, barre your index finger across the top three strings at fret 9, adding your pinky for the note at fret 12. A total of five chord voicings are used for this lick—three for A, and one each for D and E. Adjust your fret hand only when changing voicings—not when playing the upper strings (second triplet) of each chord shape.

LICK 2

This "triad roll" begins on the sixth string (rather than the fourth, as in the previous lick) and utilizes a five-string A chord voicing to kick off the figure. Notice that, unlike Lick 1, this example doesn't shift to a new A chord voicing until beat 4 of measure 1. Also, first-inversion (3rd on top) voicings are utilized for the D and E chord changes. Once again, your pick hand should use a pick-middle-ring finger combination throughout.

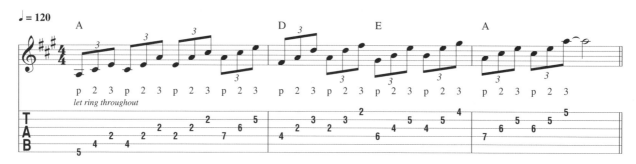

LICK 3

This major-arpeggio figure is inspired by the fast pull-off licks of Keith Urban, and like Keith, has a strong rock influence. In measure 1, a descending, root-position G major arpeggio (G–B–D) is played over the I (G) chord. In measure 2, the IV (C) and V (D) chords are outlined with descending, second-inversion C major (G–C–E) and D major (A–D–F♯) arpeggios, which resolve to a high G note (first string, fret 15) for the G chord's return.

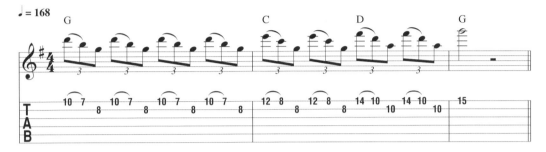

LICK 4

Country guitarists constantly strive to discover new and creative ways to mimic the distinct sound of the pedal steel guitar. One of the most common approaches is to match whole-step bends on the third string with major-triad notes on strings 1–2. Here, a single arpeggio lick is moved along the neck to outline a V–IV–I progression in the key of C major (G–F–C). The root and 5th of each chord is fretted on the first and second strings, respectively, while a pre-bend fluctuates between each chord's 3rd and 2nd. Experiment with your fret-hand fingerings, as several options are available.

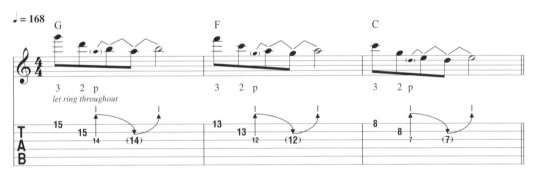

LICK 5

Similar to Lick 4, this figure is inspired by the pedal steel guitar as well. To outline the I–IV–V–I progression in G major (G–C–D–G), the top three notes of a major barre-chord shape are played as descending arpeggios, with the bottom notes (each chord's 3rd) briefly bent a half step before being returned to their original pitches. The bends temporarily change the quality of the chords from major to suspended (e.g., G to Gsus4).

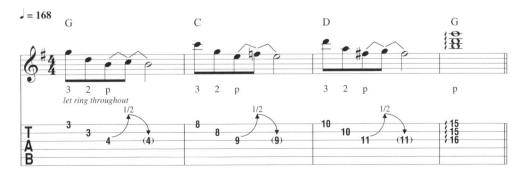

LESSON #10: MINOR ARPEGGIOS

Though not as common in country music as major arpeggios (due to an abundance of major-key songs), minor arpeggios are nonetheless requisite material for aspiring country guitarists. Why? Because minor chords (especially a major key's relative minor) appear in countless songs. To effectively navigate these minor chords, it's imperative to be equipped with an arsenal of licks that effectively outline the chord tones of these changes. And nothing outlines chord tones better than an arpeggio—the notes of a chord played individually.

The following licks present five disparate approaches to using minor arpeggios to navigate minor chords within the context of diatonic progressions in the key of C major. The relative minor, Am, is used in all five examples, while the ii chord, Dm, is incorporated into Licks 2–5.

LICK 1

All of the arpeggios in this example are based on four-string major and minor triads. The C and Am arpeggios are derived from root-position chords (root in the bass), while the F and G chord changes are outlined with first-inversion triad arpeggios (3rd in the bass). For your pick hand, use a strict pick-middle-ring finger combination throughout.

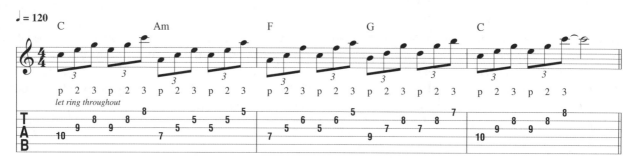

LICK 2

This lick is similar to the previous example with two slight changes. First, the root of the C chord in measure 1 is now on string 6. Second, the F chord has been substituted with the ii chord, Dm. Let all of the notes ring out clearly, like a banjo.

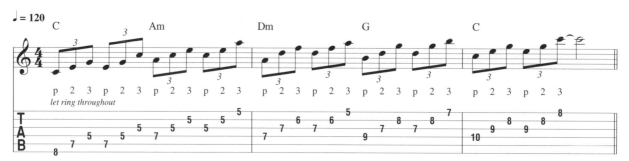

LICK 3

Borrowing the C–Am–Dm–G–C progression from Lick 2, this example outlines its changes with swift pull-off arpeggios. Descending root-position arpeggios are implemented to navigate the C–Am change in measure 1, followed in measure 2 by second-inversion and root-position arpeggios for the Dm and G chords, respectively. The lick resolves in measure 3 via a second-inversion C major arpeggio that is played in eighth position.

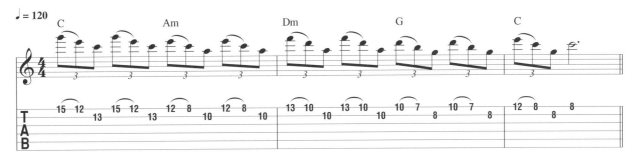

LICK 4

This lick uses simple triad arpeggios executed with half- and whole-step pre-bends along string 3 to mimic the expressive nature of the pedal steel guitar. Although the fret-hand shapes remain constant throughout, the bends alternate between whole steps (major chords) and half steps (minor chords), dictated by the quality of each chord change.

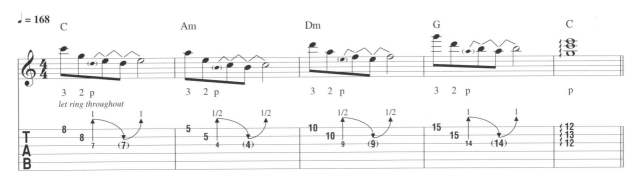

LICK 5

Here is another pedal steel-inspired lick. To outline the C major I–vi–ii–V–I progression (C–Am–Dm–G–C), major and minor triad shapes are played as descending arpeggios along strings 1–3, with the bottom note (the 3rd for major chords and the 5th for minor) briefly bent a half step before returning to its original pitch.

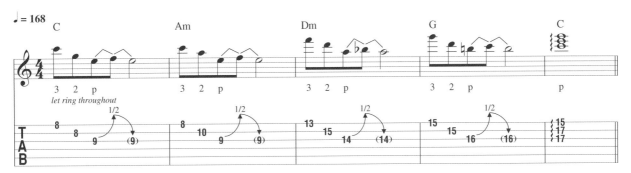

LESSON #11: DOMINANT ARPEGGIOS

Dominant arpeggios differ from their major and minor counterparts in that, unlike the three-note major and minor versions, dominant arpeggios are derived from dominant seventh chords, which contain *four* notes: the root, 3rd, 5th, and ♭7th. Dominant arpeggios are also extremely versatile. Like major arpeggios, dominant arpeggios contain a major 3rd. Therefore, they not only can be played over dominant chords, but major chords as well. With so many country songs written in major keys, guitarists have ample opportunity to incorporate dominant arpeggios into their lead lines.

In this lesson, dominant arpeggios are showcased in five distinct ways—from banjo rolls and pedal steel bends to pull-off passages and open-string cascades. As alluded to earlier, major and dominant tonalities are essentially interchangeable. Therefore, dominant chords and arpeggios can be substituted for major chords/arpeggios, and vice versa. The only difference between the two chord qualities is the bluesy sound of the dominant chord's ♭7th. Although dominant chords often appear as the V chord in major progressions, dominant tonalities work well in most instances that call for a major chord as well.

LICK 1

This example features forward banjo rolls that are played over a V7–I–V7–I progression in the key of G major (D7–G–D7–G). The phrase starts with a first-inversion (3rd in the bass) D7 arpeggio (the root note is omitted), followed by a root-position G major arpeggio, a second-inversion D7 arpeggio (again, no root), and finally, a first-inversion G major arpeggio. A common theme throughout the passage is the inclusion of the open high-E string, which lends continuity to the phrase.

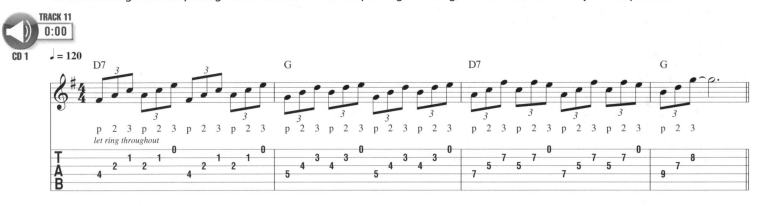

LICK 2

This example navigates an E7–C♯m–A–B7–E progression via reverse arpeggio rolls along strings 1–3. Notice the pedal steel bend in measure 3, which raises the third string's pitch from D to E, changing the chord quality from E7 to E major.

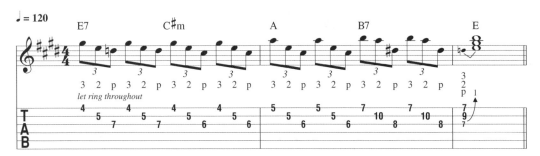

LICK 3

In a nod to Keith Urban, this rock-inspired passage flows from an E7 arpeggio (sans the root) to second-inversion, root-position, and third-inversion arpeggios for the C♯m, A, and B7 changes, respectively. Swift, descending pull-off arpeggios, played along the top two strings, form the basis of this lick.

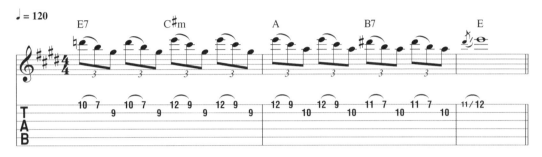

LICK 4

Here is a pedal steel-style lick. To outline the E7–C♯m–A–B7–E progression, major, minor, and dominant chord voicings are played as descending arpeggios along strings 1–3, with the bottom notes bent briefly a half or whole step before being returned to their original pitches. Note that the E7 arpeggio is the same chord shape that caps Lick 2.

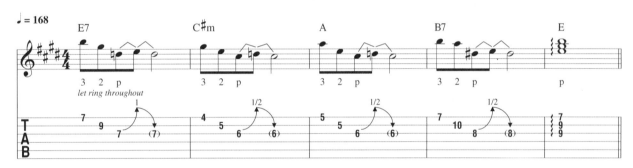

LICK 5

Of the five licks in this lesson, this open-string "cascade" perhaps is the most inventive use of a dominant arpeggio. Here, fretted notes, which outline an A7 arpeggio, are offset by open E and B strings. With the addition of the open strings, the overall tonality of the lick implies an A9 chord.

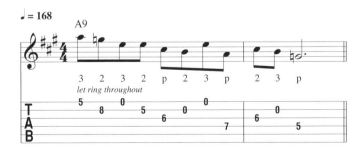

LESSON #12: INCORPORATING OPEN STRINGS INTO DOUBLE-STOP LICKS

One fact about country music that often gets overlooked is the influence that jazz had on the idiom. The jazz influence extends to country guitar as well, particularly hybrid picking—a technique that involves articulating bass notes with a pick (or thumbpick) while plucking the treble strings with the remaining fingers of the pick hand. For generations, jazz guitarists have been utilizing hybrid picking to pluck chords for chordal accompaniment (i.e., "comping"), as well as for performing chord melodies. Jazz isn't solely responsible for the hybrid-picking influence on country players, however—bluegrass guitarists and banjo players also have contributed to the hybrid-picking style used by today's country guitarists.

Often referred to as "chicken pickin'" in country music, hybrid picking not only enables guitarists to cultivate a unique sound not available with a pick, it gives them access to techniques that would otherwise be unattainable. One such technique is the incorporation of open strings into double-stop licks. Double stops are simply two notes played simultaneously and have become a staple of country guitar playing. While it's true that double stops can be articulated exclusively with a pick, the outcome can't match the speed, precision, and sound of hybrid-picked passages.

Double-Stop Shapes

In this lesson, we'll take a look at five approaches to combining open strings with common double-stop shapes. Before we get started, the following are a few common double-stop shapes, or intervals—the distance between two notes.

COMMON SHAPES ON STRING PAIRS 1–2, 3–4, 4–5 & 5–6

Note: These intervals, shown here on strings 1–2, can be transferred to every other string pair, except strings 2–3.

COMMON SHAPES ON STRINGS 2–3

Examples

LICK 1

Our first lick uses double stops along strings 4–5 to outline an E7 chord. With the exception of a brief appearance by the minor 3rd, G (beat 3 of measure 1), the entire lick is derived from the E Mixolydian mode (E–F♯–G♯–A–B–C♯–D). The open low-E string pedal tone reinforces the E dominant tonality.

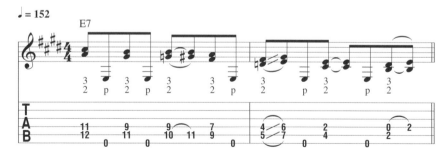

LICK 2

This lick is a nod to Brent Mason and features open-position double-stop pull-offs, a double-stop bend, and a double-stop hammer-on. Like the previous lick, this figure reinforces the harmony via an open-string pedal tone; in this case, the open A string.

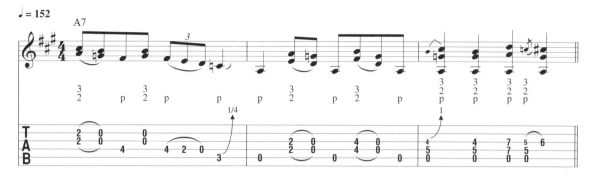

LICK 3

This lick is similar to Lick 1; however, you'll notice this phrase's pedal tone, the open D string, is on the same string as the lower notes of the double stops. For best results, pluck all of the double stops with your pick-hand's middle and ring fingers, articulating the open string with downstrokes of your pick.

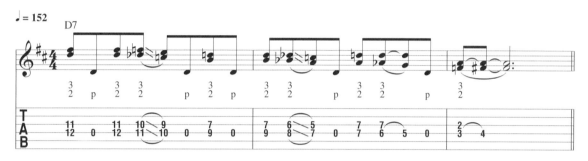

LICK 4

Here is an approach to double stops that is commonly used by country guitarists. As bass notes descend string 4, double-stop shapes along strings 2–3 are pulled off to open strings. The overall shapes are first inversion (measure 1) and root-position (measure 2) G major and F major triads, respectively.

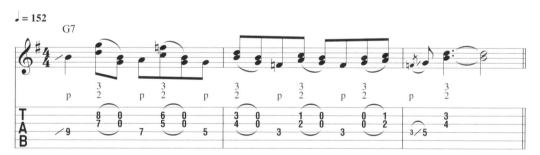

LICK 5

This example is a variation of the double-stop concept from Lick 4. Here, the double-stop shapes are positioned on strings 1–2. The fingerings are a bit trickier, so practice the lick slowly at first, increasing your speed incrementally.

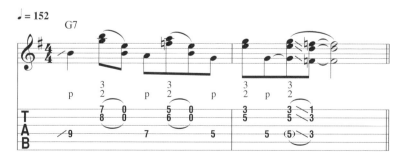

LESSON #13:

INCORPORATING OPEN STRINGS INTO PENTATONIC LICKS

Open strings are to country guitarists what Marshall stacks are to rock 'n' roll—inseparable. Consequently, country players constantly are devising new and inventive ways to incorporate open strings into their lead lines. The popularity of open strings stems from the fact that the guitar's open strings (E, A, D, G, and B) work well in country music's most popular keys—A, C, D, E, and G major—and, well open strings just sound good!

Mixing Shapes up the Neck with Open Strings

One of today's most creative practitioners and proponents of open-string playing happens to be one of Nashville's biggest stars, Brad Paisley. While open strings are naturally incorporated into open-position licks, players like Paisley have taken that practice a step further, adding open strings to pentatonic licks that are played further up the fretboard. This lesson explores the concept of incorporating open strings into common pentatonic licks that are played beyond open position. But first, let's preview the basic "box" patterns of the major and minor pentatonic scales.

MAJOR PENTATONIC SCALE

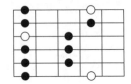

MINOR PENTATONIC SCALE

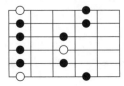

Examples

LICK 1

Our first lick is rooted in the A major pentatonic scale (A–B–C♯–E–F♯) and features several three-note hammer-ons and pull-offs. While it qualifies as an "open-position" lick because its root note, A, is the open fifth string, the pattern is technically in second position, with the root note located on fret 5 of the sixth string. With the addition of the open strings, the lick has a distinct A Mixolydian (A–B–C♯–D–E–F♯–G) sound.

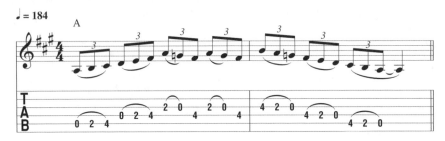

LICK 2

The G minor pentatonic scale (G–B♭–C–D–F) provides the framework for this descending legato lick. With the addition of open strings (E, B, G, and D), both the minor 3rd (B♭) and major 3rd (B) are present, giving the passage a minor-against-major sound that is so prevalent in country music.

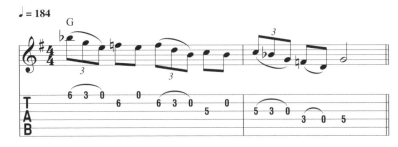

LICK 3

This example is similar to Lick 2; however, this phrase is derived from the C major pentatonic scale (C–D–E–G–A) and is solidly major, as only the major 3rd (E) is present. That said, the lick works well over an Am harmony (the relative minor of C major) as well.

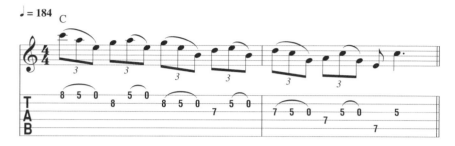

LICK 4

The A minor pentatonic scale (A–C–D–E–G) provides the framework for this lick. After a pivot-note passage in measure 1, the phrase utilizes open-string pull-offs to descend the pattern.

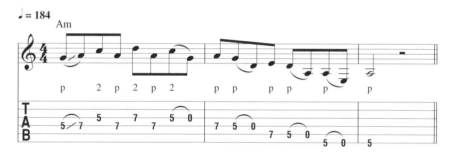

LICK 5

The last lick of this lesson involves the D major pentatonic scale (D–E–F♯–A–B) and four open strings (E, B, G, and D). As you can see, three of the four open strings are part of the scale; the other note, G, is found in several scales/modes in the key of D as well.

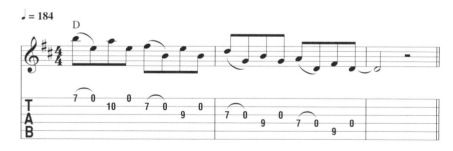

To further practice this concept, try incorporating open strings into other pentatonic licks that you already know and let your ear decide whether the open strings work in any given phrase.

LESSON #14: BASS-STRING BENDS

If guitar playing was a strength sport, country guitarists would, without a doubt, be world champions. Why? Because no other genre requires as much fretboard stamina as country guitar does. In addition to speed and dexterity, country guitarists are expected to emulate pedal steel guitar with bends that incorporate one, two, and sometimes three strings!

As if multi-string bending wasn't enough, country players have taken bass-string bends to a new level. While blues and rock players stick mainly to quarter- and half-step bends on the bottom two strings, country pickers are known to regularly nudge bass strings up a whole step, often near the nut, where the tension is knuckle-busting. This lesson focuses on five common country approaches to bass-string bends. Some require special attention to pitch precision, while others require—you guessed it—strength. Let's get started.

LICK 1

Rooted in the E major pentatonic/E blues hybrid scale, this lick features whole-step bends of the fourth and sixth strings. Both bends occur near the nut, so extra fret-hand strength is required. Execute the first bend with your ring finger, reinforcing it with your middle and index fingers. Use your middle finger to bend the sixth string down (towards the floor), reinforcing it with your index finger.

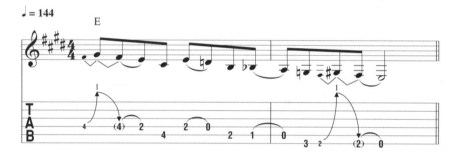

LICK 2

Here is a banjo-roll lick that incorporates half-step bends of the D string. To avoid interference with the open strings, bend the string upward (toward the ceiling). The final, low-E string bend should be pulled downward (toward the floor), altering the pitch from F♯ to the root, G.

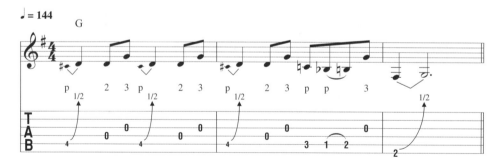

LICK 3

Double-stop oblique bends form the basis of this lick. After establishing a motif over the V (B) chord, the sequence is moved down the fretboard to outline the IV (A) and I (E) chords. Bend the fourth string with your ring finger (reinforcing it with your middle and index fingers), fretting the stationary notes on string 3 with your pinky.

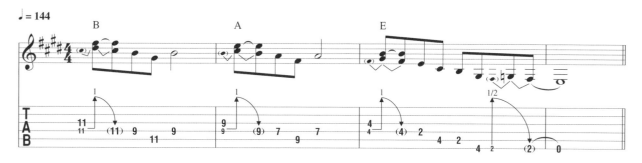

LICK 4

This short lick packs a lot of punch. In measure 1, whole-step bends emphasize the 3rds of the V (D) and IV (C) chords, which are followed by pull-offs to each chord's root note. In measure 2, a sixth-string slide puts your fret hand in place for a half-step bend from the minor 3rd (B♭) to the major 3rd (B) of the I (G) chord, which is followed by an open-string double stop.

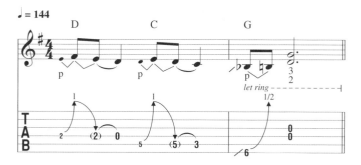

LICK 5

Here, a V–I chord progression is outlined with a fourth-string oblique bend (measure 1) and a fifth-string half-step bend from the minor 3rd (E♭) to the major 3rd (E) of the I (C) chord (measure 2). For the oblique bend, use your ring finger to nudge the string upward, playing the third-string notes with your pinky and index fingers. This approach frees up your middle finger to help with the bend.

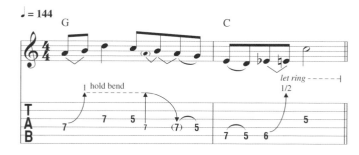

LESSON #15: TRIPLE STOPS

Although they don't garner as much attention as their two-string counterparts, triple stops are no less important to the overall sound of country guitar. Like double stops, triple stops are voiced in a variety of ways and often have a singular purpose—to simulate a pedal steel guitar. Triple stops can be close-voiced (adjacent strings) or open-voiced (non-adjacent strings), and often include string bends to further accentuate the pedal steel sound. Country guitarists have been using them for generations. In fact, country/jazz guitarist Scotty Anderson has such an affinity for the technique that he named his 2001 album—what else?—*Triple Stop*.

Since triple stops contain three notes, they are technically chords. However, due to the way in which they're used (as bends, chord partials, pedal steel simulations, etc.), "triplet stops" is a more apt title. In this lesson, we'll explore adjacent and non-adjacent triple-stop voicings along various string sets, as well as a few ways that bends can be incorporated into triple-stop passages to effectively mimic a pedal steel guitar.

LICK 1

This lick outlines a I7–IV7–V7–I progression in E major (E7–A7–B7–E) exclusively with adjacent-string triple stops. The first voicing, an E7 chord sans its 5th (B), is restated further up the neck to emphasize the A7 and B7 changes. The phrase ends with a common E major triad.

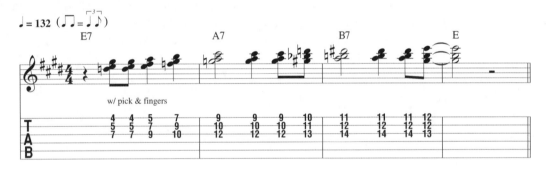

LICK 2

In this example, simple, close-voiced triple stops played along the top strings emphasize the G7 harmony. At the end of measure 2, a common C major triad is played in anticipation of the I (C) chord.

LICK 3

The triple stops in this example, played exclusively on strings 2–4, are essentially common triad shapes, although the bends obscure that fact. In measure 1, the half-step bends raise the pitch from F♯ to G and, when combined with the lower fretted notes, spell out a C major chord (C–E–G). Similarly in measure 2, the bends raise the pitch from D♯ to E, spelling out an A minor chord (A–C–E). To avoid clashing with the other notes of the triple stop, pull the bends downward (toward the floor).

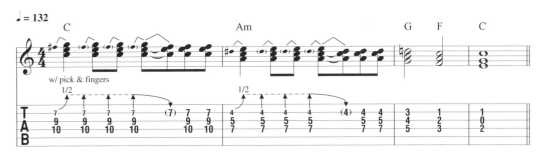

LICK 4

In this example, open-voiced triple stops are used exclusively to outline the D7–G (V7–I) progression. The voicings are a marriage of disparate intervals—specifically, minor 6ths and major 3rds and major 6ths and minor 3rds. Like you did on the other licks, employ hybrid picking throughout.

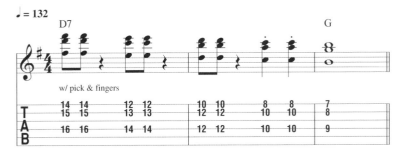

LICK 5

Close-voiced triple stops played along strings 3–5 are used exclusively to outline this D–G–A7–D (I–IV–V7–I) progression. Whole-step and half-step bends played on strings 3 and 5, respectively, impart a more genuine pedal steel sound to the lick than stationary notes alone can offer. The whole-step bend should be pulled downward so as to avoid clashing with the stationary notes; the half-step bend, however, should be nudged upward with your fret-hand's middle finger.

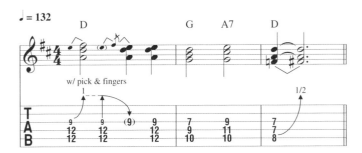

LESSON #16: UNISON BENDS

The role that string bending plays in country guitar cannot be overstated. Without bends, simulation of the pedal steel guitar, a quintessential sound of country playing, would be nearly impossible. Common half- and whole-step bends into— and out of—chord tones lend an expressive, vocal-like quality to guitar lines and can be used to effectively mimic the slide bar of the pedal steel.

While perhaps the most commonly used bend by country, rock, and blues guitarists, the unison bend doesn't garner the attention it rightly deserves relative to other bends (oblique, double stop, triple stop, etc.). This short shrift is perhaps due to its monotonic nature. Unlike the other, multi-tone bends, a unison bend involves bending one string to match the pitch of a note on an adjacent string (i.e., they're played "in unison"). These notes can be played either simultaneously or sequentially.

Exercises

Before we get into practical application of unison bends, here are a couple of exercises to get you familiar with the technique. The first exercise is a sequence of unison bends that climb the G major scale (G–A–B–C–D–E–F♯) along strings 1–2; the second is in D major (D–E–F♯–G–A–B–C♯) and ascends strings 2–3. Strive for pitch accuracy while you play these exercises; that is, be sure to match the bent pitch with the pitch of the stationary note on the higher string.

EXERCISE 1

EXERCISE 2

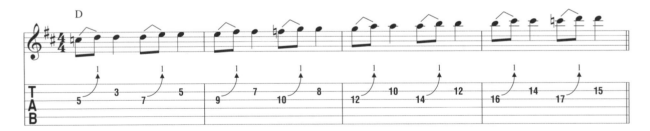

Examples
LICK 1

This first lick combines elements from both Exercises 1 and 2. In the first two measures, "pitch-matching" unison bends outline the notes of the G7 chord (G–B–D–F) as they ascend strings 1–2. In measure 3, the I (C) chord is emphasized via a C-note unison bend whose notes are played simultaneously.

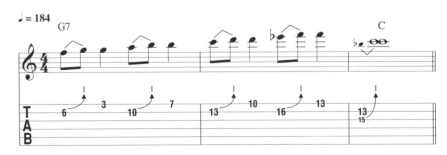

LICK 2

Oblique- and unison-bending techniques are combined in this example to create a melodic motif that is restated in measures 2 and 3. Make sure you hold the bend as you play the adjacent-string notes, after which you should rearticulate and release the bent note.

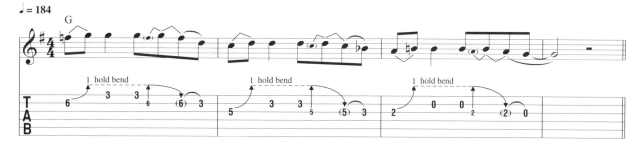

LICK 3

This bass-string unison-bending lick is relatively easy to perform. After you bend string 4 upward (toward the ceiling) a half step, pluck the open third string, repeating the sequence five times. At measure 3, shift your fret hand to string 5 and repeat. The pitches produced in measures 1 and 2 are G notes, which are the ♭7th of A7 and the root of G major; the root of D major is produced in measure 3.

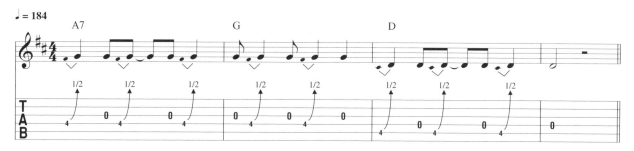

LICK 4

Unison bends are used both in common and uncommon ways in this rock- and blues-inspired line. A Chuck Berry-esque unison bend kicks off the lick, followed by a whole-step unison bend on string 2. After a rather extensive legato figure that traverses one-and-a-half measures, the low-E string is bent a half step from F♯ to G to match the pitch of the subsequent open G string.

LICK 5

This C dominant lick features some more oblique/unison bending. This time G notes, the 5th of C7, are matched and rapidly alternated on strings 2 and 3, comprising a majority of the lick. Note that the lick ends not on the root (C), but on the ♭7th (B♭).

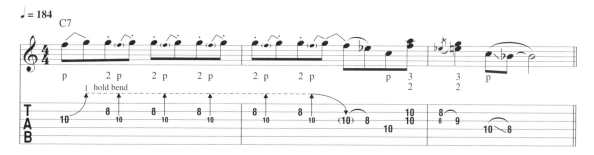

LESSON #17: ASCENDING OPEN-STRING SCALES

Modern country guitarists love to incorporate open strings into their lead lines—a technique that traces back to early bluegrass banjo and guitar players. Because the application of the guitar's open strings—E, A, D, G, and B—are limited to certain chords and keys, guitarists must use proper discretion. Fortunately, an overwhelming majority of country songs are written in keys that are friendly to open strings—specifically, C, D, E, G, and A. This begs the proverbial question: what came first, the chicken or the egg? Did country artists write songs in specific keys so they could use open strings? Or did they incorporate open strings because they fit the keys of many of their songs? Regardless of the answer, open strings have become a staple of country music.

One of the most common applications of open strings in country music is to pair them with fretted notes to create scales and scale-based licks. This approach, when applied to the aforementioned keys, enables guitarists to play major and dominant (Mixolydian) scales in as many as two complete octaves, which is the focus of this lesson. The following five licks illustrate how major and dominant scales in the keys of E, A, D, G, and C can be constructed from a combination of fretted notes and open strings.

LICK 1

Here is the E Mixolydian mode (E–F#–G#–A–B–C#–D) played in two complete octaves. It incorporates every open string, except for G. Take this one slowly at first, as the fingerings are tricky, and let the open strings ring out as long as possible before shifting your fret hand.

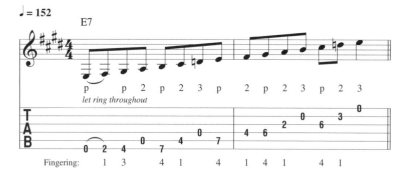

LICK 2

Also presented in two octaves, here is the A Mixolydian mode (A–B–C#–D–E–F#–G). Again, let the open strings ring out as long as possible.

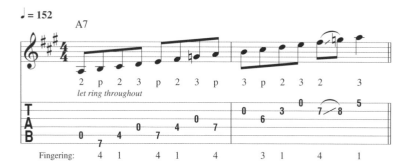

LICK 3

This arrangement of the D Mixolydian mode (D–E–F♯–G–A–B–C) is similar to the A Mixolydian pattern, but starts on the open D string (duh!) and ends on the scale's fifth degree, A, rather than its root.

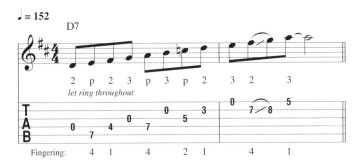

LICK 4

Here is an open-string arrangement of the G Mixolydian mode (G–A–B–C–D–E–F). This pattern requires some wide finger stretches, so take it slowly at first, increasing your speed incrementally. Also, pay close attention to the fret-hand fingerings that are included under the tab staff.

LICK 5

Here is this lesson's sole major-scale arrangement, C major (C–D–E–F–G–A–B). The pattern is similar to the G Mixolydian scale, but ends on the major scale's 5th, G, rather than its root, C.

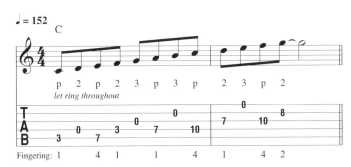

Although open-string scales sound more "musical" than standard fretted scales, once you have these patterns memorized, increase their melodic interest by including some pitches found outside of the scale (i.e., non-diatonic tones). Combining the minor and major 3rds of major or dominant scales always works well. For example, add E♭ (the minor 3rd) to the C major scale.

LESSON #18: DESCENDING OPEN-STRING SCALES

An overwhelming majority of country songs are composed in major keys. In fact, any survey of classic and/or contemporary country tunes would return the same results—that most country songs are written in one of five major keys—A, C, D, E, or G. Because of this fact, country guitarists have been incorporating their instrument's open strings—E, A, D, G, and B—into their lead lines for generations, as most (or all) of the open strings are diatonic to those five keys. Open strings not only increase the "twang" factor, but also create natural dissonance when paired with fretted notes due to the narrow intervals (e.g., minor and major 2nds) that naturally separate many of these pitches. The resultant tension (and subsequent resolution) is a key component of bluegrass and country guitar.

In this lesson, we'll take a look at how descending major and dominant (Mixolydian) scales can be created by combining fretted notes with open strings. All of the popular country keys—E, A, D, G, and C—are covered. Let's get started.

LICK 1

Here is a two-octave arrangement of the E Mixolydian mode (E–F♯–G♯–A–B–C♯–D). The fingering is a bit challenging, so take it very slowly at first, increasing your tempo incrementally. Also, be sure to let the open strings ring loud and proud!

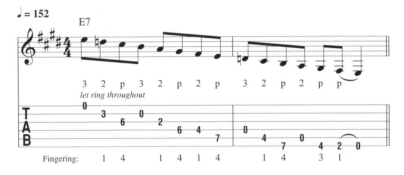

LICK 2

This A Mixolydian (A–B–C♯–D–E–F♯–G) pattern starts with three fretted notes, but quickly turns into a cascade of open and fretted pitches. This lick works well over both A major and A dominant chords.

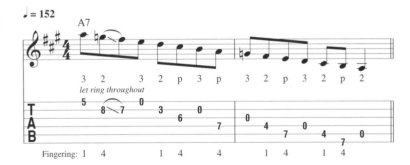

LICK 3

Starting on the scale's fifth degree, A, this D Mixolydian (D–E–F♯–G–A–B–C) pattern is similar to Lick 2 (A Mixolydian), but concludes on—what else?—the open D string. Pay strict attention to the pick- and fret-hand patterns, which are located between and below the staves, respectively.

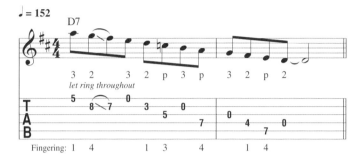

LICK 4

Here is a two-octave open-string arrangement of the G Mixolydian mode (G–A–B–C–D–E–F). The wide finger stretches in measure 2 are challenging, so go slowly, taking care to let the open strings ring out.

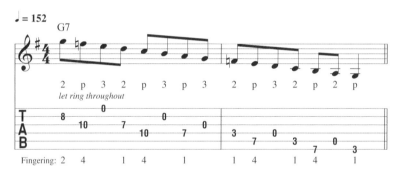

LICK 5

The only major scale of the group, this C major (C–D–E–F–G–A–B) arrangement commences on the scale's fifth degree, G, and follows a pattern that is similar to Lick 4 (G Mixolydian). Once you get the picking pattern down cold, the rest should fall into place.

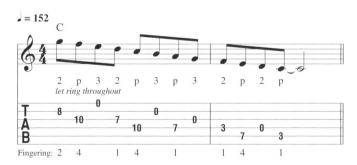

If these descending open-string scales sound too rudimentary, you can increase their melodic interest by incorporating chromatic passing tones from their relative blues scale (e.g., the ♭3rd or ♭5th). For example, play the C major scale with the notes E♭ (the ♭3rd) and G♭ (the ♭5th).

OPEN-STRING SCALE LICKS

Open-string scale licks are exactly that—licks that are derived from a specific scale that is comprised of both fretted and open-string pitches. Country and bluegrass guitarists have been incorporating open strings into their lead lines for decades and the technique has since become a staple of the genre. It also helps that a majority of country songs are written in A, C, D, E, or G major—keys that are very accommodating to open strings.

Sometimes called "harp" or "cascade" licks, open-string scale licks are distinctly country and, thus, can impart a genuine country sound to any lead line. In this lesson, we'll explore five creative ways to outline various chords and progressions with a combination of open and fretted tones.

LICK 1

Utilizing a generous helping of hammer-ons, this ascending lick intersperses open strings among fretted notes that are derived from the A Mixolydian mode (A–B–C♯–D–E–F♯–G). To increase the bluesy quality of the line, both the major 3rd (C♯) and minor 3rd (C), borrowed from the A minor/blues scale, are present.

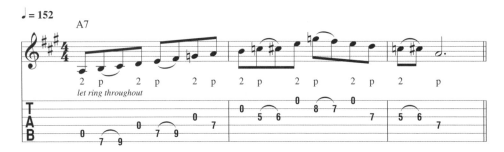

LICK 2

This G dominant lick covers a lot of fretboard territory, moving all the way from seventh position to open position. Smooth, seamless position shifting is a byproduct of using open strings in your lead lines.

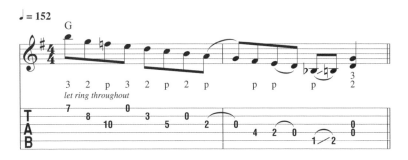

LICK 3

This lick works well over D7 chords. It's constructed from a combination of the D major pentatonic (D–E–F♯–A–B) and D blues (D–F–G–A♭–A–C) scales (as well as one chromatic passing tone, B♭) and employs hammer-ons, pull-offs, and slides to work its way down the fretboard.

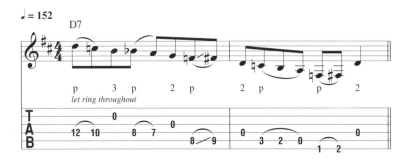

LICK 4

In this example, a V7–I (G7–C) progression is outlined with a (mostly) ascending lick that combines five of the guitar's open strings with notes from the G major pentatonic (G–A–B–D–E) and G blues (G–Bb–C–Db–D–F) scales. In measure 2, the notes are derived from the C major scale (C–D–E–F–G–A–B).

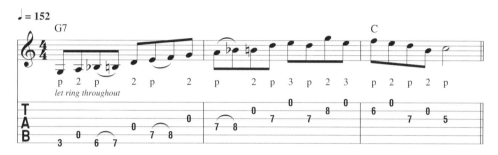

LICK 5

In measure 1, fretted pitches from the E minor pentatonic scale (E–G–A–B–D) are interspersed among the open high-E, B, and G strings. In measure 2, the G major pentatonic scale (G–A–B–D–E), E minor's relative major, is employed to outline the I (G) chord. Note that one non-diatonic pitch, Bb, makes an appearance on beat 3 of the third measure, briefly adding a bluesy quality to the lick before it resolves to a G/D dyad on beat 4.

Once you're comfortable with these five licks, try incorporating open strings into some of the licks that you already know in the keys of A, C, D, E, and G major. The higher the licks are up the neck, the more jangly and dissonant the sound. Creating and resolving tension is a common theme in country guitar playing.

LESSON #20: REPETITIVE LICKS

The sign of a good guitar solo is one that captivates the audience. One way to hold the attention of your audience is to vary the intensity of your solo. Varying the intensity of a solo can be as simple as manipulating your guitar's volume, increasing/decreasing your note output, or perhaps most effective, playing repetitive licks. Repetitive licks are simply melodic patterns that are repeated two or more times.

Repetitive licks come in all shapes and sizes. However, in this lesson, we're going to focus on single-note and double-stop licks, with an emphasis on the latter. The great thing about repetitive licks is that you can alter their repetitions at will to fit the chord you're soloing over, whether it lasts two bars, three bars, four bars, etc.

LICK 1

This type of repetitive lick is a favorite of hot country picker Brent Mason. To outline the A7 chord, open-string and 2nd-fret double stops alternate with single notes that are played on string 4.

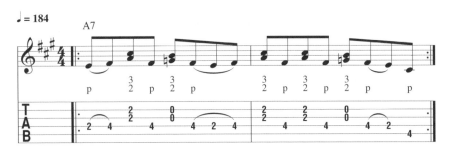

LICK 2

This single-note lick is performed exclusively with third- and fourth-string pull-offs. The notes are derived from the D Mixolydian mode (D–E–F♯–G–A–B–C), with B being the only note that is excluded. Notice how the six-note sequences begin on the ♭7th (C) and end on the open root note (D).

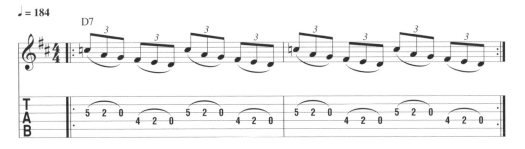

LICK 3

Here is a double-stop pull-off lick that employs the open B and G strings as common tones to lend continuity to the line as it moves from C7 (V7 chord) to F7 (I7 chord). The fourth-string B♭ note (♭7th of C7) in measures 1–2 and the A note (3rd of F7) in measures 3–4 emphasize the quality of the chord changes.

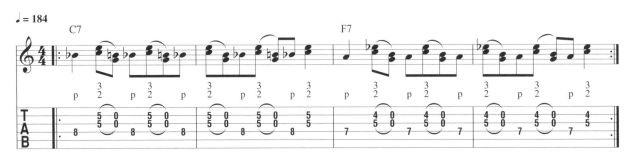

LICK 4

To effectively perform this double-stop lick, you'll need to give your fret hand some extra attention. In measures 1–2, fret the top three strings like a standard major triad, using your pinky to pull off from the 11th fret to your barred index finger (at fret 8). In measures 3–4, use your middle, ring, and pinky fingers to voice a standard open D chord, playing it here three frets higher. Then, pull off with your pinky from the 6th fret to your index finger (at fret 4).

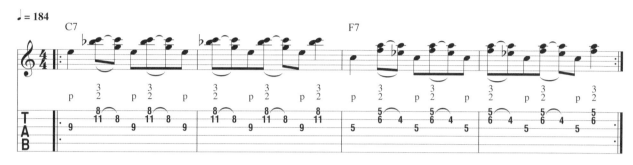

LICK 5

This is a standard country double-stop lick that combines pitches from the A major pentatonic (A–B–C♯–E–F♯) and A blues (A–C–D–E♭–E–G) scales. After playing the pattern in fifth position for the A7 chord, shift it up to tenth position to outline the D7 chord. All of the double stops should be plucked with a combination of your pick-hand's middle and ring fingers.

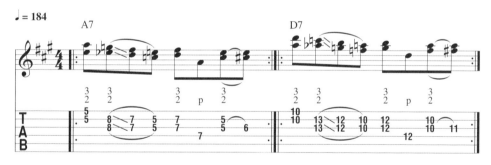

LESSON #21: 6TH-TO-♭7TH BENDS

Similar to blues music, the ♭7th plays an important role in country. It's the ♭7th tone that defines the dominant quality of a chord, and the dominant scale—the Mixolydian mode (1–2–3–4–5–6–♭7)—is perhaps the most diverse scale in Western music. Due to its unique structure, in which both the major 3rd and minor 7th are present, the Mixolydian mode can be employed to outline both major triads (1–3–5) and dominant seventh (1–3–5–♭7) chords. The presence of that one note (the ♭7th) lends a bluesy quality to the "happy" sound of major triads—a quality that is inherent in dominant seventh chords.

Through the years, country guitarists have developed creative ways to emphasize the ♭7th tone while soloing over major or dominant chords. One approach that has become a hallmark of country lead playing is bending the sixth degree (the major 6th) of the Mixolydian mode up to the ♭7th. For example, in the key of D, the note B is bent upward a half step, to C (the ♭7th). It's important to note that the 6th-to-♭7th bend is always a half step—a whole-step bend will sound the major 7th (in this case, C♯), which will give your line a much brighter, happier (i.e., major) sound. To locate the major 6th of a given scale, simply slide down three frets from the root note. Let's take a look at five examples of the 6th-to-♭7th bend in action.

LICK 1

Over the IV7 (D7) chord, the 6th (B) is bent up to the ♭7th (C) and held while E and D notes are articulated on the second string. The lick concludes with a pull-off sequence that leads to the open A string, the root of the A7 (I7) chord.

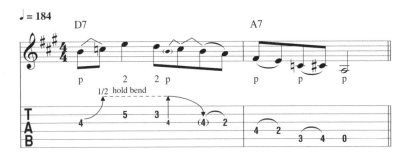

LICK 2

In this lick, a 6th-to-♭7th (F♯-to-G) bend acts as a pedal tone while the root note, A, is articulated on string 3. The multiple iterations of A and G notes really emphasizes the dominant quality of the A7 chord.

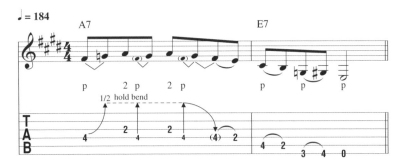

LICK 3

This A dominant lick features a cool approach to the 6th-to-♭7th lick. On beat 2 of the first measure, a non-bent ♭7th (G) note is played, immediately preceding multiple bends from F♯ (the 6th) to G. You can use the fretted G to help with the accuracy/intonation of your half-step bends.

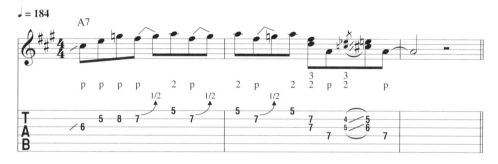

LICK 4

This example features a couple of oblique bends. The first bend is standard country fare and emphasizes the 3rd (B) and 5th (D) of the G7 chord; the second bend is a 6th-to-♭7th bend that outlines the root (G, second string) and of course, the ♭7th (F). A cool dominant trick occurs at the end of the phrase, where another 6th-to-♭7th (E-to-F) bend is implemented. When playing over a dominant chord, ending a phrase on the ♭7th is common practice in country, as well as in blues.

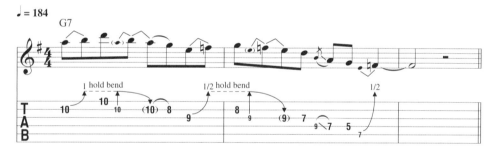

LICK 5

An open-position 6th-to-♭7th (C♯-to-D) oblique bend kicks off this E7 lick. In measure 2, the C♯-to-D bend is recreated on the fifth string and immediately followed by the open D string, creating unison D pitches—a common technique used by country guitarists. Be sure to bend the string upward (toward to the ceiling) to avoid obstructing the open string.

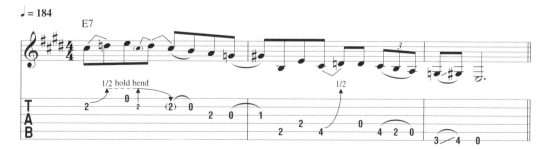

LESSON #22: INCORPORATING OPEN STRINGS INTO CHORD PROGRESSIONS

Open strings, long a staple of country lead guitar playing, do not have to be limited to single-note lines. On the contrary, open strings work quite well in several rhythm guitar settings, as well as in banjo rolls—a lead guitar technique whereby chords are rapidly arpeggiated via a repetitive hybrid-picking pattern to mimic a banjo (hence, the name). In these settings, typically one or two open strings are played throughout the progression, acting as a common tone to lend continuity to the chord changes.

The first three examples of this lesson are banjo rolls that utilize common major and minor triad shapes and open strings to outline a C–Am–F–G–C progression. Each example offers a varied approach to the chord voicings and which open strings are employed. The fourth example is a rhythm guitar approach to a G–Em–D–C–G progression that utilizes "Travis picking" and the open G string. And finally, the fifth example is a strummed rhythm pattern in 6/8 time that juxtaposes the open D string and chord voicings that are derived from six-string barre-chord shapes.

EXAMPLE 1

This banjo roll pairs chords that are exclusively voiced on strings 2–4 with the open high-E string, starting with an eighth-position C major triad. Voice the Am chord with your fret-hand's middle, index, and pinky fingers on strings 2, 3, and 4, respectively, using a pick-middle-ring picking pattern throughout.

EXAMPLE 2

Like Example 1, this banjo roll lends continuity to the progression via the open high-E string; however, all of the chord shapes in this example are voiced within the first five frets. Notice that the C and Am voicings contain an E note in the bass, their 3rd and 5th, respectively.

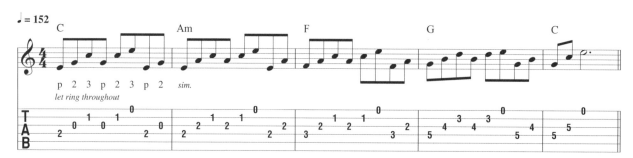

EXAMPLE 3

This banjo roll employs not one, but two open strings (G and high-E) throughout. Notice that the chord voicing remains constant for the C–Am7 change. Consequently, the Am triad of Examples 1 and 2 is replaced with a minor seventh voicing in this progression due to the presence of the open G string (the minor 7th of Am7). Again, in lieu of root notes, an E note is found in the bass of both chords.

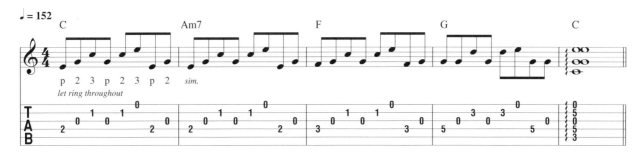

EXAMPLE 4

Shifting from banjo rolls to rhythm guitar, this example features a G–Em–D–C–G progression that is played with a "Travis picking" pattern. The chord voicings are derived from standard barre-chord shapes whose roots are located on the fifth string. Notice however, that the open G string is allowed to ring throughout. Pay strict attention to the picking pattern in measure 1, as it forms the basis of the entire example.

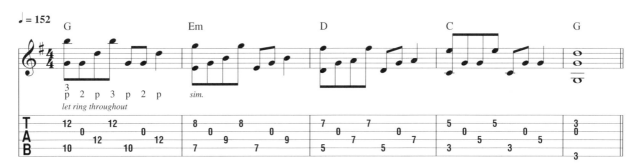

EXAMPLE 5

With chord shapes that are derived from major and minor barre chords whose roots are located on the sixth string, this example employs the open D string to act as a common tone throughout the progression and reinforce the key center, D major. The wide intervals between the fretted notes on strings 3 and 6 are a rhythm guitar technique that is found in both rock and country music. For examples, check out the Red Hot Chili Peppers' "Scar Tissue," Collective Soul's "The World I Know," and Thompson Square's "Glass."

Experiment with adding open strings to some of your favorite non-open string chord voicings. A good place to start is the common-tone approach. Let your ears guide you. Be creative!

LESSON #23: OBLIQUE-BEND DOUBLE STOPS

This lesson combines two of country guitar's most popular techniques—oblique bends and double stops. Double stops simply are two notes played simultaneously. In country, double stops typically are performed via hybrid picking, whereby the middle and ring fingers each are assigned a string. Hybrid picking not only increases the efficiency by which the double stops are performed, but also increases the "twang" factor not afforded by a pick.

An oblique bend pairs a bent note, which is held, with one or more fretted pitches that are played on a higher adjacent string, non-adjacent string, or both. To perform an oblique-bend double stop, a bent note is played simultaneously with a higher, fretted note. In this lesson, we'll explore both types of oblique-bend double stops, starting with the former.

LICK 1

This A7 lick starts with an oblique-bend double stop that emphasizes the chord's root (A) and 3rd (C♯). In measure 2, a second oblique-bend double stop is employed—this time to emphasize the 5th (E) and ♭7th (G). Focus on bending the strings precisely one whole step; otherwise, your double stops will clash with the A7 harmony. Notice that all of the A7 chord's tones (A–C♯–E–G) have been incorporated into the double stops.

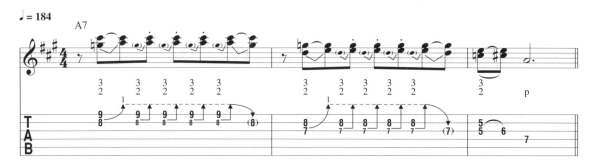

LICK 2

Another dominant lick, this example employs two oblique-bend double stops in the first measure to outline all four tones of the G7 chord—G, B, D, and F. The first bend is a B/D double stop; the second, G/F. Be sure to nudge the third-string bend up just a half step; otherwise, the F note becomes an F♯, the *major* 7th—bad!

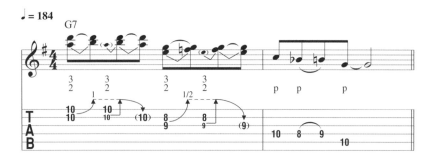

LICK 3

In this example, two distinct oblique-bend double stops are utilized to outline an E7–A (V7–I) progression. In measure 1, the E7 chord's 3rd (G♯) is played on string 2 while the third string is bent from the ♭7th (D) to the root (E). In measure 2, the A chord's 5th (E) is played on string 3 while a whole-step bend emphasizes the 3rd (C♯). Use your pinky to fret the bends' stationary pitches, your index finger for the first bend, and your ring finger for the second bend.

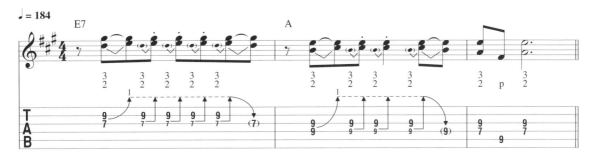

LICK 4

This example is the first of two oblique-bend double-stop licks that are played on non-adjacent strings. This lick is played over an E7 chord and features a minor 7th interval that is played along strings 1 and 3. To stay within the confines of the E Mixolydian mode (E–F♯–G♯–A–B–C♯–D), the third string is manipulated with half- and whole-step bends. Pay close attention to which type of bend (whole step or half step) is being used at any given time. Also, use a combination of your pick and middle finger to pluck the entire figure, which is a different approach from adjacent-string oblique-bend double stops.

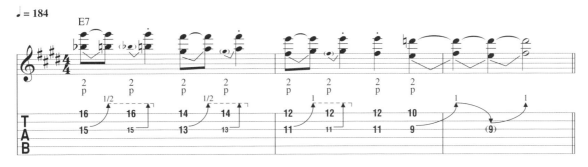

LICK 5

This phrase is similar to Lick 4, only it's played along strings 2 and 4. The notes are derived from the A Mixolydian mode (A–B–C♯–D–E–F♯–G), beginning with a C♯/E double stop (the 3rd and 5th of A7, respectively) and ending with an A/G note pair (the root and ♭7th). The whole-step bends that conclude the phrase cause the lower note to fluctuate between the pitches A and B (the 2nd/9th).

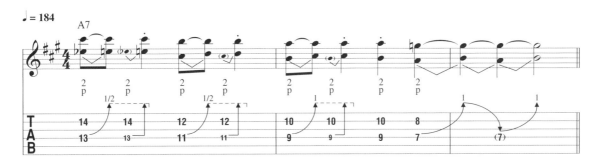

LESSON #24: TRAVIS PICKING

One of the most popular fingerstyle approaches to the guitar is Travis picking. Named after the man responsible for its widespread popularity, country artist Merle Travis, Travis picking involves playing steady quarter notes (often alternating between a chord's root and 5th) on the bass strings with the thumb while the remaining fingers pluck chord tones on the higher strings. While the quarter-note bass line lends the pattern a driving, propulsive feel, the upper strings supply its harmony and melody.

In this lesson, we're going to focus on a few basic Travis-picking patterns that utilize open chords, barre chords, and seventh chords. We'll also explore a couple of more advanced concepts—specifically, walking bass lines and chord melody.

Exercises

Before we apply Travis picking to actual chord progressions, here are some exercises that will get your fingers acclimated to the basic pattern. These exercises and examples are notated for hybrid picking with your pick, middle, and ring fingers. However, if you choose to play without a pick—as many Travis pickers do—simply use your thumb, index, and middle fingers in place of the pick, middle, and ring fingers, respectively.

EXERCISE 1

This exercise focuses solely on an alternating root/5th (D–A) bass line for a D chord. Play the line exclusively with your pick.

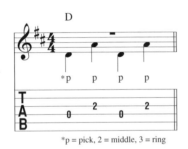

*p = pick, 2 = middle, 3 = ring

EXERCISE 2

In this exercise, a second-string D note, plucked with your middle finger, is added to the root/5th bass line.

EXERCISE 3

To further evolve the patterns from Exercises 1–2, the open D chord's high F♯ note (first string) is added, played here with the pick-hand's ring finger.

EXERCISE 4

In this example, the picking pattern is fully formed, with chord tones played in a steady stream. Pay close attention to the picking pattern, which is indicated between the notation and tab staves.

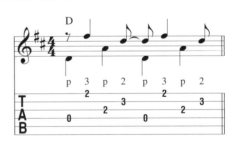

EXERCISE 5

This exercise introduces a beat 1 "pinch," whereby two notes of a chord are plucked simultaneously.

EXERCISE 6

Here, the "pinch" has been shifted from beat 1 (from Exercise 5) to beat 2.

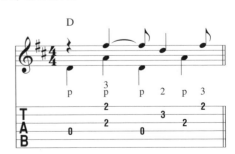

Examples

PROGRESSION 1

This example employs the picking pattern from Exercise 4 to play a D–A–D (I–V–I) progression. For the A chord, the bass line shifts from strings 3–4 to strings 4–5.

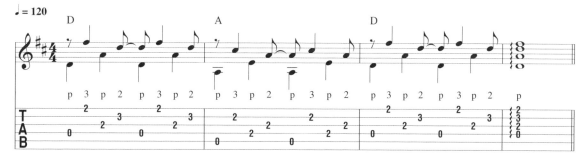

PROGRESSION 2

The picking pattern from Exercise 6 is used in this progression, which employs the same chord voicings as Progression 1.

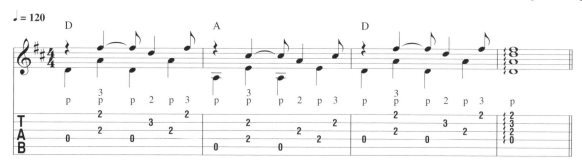

PROGRESSION 3

A variation of the picking pattern from Exercise 5, which features a "pinch" on beat 1, is used for this C–G–F–C (I–V–IV–I) progression. For the C chord, maintain the voicing's shape on the upper strings while alternating your fret-hand's ring finger between the fifth- and sixth-string bass notes.

PROGRESSION 4

For this progression, a standard C7 chord voicing is utilized for both the I7 (C7) chord and the IV7 (F7) chord. Like the C chord bass line from Progression 3, your ring finger should be employed for the root/5th bass line over both the C7 chord and the F7 chord. Notice the walking bass lines that lead into the C7 chord from both directions.

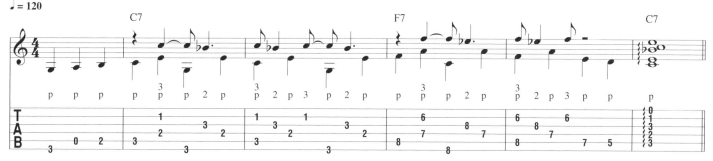

LESSON #25: FINGERSTYLE COUNTRY

The term "fingerstyle" basically refers to any picking technique that involves the pick-hand's fingers exclusively or consists of a combination of the pick and fingers (i.e., hybrid picking). Fingerstyle guitar is common in several musical genres, including classical, jazz, blues, rock, and country, among others. Although single-note lines can be executed with a fingerstyle approach, the technique is typically reserved for a rhythm guitar role.

In country music, no player elevated the fingerstyle approach more than Chet Atkins. Equally adept at chordal and single-note playing, Atkins' right-hand prowess was unparalleled during his 60-year career and has had a profound influence on generations of guitarists, country and otherwise. Utilizing a thumbpick and his index, middle, ring, and pinky finger, "Mr. Guitar" was well-versed in several styles, often intertwining multiple genres in a single song. In this lesson, we'll explore several of Chet Atkins' fingerstyle techniques, including Travis picking, chord melody, and classical.

EXAMPLE 1

This example features a basic Travis-picking approach to an A–E7–A (I–V7–I) progression. A root/5th bass line played in steady quarter notes provides a strong foundation for the chord changes, which are accented on beats 2 and 4. To break up the monotony of the root/5th pattern, short walking bass lines lead into each new chord.

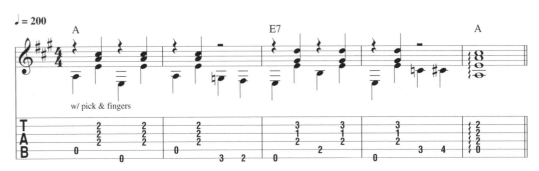

EXAMPLE 2

This picking pattern is a variation of the one found in Example 1. Unlike the previous example's strict rhythm guitar assignment, however, this example features Chet's ability to seamlessly combine chords, bass lines, and single-note melodies. This chord-melody style involves maintaining a steady quarter-note bass line while a melody (top notes) is intertwined with open A and D7 chords.

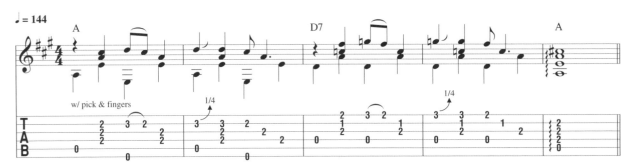

EXAMPLE 3

Featuring a more sophisticated progression (A–C#m–F#m–D–Dm–A), this example demonstrates how Chet would employ common tones to lend continuity to several chord changes. In measures 1–2, notice how he maintains the unison E notes on strings 1–2 while the chords shift from A to C#m. Similarly, in measures 3–4 the high A note (first string, fret 5) of the F#m chord is carried over to the D chord. Notice too that Chet adheres to a strict root/5th bass line throughout the progression.

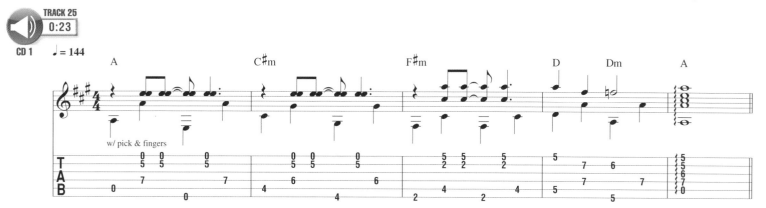

EXAMPLE 4

This progression exemplifies Chet's classical influence. Each chord change is initially stated via wide intervals, which are immediately followed by narrow-interval double stops that serve both a melodic and a harmonic role. The figure can be played exclusively with your fingers or with a combination of your pick and fingers.

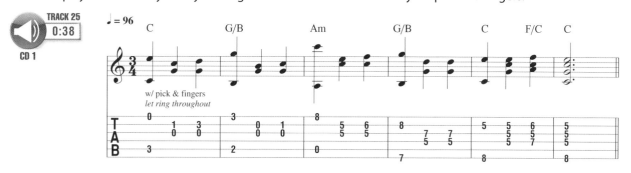

EXAMPLE 5

This figure is informed by banjo rolls and can be used in either a lead guitar role or as a rhythm guitar part. Here, arpeggiated chord tones and double stops are combined to outline an A–D–E–A (I–IV–V–I) progression. The A chord is played with the 3rd (C#) in the bass, followed by D and E chords that are based on an open C-chord shape. In measure 4, A and D triads are swiftly alternated. To execute these triads efficiently, barre your index finger across both strings 1 and 2 at the 5th fret.

OPEN-CHORD EMBELLISHMENTS

Nothing spices up an otherwise bland open-chord progression like embellishments. Sometimes referred to as chordal "ornaments," open-chord embellishments come in many forms, from legato passages to chordal suspensions (sus2 and sus4) to short melodies.

Chordal embellishment is quite popular in country music, no doubt due to the proclivity of country guitarists to use open chords. Embellishments sound particularly colorful on acoustic guitar (another staple of country), especially when played with a capo. A capo shortens the length of the strings and in turn, raises their pitches, enabling embellishments to really ring out.

In this lesson, we'll take a look at several open-chord embellishment options, played within the context of common progressions. While the first two progressions feature common hammer-on embellishments, the others get increasingly more complex.

PROGRESSION 1

Fundamentally, this example is a simple G–C progression. However, embellishments add a layer of sophistication to the changes. In measure 1, fret the G chord with your middle, ring, and pinky fingers, thereby enabling you to shift your fingers to voice the C/G chord without having to reposition your fret hand. In measure 2, use your pinky to add the 4th, the F note on fret 3 of the fourth string, for the Cadd4 chord, and keep the C chord voiced while performing the hammer-on figure at the end of the measure.

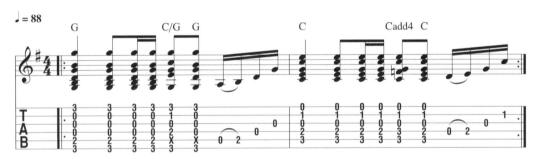

PROGRESSION 2

Perform this C–Am–F–C–G (I–vi–IV–I–V) progression with a combination of your pick and fingers (i.e., hybrid picking). The first two measures are articulated with a repetitive bass note/double stop/hammer-on/double stop picking pattern. In measure 3, the G–C/G–G changes from Progression 1 are reprised.

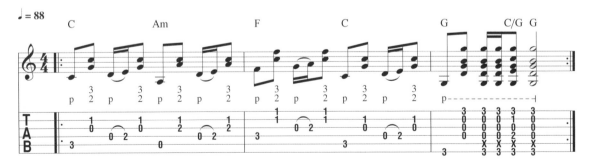

PROGRESSION 3

In this example, several embellishments are implemented to add harmonic and melodic interest to a basic E–A–B7–E (I–IV–V7–I) progression played in 6/8 time. The most notable embellishments are the hammer-on/pull-off figure at the end of measure 2 and the harmonic movement along string 1 of the B7 chord voicing and string 3 of the E chord.

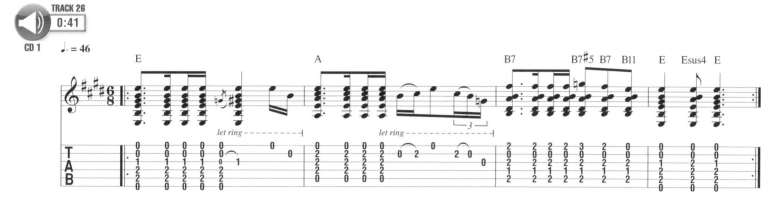

PROGRESSION 4

To spice up this D–Am–F–C–G (V–ii–VII–IV–I) progression, several legato passages are employed. Be sure not to rush the hammer-and-pull figure on beat 3 of the second measure, which should be performed in even 16th notes with your index and pinky fingers. In measure 4, voice the G chord with your ring and pinky fingers, which will put your index finger in position to play the C note (second string, fret 1) of the Gsus4 chord.

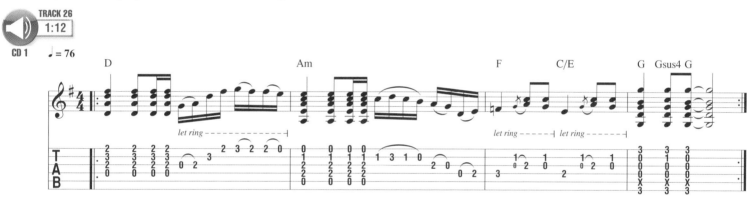

PROGRESSION 5

This example is essentially a review of several of the embellishments that were used in the first four progressions. Featuring a G–C–F–C–G (I–IV–♭VII–IV–I) progression, the figure commences with a hammer-and-pull figure and the quick G–C/G–G chord changes from Progressions 1 and 2. In measure 2, the Csus4 voicing makes another appearance, which is followed by an F–C/E–G progression that is similar to the one found at the end of Progression 4.

For additional practice, try to incorporate these embellishments into your own progressions or use them to spice up the chord changes to some of your favorite songs. Embellishments do not change the harmonic structure of a song; instead, they merely add interest to basic chord changes.

LESSON #27: SOLOING OVER STANDARD TURNAROUNDS (V–IV–I CHANGES)

A turnaround is a short chord sequence that occurs at the end of a song progression to signal a return to the top (beginning) of the tune. Turnarounds are found in a variety of musical genres, but are most evident in the chord progressions of blues, jazz, and country music. Typical turnarounds are two or four measures long and contain both the I chord and the V chord of the song's key. For example, in the key of C major (C–D–E–F–G–A–B), a standard turnaround would contain major chords built from the scale's first and fifth degrees, C and G, respectively.

Similar to blues music, country songs are often comprised of some variation of the I, IV, and V chords of the song's key (e.g., C, F, and G in the key of C major), which are played as either basic triads or as dominant seventh chords (C7, F7, and G7). Commonly found at the end of these progressions is a short V–IV–I turnaround (G–F–C in the key of C major), which is the basis of this lesson. To help you navigate these swift-moving changes, the following are five distinct approaches (pedal steel licks, single-note lines, banjo rolls, etc.) to soloing over a standard V–IV–I turnaround. Let's begin.

LICK 1

Wide-interval oblique-bend double stops are employed to outline this D–C–G turnaround progression. Pluck the entire figure with a combination of your pick and middle finger and be sure to alter your fingering on beat 4 of the second measure to effectively outline the I (G) chord.

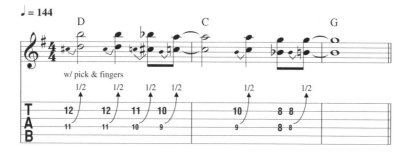

LICK 2

In this example, reverse banjo rolls are used to outline a G7–F7–C7 turnaround. For your pick hand, employ a repetitive ring-middle-pick combination. Also, because the G7 and F7 chord voicings are the same, the shape simply needs to be shifted down two frets.

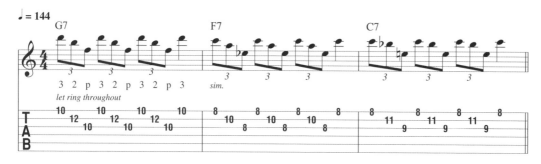

LICK 3

For this G–F–C turnaround, an oblique-bend pedal steel motif is established in fourteenth position for the G chord and shifted down to twelfth and seventh positions for the F and C chords, respectively.

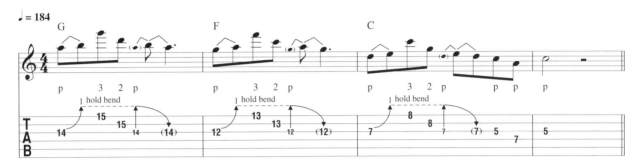

LICK 4

This example features a single-note line that employs open-chord licks exclusively. Notice that both the minor 3rd and the major 3rd are present in the licks for each chord change—D (F and F♯), C (E♭ and E), and G (B♭ and B)—a soloing device that is commonly used by country guitarists.

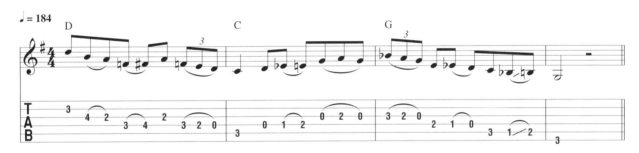

LICK 5

Another single-note line, this example establishes a melodic motif in measure 1 and restates it with slight variation in measure 2. An oblique bend is employed in measure 3 to outline the 3rd (B) and 5th (D) of the I (G) chord before resolving to the root note.

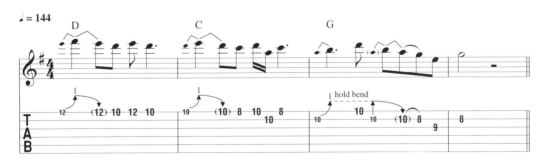

LESSON #28: WALKING BASS LINES

A common practice of rhythm guitarists in country music is to alternate chord tones (typically the root and 5th) on the bass strings on beats 1 and 3 of each measure to create a bass line while the chords are accented on the higher strings, on beats 2 and 4. Sometimes referred to as the "boom-chick" rhythm or "Carter strumming" (named after Maybelle Carter, the matriarch of the Carter Family country group), the popularity of this technique stems from the fact that it enables guitarists to simultaneously mimic cut-time bass lines and strum the chord changes.

Throughout the years, country guitarists have created variations on the basic root/5th pattern. One such variation is the incorporation of walking bass lines to connect one chord change with another. Walking bass lines are single-note lines that are typically derived from the song's key center (or chord's harmony) and played in a quarter-note rhythm. When combined with the boom-chick rhythm, walking bass lines impart a driving, propulsive feel to the song, especially in instances when the guitar is the sole rhythmic instrument.

In this lesson, we'll explore a few ways that walking bass lines can be incorporated into common Carter-strumming patterns. The first two examples focus on a standard approach to walking bass lines, while the latter two involve simultaneously playing a melody on the bass strings (in quarter notes, like a walking bass line) and accenting the chords on beat 2.

BASS LINE 1

In this example, each of the three chord changes (D, G, and A) employ the alternating root/5th bass line for one measure, followed by one measure of a walking bass line. Notice how the lines walk into the root note of each new chord by way of either a half step (one fret) or a whole step (two frets).

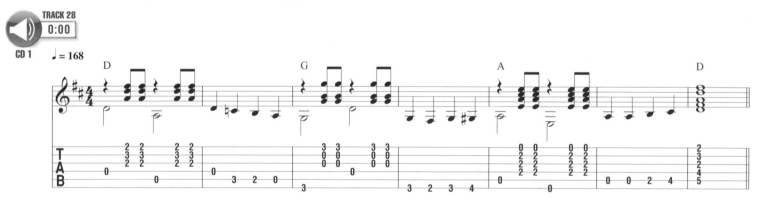

BASS LINE 2

This bass-line figure is a variation of the previous example. Here a D major chord, based on an open C chord, and six-string barre chords are used in lieu of open-position triads. In measure 1, keep the D chord voiced on strings 1–4 as you use your pinky to alternate between the fifth- and sixth-string bass notes.

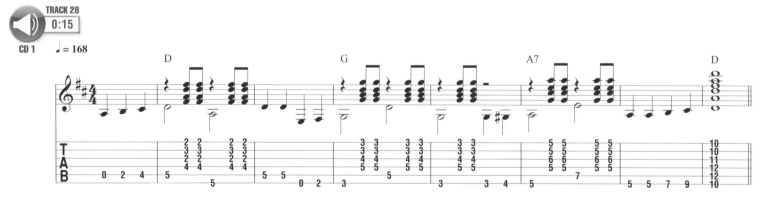

BASS LINE 3

This bass line is modeled after the Carter Family's version of "Wildwood Flower" and serves two roles: 1) it's the song's melody, and 2) it serves as the bass line. Notice how the chord voicings are strummed on beat 2 of each measure to emphasize the harmony. This approach is truly ingenious.

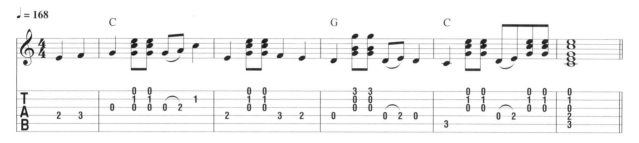

BASS LINE 4

Our final example takes the melody/bass line from the previous example and transposes it to a new key, G major. This rhythm technique works well in both keys (D major and G major) due to the presence of open strings in all of the chord voicings.

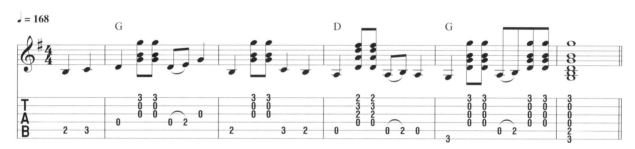

LESSON #29: SOLOING OVER I–VI PROGRESSIONS (MAJOR TO RELATIVE MINOR)

Country music songwriters make extensive use of diatonic progressions—chord changes that are entirely derived from one key center/scale. For example, the following chords are diatonic to the key of C major:

C major = I chord   D minor = ii chord   E minor = iii chord   F major = IV chord   G major = V chord

A minor = vi chord   B diminished = vii° chord

As you can see, C major (the I chord) and A minor (the vi chord) are diatonic—both chords are derived from the C major scale (C–D–E–F–G–A–B). In fact, A minor is the relative minor of C major. Although they contain different root notes, both chords share a common key signature (and thus, the same notes). Consequently, one scale can be used to solo over both chords, only the target notes (chord tones) must be altered depending on which chord is being played at a given time. Because of their diatonic relationship, major-key progressions in country music often contain the relative minor.

Relative Scales: the Country Composite and Blues Scales

Country guitarists often navigate the I–vi changes with the "country composite scale"—the major pentatonic scale with one chromatic passing tone, the minor 3rd. In the key of C, the scale is spelled: C–D–Eb–E–G–A. When the scale's notes are reordered so as to solo over the vi chord, starting from the sixth degree, A, the resultant scale becomes the composite scale's relative minor, the A blues scale (A–C–D–Eb–E–G).

C COUNTRY COMPOSITE SCALE

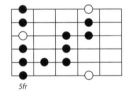

5fr

A BLUES SCALE

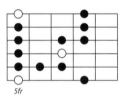

5fr

Examples

In this lesson, we'll take a look at five disparate approaches to soloing over the ubiquitous I–vi progression, from single-note lines to pedal steel bends to double-stop licks. Some of the examples put emphasis on the diatonic relationship of the I and vi chords, while others place more emphasis on practical soloing devices (bends, pull-offs, etc.) than on their theoretic relationship.

LICK 1

This double-stop figure requires just one slight finger adjustment to switch from outlining the C7 chord to outlining the Am chord. On string 4, the Bb note (the b7th of the C7) moves down one fret to A for the vi (Am) chord. The 5th-fret double stops and open strings lend continuity to the overall phrase.

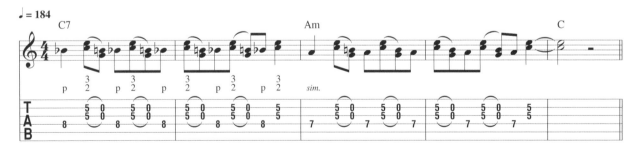

LICK 2

The following single-note line employs the C country composite scale (C–D–Eb–E–G–A) over the C chord and the A blues scale (A–C–D–Eb–E–G) over the Am chord. Notice that, although their orders are different, both scales contain the same notes (i.e., they're relative). In measure 3, notes from the C major scale are borrowed for the lick's resolution.

LICK 3

In this example, triple-stop pedal steel bends are employed to outline the D–Bm chord progression. Pluck the chord shapes with a combination of your pick, middle, and ring fingers, paying special attention to the distance of the bends. For the D major chord, the bend is a whole step (E to F♯, 2nd to major 3rd); for Bm, the bend is just a half step (C♯ to D, 2nd to minor 3rd).

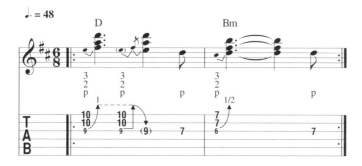

LICK 4

Major- and minor-6th intervals and the open high-E string comprise this four-measure lick, which outlines an E–C♯m–A–E (I–vi–IV–I) progression. Pluck strings 3 and 1 with your pick and middle finger, respectively. As for your fret hand, voice the notes on string 3 with your middle finger, alternating your ring and index fingers for the notes on string 1.

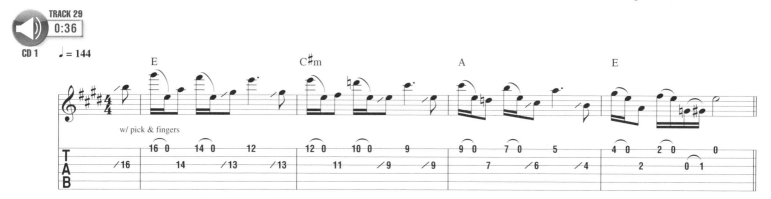

LICK 5

This lick is another example of utilizing relative scales to outline diatonic chord changes. Here, the A country composite scale (A–B–C–C♯–E–F♯) is employed for the A major chord, while the F♯ blues scale (F♯–A–B–C–C♯–E) is used over the F♯m chord. Again, both scales contain exactly the same notes.

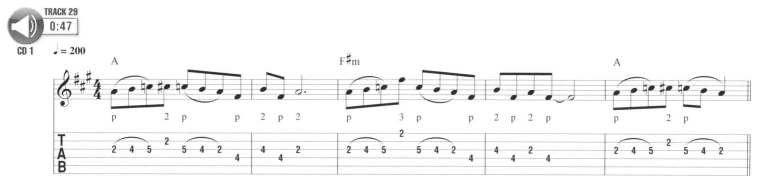

Once you feel comfortable with the relationship between the country composite scale and its relative blues scale, practice soloing over I–vi progressions in other keys. As the chord's change, all you need to do is refocus your attention on the new target notes. Use Lick 5 as a guide.

USING THE MIXOLYDIAN MODE TO SOLO OVER DOMINANT CHORDS

In country music, major chords dominate the chordal landscape. Coming in a close second, however, are dominant chords. Unlike major triads—three-note chords built from the root, third, and fifth degrees of their corresponding major scales—dominant chords are seventh chords, which contain four notes—the root, 3rd, 5th, and ♭7th.

The Mixolydian Mode

Country guitarists use several approaches to solo over dominant seventh chords, one of which involves the Mixolydian mode. The Mixolydian mode is a seven-note scale whose first note is the fifth note of its relative major scale. In other words, the Mixolydian mode contains exactly the same pitches as the major scale, only starting from different pitches. Here is the F major scale and the mode that is constructed from its fifth degree, C Mixolydian:

F Major

Pitches:	F	G	A	B♭	C	D	E
Scale Degrees:	1	2	3	4	5	6	7

C Mixolydian

Pitches:	C	D	E	F	G	A	B♭
Scale Degrees:	1	2	3	4	5	6	♭7

The unique aspect of the Mixolydian mode is the presence of a half step between the scale's sixth and seventh degrees (in the case of C Mixolydian, A and B♭), compared to the whole step that exists between the sixth and seventh degrees of the major scale (D and E in F major). This minor 7th pitch (B♭) is what makes the Mixolydian mode a perfect choice for soloing over dominant seventh chords (1–3–5–♭7). While its primary application is over V7 chords (e.g., C7 in the key of F major), the Mixolydian mode also works well over major triads due to the presence of the major 3rd. Consequently, the Mixolydian mode can be used over the I, IV, and/or V chords of country music, where those chords are typically major or dominant.

In this lesson, five licks, all derived from the C Mixolydian mode, are employed to solo over five C7 chord voicings that are played at various locations along the fretboard. Use the chord shapes to familiarize yourself with the target notes (chord tones), the licks' most important pitches, and the scale patterns to familiarize yourself with *all* of the pitches from which the licks are derived:

C MIXOLYDIAN MODE

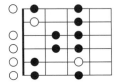 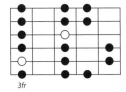 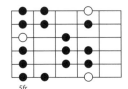 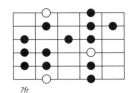 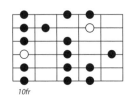

3fr   5fr   7fr   10fr

Examples

LICK 1

This open-position lick outlines a standard open-position C7 (V7) chord. All of the pitches are diatonic to the C Mixolydian mode and lead to the root note of the I chord, F. Don't rush the legato figures!

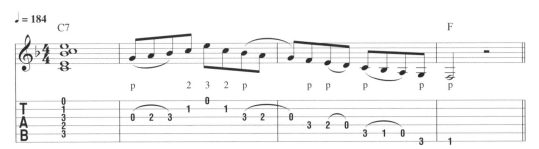

LICK 2

Here, C7 acts as the I chord, rather than the V7 chord. Beginning with a pre-bend, the phrase utilizes hammer-ons, pull-offs, and slides to descend the C Mixolydian mode in third position. This phrase incorporates one note that is not diatonic to the scale—Eb, the minor 3rd—a common soloing device in country.

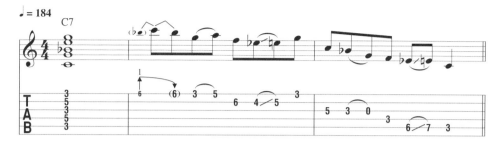

LICK 3

Another lick in which C7 plays the role of the I chord, this phrase is rooted in fifth position and employs an oblique bend and hammer-on passages to outline the chord's dominant harmony. For the bend, push the third string up with your middle finger, playing the stationary notes with your pinky and index fingers.

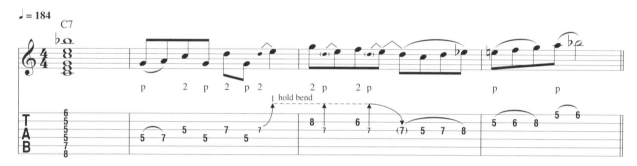

LICK 4

Double stops are the primary focus of this C7 lick. Perform the oblique pre-bend with your fret-hand's ring and pinky fingers, barring the 8th- and 10th-fret double stops with your index and ring fingers, respectively. Notice that, like Lick 2, both the minor 3rd (Eb) and major 3rd (E) are present in this example. Another cool characteristic of this lick is the final double stop, which forgoes the root note in favor of a Bb/E (b7th/3rd) dyad.

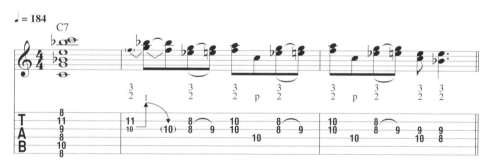

LICK 5

Here, the C7 once again is cast as the V7 chord. Similar to Licks 2 and 4, both the minor 3rd (Eb) and major 3rd (E) are implemented in this phrase, played on beat 1 of both measures 1 and 2. Similar to Lick 1, this example resolves to the root of the I (F) chord.

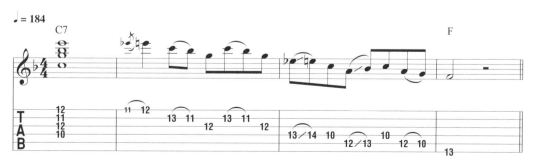

LESSON #31: 2ND-TO-3RD BENDS

Due to the preponderance of major-key songs, the major 3rd plays an important role in country music. After all, it's the major 3rd that defines the major quality of a chord or a song. The major 3rd is found in several popular scales in country music, including the major scale, major pentatonic, country composite (major pentatonic with a minor 3rd passing tone), and Mixolydian mode. The major 3rd lends a bright, "happy" sound to lead lines and can be played over both major triads (1–3–5) and dominant seventh chords (1–3–5–♭7).

Like the prevalence of the major 3rd, string bending has become a hallmark of country lead playing. What better way then to emphasize the major tonality of a chord or song than with a bend from the major 2nd to the major 3rd? A 2nd-to-3rd bend is *always* a whole step—a half-step bend will raise the pitch to the *minor* 3rd, imparting a bluesy, more somber (i.e., minor) sound to your licks. To locate the major 2nd of a given scale, simply slide up two frets from the root note. Let's take a look at five examples of the 2nd-to-3rd bend in action.

LICK 1

In this example, the 2nd-to-3rd bend is performed in two different octaves, played over an A major triad. In measure 1, an oblique bend outlines the A triad via two chord tones, C♯ (the 3rd) and E (the 5th). In measure 3, perform the 2nd-to-3rd bend with your fret-hand's index finger, bending the string from B to C♯, followed by resolution to the open A note.

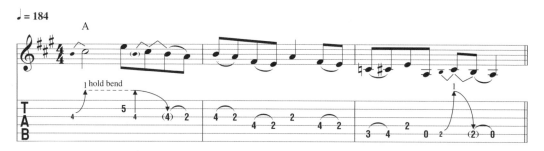

LICK 2

Played over a D major triad, this phrase is similar to Lick 1, as it contains both an oblique bend and a bass-string bend. Unlike Lick 1, however, the oblique-bend in this example features *two* stationary notes on the higher, adjacent string. In measure 3, a 2nd-to-3rd bend segues to a pull-off to the open D string.

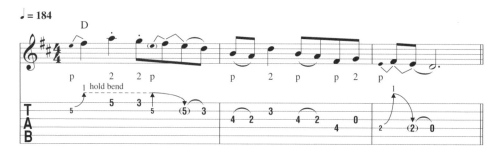

LICK 3

Bass-string bends drive this lick. In measure 1, the 2nd (A) is bent to the 3rd (B) on string 6, where it is held and re-attacked several times. After a climb up the G major pentatonic scale (G–A–B–D–E), an oblique bend caps the festivities.

LICK 4

This example features an oblique-bend motif that is established over the V7 (G7) chord in measure 1, restated over the IV (F) chord, and with a string shift and slight variation, played over the I (C) chord. Perform the first two bends with your fret-hand's middle finger, fretting the first-string notes with your pinky and ring fingers. In measure 3, perform the bend with your middle finger, playing the adjacent-string notes with your pinky and index fingers.

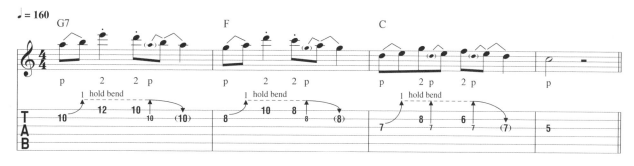

LICK 5

This slippery lick is played exclusively on the bass strings and features 2nd-to-3rd bends over each of the three chords, E7, D, and A. The bends in measures 1 and 3 are pre-bends—that is, the strings must be bent a whole step before they are articulated with your pick. Be sure not to rush the legato passage that leads into the D chord, which should be played in steady 8th notes.

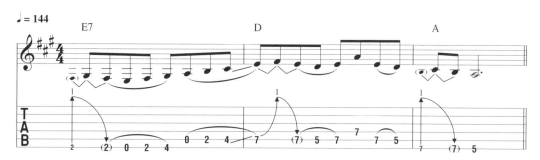

The 2nd-to-3rd bend can be easily incorporated into any of the major or dominant lead licks that you already know. Simply find the root, move your finger up a whole step (two frets) to the 2nd, and bend the string up a whole step to the 3rd. Good luck!

LESSON #32: LEGATO PLAYING

Legato playing is an indispensable technique for guitar players of all stripes, from rock and blues to jazz and of course, country. In music, legato is defined as successive notes played smoothly and connectedly. On the guitar, legato is typically achieved via three fret-hand techniques: hammer-ons, pull-offs, and slides. Legato technique can be applied to as few as two notes or, theoretically, can sustain a phrase indefinitely. When the three techniques are combined, pick- and fret-hand efficiency is achieved, resulting in smooth, flowing lines not achievable by strict alternate picking.

In this lesson, we'll explore several applications of slides, hammer-ons, and pull-offs to country licks. The objective of these licks is to demonstrate how legato affects the phrasing and sound of single-note lines and how hammer-ons, pull-offs, and slides can be seamlessly entwined with techniques that are fundamental to country guitar playing (double stops, bends, hybrid picking, etc.).

LICK 1

This phrase utilizes a rhythmic (triplet and two 8th notes) motif, pitches from the hybrid G major/G minor pentatonic scale, and a heavy dose of legato to create a smooth, descending open-chord lick.

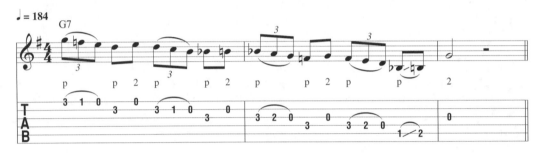

LICK 2

This figure kicks off with a whole-step bend/pull-off motif that is repeated as it shifts down one string set. Measure 2 features pull-offs that facilitate a shift from third position to open position and a half-step bend to the chord's root, G, to resolve the figure.

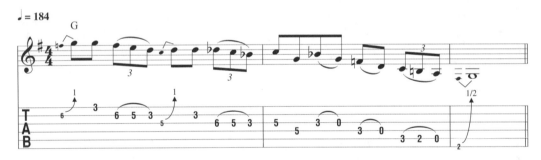

LICK 3

In this example, third-string legato passages are combined with first- and second-string double stops to create a flowing line that effectively outlines the C7 harmony. Use your pick to articulate the first note of each legato line and a combination of your fret-hand's middle and ring fingers for the double stops. Watch out for the triplet rhythm in measure 3, which follows a heavy helping of 8th notes.

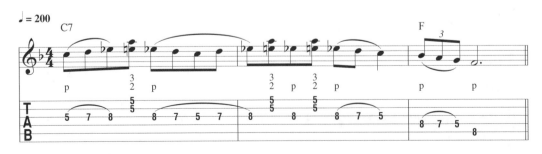

LICK 4

Like Lick 3, this phrase features a heavy dose of double stops; however, the double stops in this example are played along strings 2–3. In measure 1, a C#/E double stop (the 3rd and 5th of A7) is offset by a fourth-string legato line that slides back-and-forth between the root (A) and ♭7th (G). After the double stops make their way down the fretboard, a short, two-beat legato figure flows to the open A string to punctuate the phrase.

LICK 5

In this example, open-string pull-offs are used exclusively to outline a B7–A7–E7 (V7–IV7–I7) progression. The fretted notes emphasize chord tones, while the open high-E string lends continuity to the lick and reinforces its key center (E major).

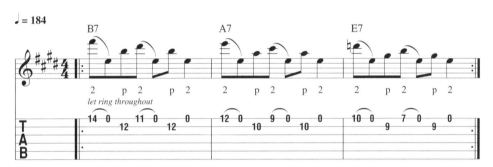

If legato isn't a regular part of your guitar technique, I highly recommended that you add it. In addition to learning the licks from this lesson, try adding slides, hammer-ons, and pull-offs to single-note lines that you regularly perform with alternate picking.

LESSON #33: POSITIONAL PLAYING

Every guitarist, regardless of musical style, should aspire to have total command of the fretboard—the ability to visualize the guitar's neck and instinctively navigate from one melodic idea to the next. Guitarists who move fluidly from one phrase to the next with nary a pause are players who have developed an effective approach to connecting musical thoughts.

Several approaches to visualizing and navigating the fretboard exist (scales, arpeggios, chord shapes, etc.); however, because not every guitarist learns the same, a "one size fits all" approach doesn't work. Consequently, it's prudent for every developing guitarist to experiment with the various concepts until he finds one that works best for him, supplementing it with other devices. Ultimately, the goal is to be able to play what you hear in your head in any position on the neck, without having to jump around the neck to connect your melodic creations.

Positional playing involves staying in one position of the fretboard while fluidly connecting several musical ideas. Although not desired in every situation, playing "in position" increases fret-hand efficiency and, in turn, speed! This lesson contains five licks that are played in position, as well as the devices (scales, chord shapes, etc.) from which the phrases are derived. Let's take a look.

LICK 1

This lick is played exclusively in open position and utilizes the following chord voicings to visualize and navigate the G–D7–C–G (I–V7–IV–I) chord changes:

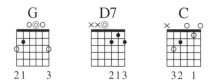

Use the shapes as a roadmap to guide your lines from chord to chord, paying particular attention to the root notes. The notes themselves are derived from the G country composite (G–A–Bb–B–D–E), D country composite (D–E–F–F#–A–B), and C Mixolydian (C–D–E–F–G–A–Bb) scales.

LICK 2

Similar to Lick 1, chord shapes (G/B, F/A, and C/E) guide this double-stop lick:

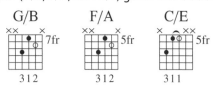

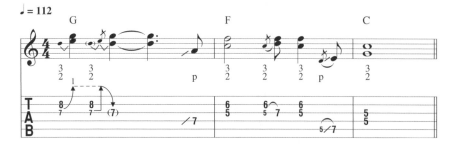

The phrase is played exclusively in fifth position and uses the chord shapes to form the double stops. Notice that the oblique bend (measure 1) and hammer-on (measure 2) briefly move their respective third-string pitches out of the framework of the chord shapes.

LICK 3

This lick is based on the D major pentatonic (D–E–F♯–A–B) and B minor pentatonic (B–D–E–F♯–A) scales, relative scales that share notes, and thus, the same pattern.

Played entirely in seventh position, this lick emphasizes chord tones in measures 1–2, with the root note of the Bm chord articulated four times. In measure 3, some adjustment is need to outline the A chord. Here, three notes that are not part of the D major/B minor pentatonic scale are included—C, C♯, and G.

LICK 4

This figure is based more on a pull-off pattern and open strings than on any scales or chord shapes. Notice that, as the pull-off pattern moves from the B7 (V7) chord to the A (IV) chord, the D♯ note (second string, fret 4) is replaced by D natural. The former is the 3rd of the B7 chord, while the latter is derived from the A major scale. In measure 3, notes are borrowed from the E Mixolydian mode (E–F♯–G♯–A–B–C♯–D) as the pattern descends to its ultimate destination—the open low-E string.

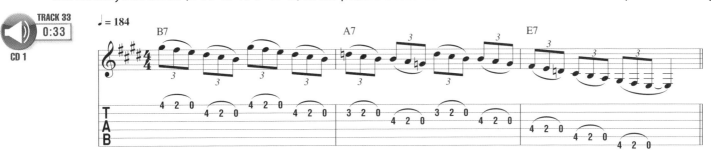

LICK 5

This lick, played exclusively in fifth position, derives its notes from a hybrid of the A major pentatonic (A–B–C♯–E–F♯) and A minor pentatonic (A–C–D–E–G) scales.

Hybrid A Major/A Minor Pentatonic Scale

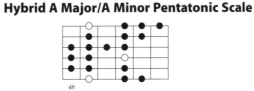

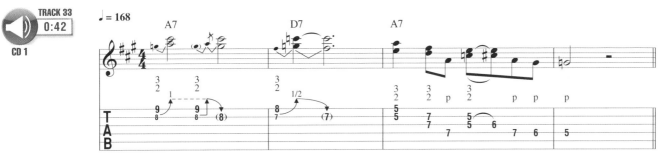

In measure 1, the A7 (I7) chord is outlined with an A/C♯ oblique-bend double stop, followed in measure 2 by an F♯/C oblique-bend double stop that emphasizes D7 (IV7) chord tones. Pay attention to each bend's distance—the first bend is a whole step, while the second is bent just a half step. After double stops descend the scale in measure 3, a chromatic passing tone (G♯) is used to connect the root note of the A7 chord (A) with its ♭7th (G).

LESSON #34: TARGETING CHORD TONES WITH PRE-BENDS

String bending is a vital component of the overall sound of the guitar, particularly in musical genres such as rock, blues, and country. What differentiates country string bending from that of blues or rock music, however, can be summed up in one word—accuracy. Unlike blues and rock, in which blending minor and major tonalities is often the goal, country bending involves precise, in-tune bending into—and out of—chord tones. In fact, the goal of much of country bending is to mimic the sound of the pedal steel guitar, which sometimes can mean bending strings to form complete major or minor triads. Therefore, much of country string bending revolves around accurate half- and whole-step bends, rather than the micro-tonal (i.e., quarter-step) bends that are frequently found in blues and rock.

In this lesson, we'll explore a string-bending technique that is quite popular among country guitarists—the pre-bend. A pre-bend involves bending a string to a desired pitch *before* the string is struck. That is, the pitch that you want to articulate is the destination note—not the initial, fretted pitch. The following five licks represent several ways to target chord tones with pre-bends to create fluid lines that sound right at home in any country setting.

LICK 1

This example employs a triple-stop pre-bend in measure 1 to mimic a pedal steel guitar and outline an A major triad (A–C#–E). After a few single notes, derived from the A major pentatonic scale (A–B–C#–E–F#), a half-step pre-bend targets the A chord's major 3rd, C#, before resolving to an A5 chord voicing.

LICK 2

This repetitive pre-bend lick is comprised entirely of D7 chord tones (D–F#–A–C). The pre-bend, framed by a second-string F# note (the 3rd) and fourth-string A note (the 5th), fluctuates between the ♭7th (C) and the root (D). Play the pre-bend with your index finger and the F# and A notes with your pinky and ring fingers, respectively.

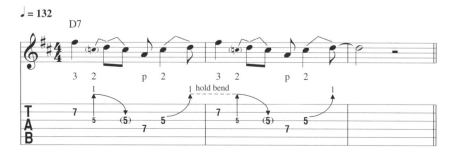

LICK 3

A pre-bend and multiple double stops are used to establish a melodic and rhythmic motif over the D (V) chord in measure 1, which is restated in tenth and fifth positions to outline the C (IV) and G (I) chords, respectively. Play all of the third-string notes with your pinky, employing your ring finger for the pre-bends.

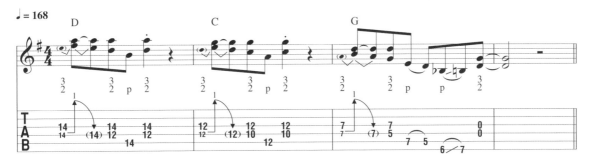

LICK 4

To outline the A7 chord, this lick begins with a pre-bent double stop that targets the chord's 3rd (C#) and 5th (E). At the end of measure 1, a half-step pre-bend targets the ♭7th (G) before being released and giving way to single notes that work their way down to a pre-bend on string 5, which also targets the A7 chord's 3rd, C#.

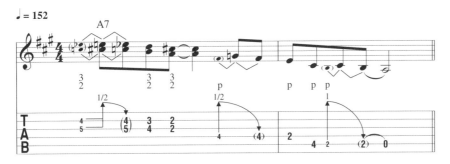

LICK 5

In this example, major- and minor-6th double stops are used exclusively to outline the G–C (V–I) chord progression. Double-stop pre-bends commence each of the two measures, targeting the 5th (D) and 3rd (B) of the G chord and the 5th (G) and the 3rd (E) of the C chord. Notice the extensive use of chromaticism in this figure.

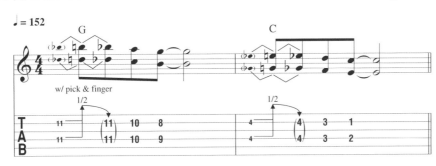

Beyond these five licks, a good way to practice pre-bends is to play a scale that you already know, replacing the fretted pitches with half- and/or whole-step pre-bends. The key is to make sure that each bend is accurate (i.e., that it matches the pitch of the fretted tone that it targets).

LESSON #35: PEDAL STEEL CHORD MELODIES

One instrument that contributes greatly to country music's instantly identifiable sound is the pedal steel guitar. It's no wonder then why country guitarists have been simulating its sound for generations. However, with only six strings to work with, guitarists are at a distinct disadvantage when trying to mimic the pedal steel's 8–14 strings and four levers, which can raise the string pitch by a half or whole step. Nonetheless, with a little ingenuity, country pickers have come up with some creative approaches to emulate the sounds of this distinctly country instrument throughout the years.

In this lesson, we'll focus on how a few common guitar techniques—bends, double stops, triple stops, and arpeggios—can be combined to create chord melodies that mimic the sound of the pedal steel guitar. As with all string bending in country music, pay close attention to the accuracy of your bends. Because country string bending involves chord tones, each bend must travel precisely a half or a whole step. Let's see them in action…

CHORD MELODY 1

This harmonic phrase involves bending the bottom (third-string) notes of double and triple stops to outline an E7–D7–A (V7–IV7–I) progression. In measures 1 and 2, the whole-step bends raise the pitch of each chord's ♭7th to its root and back again. In measure 3, the bottom note of a standard A triad is raised by a half step, briefly changing the chord's quality from major to suspended (Asus4). In measure 4, the third-string manipulation continues. Here, an A major triad is created by bending from the chord's 2nd (B) to its 3rd (C♯).

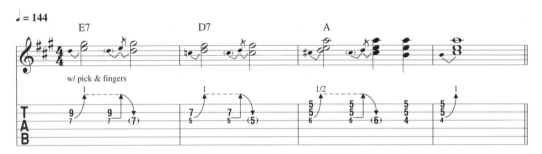

CHORD MELODY 2

The unique aspect of this example is that the whole-step bends are performed by pulling the strings downward (toward the floor), rather than upward. To execute each measure's arpeggio, voice all three of the fretted pitches simultaneously, picking the strings with a combination of your pick, middle finger, and ring finger and using your fret-hand's index finger to bend and release string 3. Be sure to let the strings ring out.

CHORD MELODY 3

This example employs double stops and triple stops, both common and uncommon, to outline a D–A–G–D (I–V–IV–I) progression. In measures 1 and 2, common chord shapes are manipulated with half- and whole-step bends to weave out of—and back into—the basic triad harmonies. In measure 3, oblique-bend double stops imply harmonic movement of G6 to G5, followed in measure 4 by a half-step triple-stop bend that spells out a first-inversion D major triad (F#–A–D).

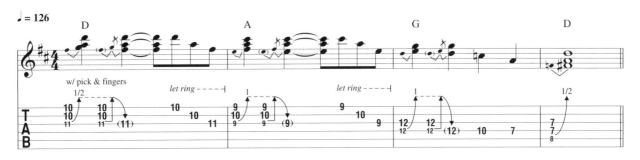

CHORD MELODY 4

Triple stops played along strings 1–3 are used exclusively to create a chord melody that outlines a G–D7–C–G (I–V7–IV–I) harmony. To perform the whole-step bends in measures 1 and 3, voice the chords from top to bottom with your index, pinky, and ring fingers, reinforcing the bend with your middle finger. For the D7 chord, fret the voicing from top to bottom with your ring, middle, and index fingers. Be sure to keep the non-bent notes stationary while executing the third-string bends.

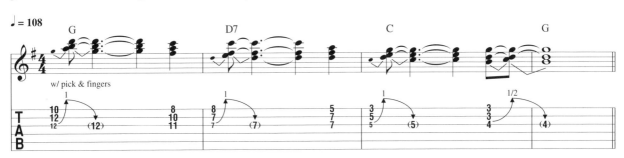

CHORD MELODY 5

This example is similar to Chord Melody 2, only the chord voicings here are plucked with your pick and fingers, rather than arpeggiated. The first three bends should be performed with a downward (toward-the-floor) bend, while the final bend must be bent upward (toward the ceiling) to avoid clashing with the stationary tones.

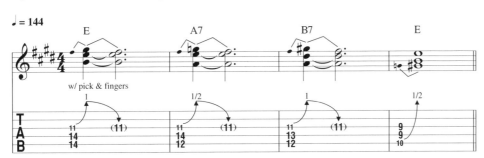

LESSON #36: FAUX G-BENDER LICKS

In 1967, Gene Parsons and Clarence White of the country-rock group the Byrds created a device that would become known as the B-Bender—a mechanical device that enables the user to raise the pitch of his guitar's B string by a whole step, to C♯, by pushing down on the neck. The advent of the B-Bender made it easier for players to simulate the sound of the pedal steel guitar and perform string bends that were otherwise impossible.

An offshoot of the B-Bender, the G-Bender enables the user to raise the pitch of his guitar's G string by a whole step, to A, and has become increasingly popular among country guitarists, including superstar Brad Paisley. The popularity of the G-Bender is no doubt due to the abundance of pedal steel bends that incorporate the guitar's G string.

While a G-Bender can alleviate some of the finger stress that results from performing pedal steel licks, possessing a guitar that is equipped with one is not requisite to perform these licks. With that in mind, this lesson presents five faux G-Bender licks—five phrases that substitute the G-Bender with good old-fashioned string bending to simulate the sound of the pedal steel guitar.

LICK 1

This open-position lick works a whole-step G-string pre-bend into its descending pattern. The notes are derived from a hybrid of the E major pentatonic (E–F♯–G♯–B–C♯) and E blues (E–G–A–B♭–B–D) scales.

LICK 2

This lick is a nod to Brad Paisley and requires some extra fret-hand strength. To outline the first F chord, use your index finger to bend the G string a whole step, holding it while the second-string F note is struck. The result is a C/F double stop. In measures 2 and 3, employ your fret-hand's ring and pinky fingers for the oblique-bend double stops.

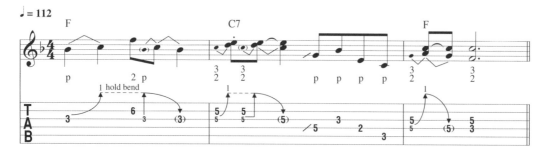

LICK 3

Here, a G-string pivot-note bend is held while notes descend the C Mixolydian mode (C–D–E–F–G–A–B♭) along strings 1–2. Bend the G string with your fret-hand's middle finger, using your pinky and index fingers to play the stationary notes.

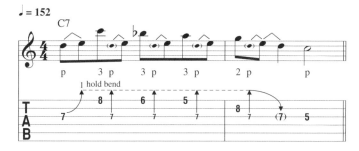

LICK 4

In this example, an oblique-bend pedal steel motif is established over the E (V) chord and restated over the D (IV) chord. In measure 3, a variation of the motif, including an additional stationary note on string 2, emphasizes tones from the A (I) chord. Perform the bends with your ring finger (reinforcing it with your middle and index fingers), playing the second-string notes with your pinky and index fingers.

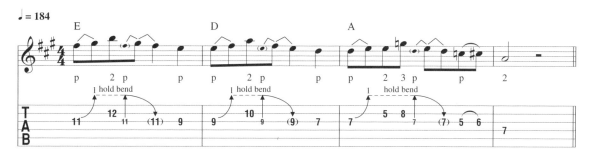

LICK 5

This lick employs whole-step G-string bends and wide-interval shapes to descend strings 1 and 3 and outline a D7–A7 (IV7–I7) chord progression. In measures 1–3, bend the G string with your fret-hand's index finger, voicing the first-string notes with your pinky. In measure 4, perform the bend with your middle finger, fretting the stationary notes on string 1 with your pinky and index fingers.

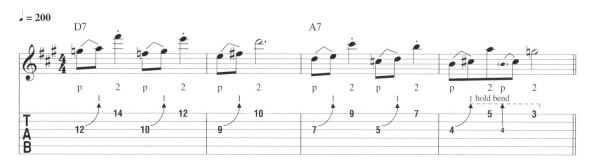

LESSON #37: COUNTRIFIED BOOGIE PATTERNS

The sound of modern country guitar has been shaped and influenced by a variety of musical styles, everything from jazz and bluegrass to rock and blues. The influence of bluegrass is most apparent in the popularity of open-position playing and the incorporation of opens strings into lead lines. Similarly, the prevalence of hybrid picking and chromaticism are in part due to the influence of jazz. And the increasingly common use of distortion and Drop D tuning in contemporary country? Yep—rock.

Like jazz, bluegrass, and rock, the blues has had a significant impact on country music, as well. In addition to its influence on lead playing, the blues also has shaped country rhythm guitar, especially the incorporations of boogie-woogie patterns. In this lesson, we'll explore several ways to "countrify" blues-based boogie patterns.

BOOGIE PATTERN 1

Several aspects of this boogie pattern give it a country feel, including the fast tempo (152 bpm), the single-note pattern (in lieu of dyads, common in blues), and the incorporation of both the minor 3rd and the major 3rd over both chords (E and A).

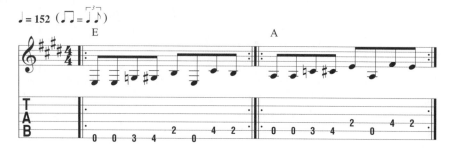

BOOGIE PATTERN 2

This example is an offshoot of Pattern 1. Here, the second note of the pattern has been transposed up one octave, moving it from the open low-E string to fret 2 of the D string. You can pluck this new note either with your pick or with the middle finger of your pick hand (i.e., with hybrid picking).

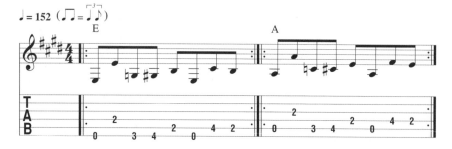

BOOGIE PATTERN 3

This example borrows its first measure from Pattern 2 and features a popular country guitar technique in measure 2— matching fretted pitches with open strings. Here, a slide from C♯ to D on the fifth string is matched with the open D string (the pattern is moved up one string set for the A chord).

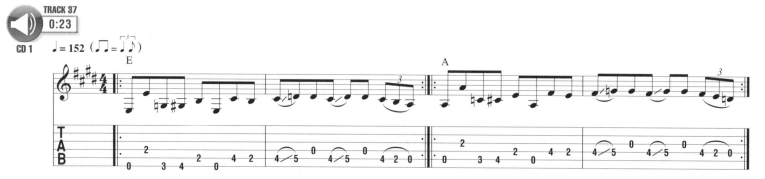

BOOGIE PATTERN 4

A variation of Patterns 1–3, this two-measure figure climbs the E country composite scale (the major pentatonic scale with a minor 3rd passing tone) in measure 1 before working its way back down the scale in measure 2. Be sure to hold the E note at fret 2 of the fourth string as the pattern moves from measure 1 to measure 2. Shift the pattern up one string set for the A major chord.

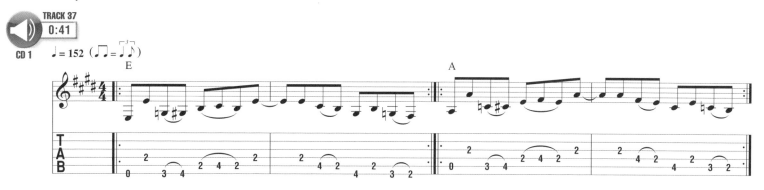

BOOGIE PATTERN 5

This boogie pattern is influenced by Chicago blues legend Buddy Guy. Although played as double stops, with your thumb fretting the root notes on string 6, you can hear the skeleton pattern by playing the first two root notes, followed by the bottom note of each double stop. The double stops and the inclusion of both the major 3rd and the minor 3rd "countrify" the pattern, as does the use of a hybrid-picking pattern, which is notated between the notation and tab staves.

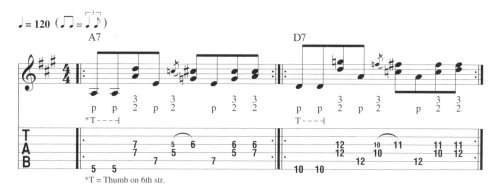

*T = Thumb on 6th str.

Bluegrass and jazz has had a profound effect on the lead playing of modern country guitarists. For a prime example of their influence, look no further than the extensive use of chromaticism in country solos—a common melodic approach in bluegrass and jazz. Chromaticism means to use a series of notes, each separated by a semitone (one fret). Chromatic lines contain scale tones and non-scale tones alike. In country, a common chromatic practice is to blend two different scales to create one composite scale, resulting in various chromatic passages within the new "hybrid" scale.

In this lesson, we'll take a look at five licks that exemplify how country guitarists construct chromatic single-note lines. The first two examples are chromatic "open-chord" licks that are inspired by bluegrass players, while the last three figures are performed further up the neck and contain distinct jazz qualities.

LICK 1

This descending C major lick is comprised of three separate chromatic passages. The first passage, E–Eb–D, opens the lick and contains an open (E) string and two fretted pitches (Eb and D). The second passage is an A–Ab–G passage that crosses the bar line, moving from measure 1 to measure 2. The triplet in measure 2 contains the third passage, E–Eb–D, which is a restatement of the opening chromatic series, only it's played here an octave lower.

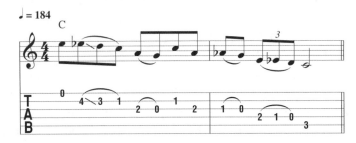

LICK 2

Another open-chord lick, this example is played over a G major triad and contains two separate chromatic lines. The first chromatic passage, Db–C–B–Bb–A, begins in measure 1 (on the "and" of beat 3) and flows into the opening triplet of measure 2. The second chromatic series, B–Bb–A, is played on beat 3 of the second measure and represents the 2nd (A), minor 3rd (Bb), and major 3rd (B) of the G key center.

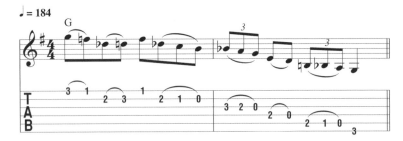

LICK 3

The notes that comprise this chromatic lick are derived exclusively from the D country composite scale (D–E–F–F♯–A–B). The country composite scale is the major pentatonic scale with one chromatic passing tone, the minor 3rd. Here, a seven-note pattern containing one chromatic passage (E–F–F♯) is played in two octaves.

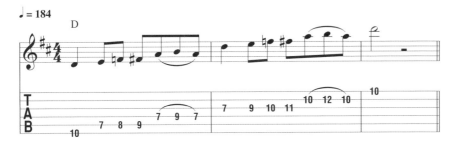

LICK 4

This lick abounds with chromatic lines and would feel right at home in either a country or a jazz setting. Once you are able to play this example with straight 8th notes, switch to a shuffle rhythm (swung 8ths) to hear how it would sound in a jazz or Western swing context. Notice that the phrase ends on the ♭7th (G) of the A7 chord, rather than the root. This approach is common in blues and jazz music.

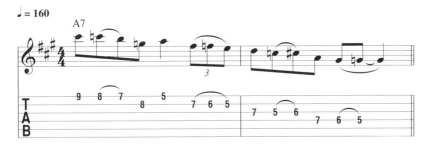

LICK 5

The pre-bend in measure 1 lends this lick a distinct pedal steel feel. After a descending chromatic line, B–B♭–A (the 5th, ♭5th, and 4th of E major), and pre-bend/release, a C♯–C–B chromatic passage (the 3rd, ♭3rd, and 2nd of A major) takes over in measure 2. The phrase ultimately resolves to the root note of the I (A) chord.

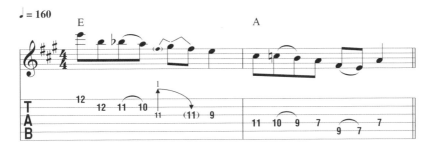

LESSON #39: MULTI-OCTAVE MELODIC MOTIFS

When it comes to playing solos, guitarists often get so caught up in the technical, or "flashy," components of playing lead (scales, arpeggios, sweep picking, etc.) that we sometimes forget to focus on what is most important—the audience. While technical prowess certainly is impressive, showcasing too much of it within the context of a short solo will lose your audience's attention. On the other hand, solos that are equal parts style (flash) and substance (melody) will leave your audience wanting more.

If your goal is to create solos that your audience will remember, then go heavy on melody—give them something to latch onto, something to hum in the shower. One approach to melodic soloing is to establish a motif early in the solo and restate it in multiple octaves to reinforce the idea. A motif is simply a short melodic, rhythmic, or harmonic phrase that acts as the solo's "theme" and is often restated at random points throughout the lead. In this lesson, we'll focus on melodic motifs and how they can be restated in multiple octaves along the fretboard. The following are five disparate examples to get you acclimated to the concept.

LICK 1

This example is derived entirely from the extended G major pentatonic scale (G–A–B–D–E), with the addition of one chromatic pitch, B♭, resulting in a hybrid scale known as the "country composite scale." Notice how the eight-note phrase is restated twice as it shifts from tenth position to seventh position, and finally, to fifth position.

LICK 2

Similar to Lick 1, this example derives its notes exclusively from the extended E major pentatonic scale (E–F♯–G♯–B–C♯) to create a pre-bend/legato phrase that ascends the neck from open position to seventh position. In measure 4, a G♯/D double stop caps the lick, reinforcing the lick's E7 (E–G♯–B–D) harmony.

LICK 3

Like Lick 2, the extended E major pentatonic scale provides the pitches for this five-note multi-octave motif. Use a combination of your pick and middle finger to articulate the phrase (the picking pattern is indicated between the notation and tab staves).

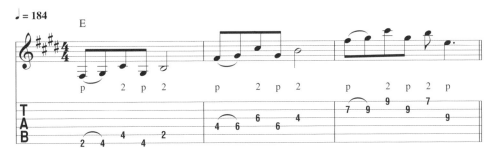

LICK 4

Here, a pedal steel-style lick is employed to outline the D major harmony. In measure 1, single notes and a pre-bend and release are used to create a four-note motif, which is restated an octave lower in measure 2. Although a slide is utilized in lieu of the pre-bend to cap the lick, the four-note motif remains intact.

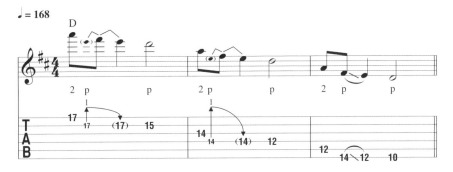

LICK 5

This lick works well at the end of a solo—in this case, a solo that ends with a G major chord. Here, a four-note motif is comprised of a triplet-based hammer-on and a wide-interval jump to a non-adjacent string to sound the root note (G). Articulate the hammer-ons with your pick, plucking the higher non-adjacent string with your pick-hand's middle finger.

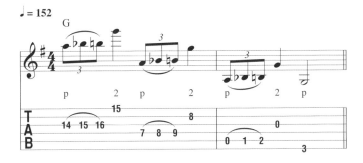

Although the motifs in these examples are played at a brisk tempo, their repetitive nature is sure to grab your audience's attention. To make them even more effective, repeat the motifs at random points throughout your solo, altering them to work over other chord qualities.

LESSON #40: STRING-SKIPPING LICKS

Though most often associated with rock and metal, string skipping comes in quite handy while performing country licks. As the name implies, string skipping is a guitar technique that involves bypassing one or more strings while moving from one string to another, either higher or lower. The act of moving to a non-adjacent string creates a wider interval between successive notes, and in the process, lends melodic interest to lead lines.

Unlike rock and metal, where string skipping is typically performed exclusively with the guitar pick, most string skipping in country involves hybrid picking—a combination of the pick and middle, ring, and pinky fingers. In this lesson, we'll explore several applications of string skipping in country, including pedal steel licks, double-stop licks, and legato phrases.

LICK 1

Although this phrase has a bit of a rock feel, the scale of choice, the C country composite scale (C–D–Eb–E–G–A), gives it a distinct country sound. Articulate the third-string legato passages with your pick, plucking the first- and second-string notes with your pick-hand's ring and middle fingers, respectively.

LICK 2

This lick is a nod to British country guitarist Albert Lee, who is known to incorporate this type of chicken pickin' phrase to his single-note lines. Fret the third-string notes with your index, middle, and ring fingers, grabbing the initial first-string note with your middle finger, and the subsequent first-string notes with your pinky. As for your pick hand, use alternate picking for the triplet figures, plucking the first-string notes with your ring finger.

*⊓ = downstroke, V = upstroke

LICK 3

This example presents an approach to double stops that is quite popular among country guitarists. Here, double stops, plucked with your pick-hand's middle and ring fingers, descend strings 1–2 while pedal tones, articulated with your pick, are played on a non-adjacent string—in this case string 4.

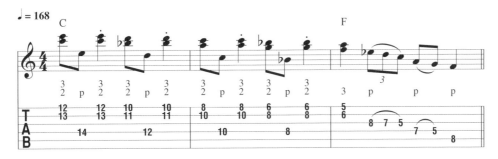

LICK 4

A common technique for simulating a pedal steel guitar, this example involves outlining an E7–D7–A (V7–IV7–A) progression with non-adjacent oblique bends. While your fret-hand's middle finger holds the whole-step bends, employ your pinky and index fingers to voice the notes on string 1. This fingering approach should be used for the bends in each of the three measures.

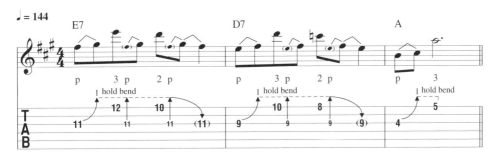

LICK 5

This two-bar A7 lick is played mostly with double stops and features string skipping in both measures. Pluck each of the double stops with your pick-hand's middle and ring fingers, using your pick for the single notes.

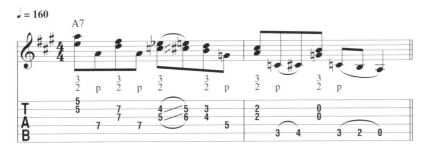

LESSON #41: BASS-STRING LICKS

The guitar's bass strings have long been a fixture in country music. In fact, country artists and producers have, throughout the years, incorporated the baritone guitar into their songs to fill the sonic void that exists between a standard-tuned guitar and the bass guitar. In addition to adding low end to a song, bass strings, particularly when played as open strings, increase its overall "twang"—the low-end jangle that is highly coveted in country music. Prime examples of the power of bass strings can be found in the main riff to Alan Jackson's country classic "Chattahoochee" (played by Brent Mason), as well as in nearly every solo by Brad Paisley, who's a strong proponent of the guitar's low-end capabilities.

In this lesson, we'll take a look at five bass-string licks. For maximum effect, all of the phrases are played in open position and incorporate a healthy dose of open strings.

LICK 1

This phrase incorporates all three of the guitar's bass strings (E, A, and D) and derives its notes from a hybrid of the E major pentatonic (E–F♯–G♯–B–C♯) and E blues (E–G–A–B♭–B–D) scales. In measure 2, notice how G-to-G♯ (minor 3rd-to-major 3rd) legato passages are offset by iterations of the root note, E, which are played in two different octaves.

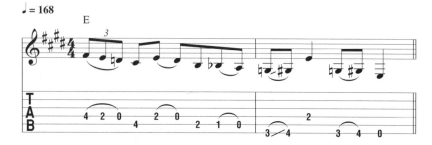

LICK 2

This A major lick is constructed from the A country composite scale (A–B–C–C♯–E–F♯), which simply is the A major pentatonic scale with a chromatic passing tone, the minor 3rd (C). You can play this phrase exclusively with your pick or with a combination of your pick and middle finger (for the fourth-string notes).

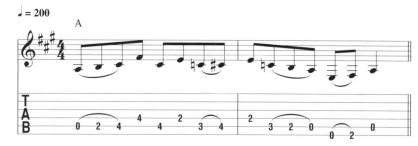

LICK 3

This D major lick flows from the open D string to the low-E string and back again. The phrase derives its notes from the D major pentatonic (D–E–F♯–A–B) and D minor pentatonic (D–F–G–A–C) scales and includes one passing tone, B♭, which creates a chromatic line between the scale's 6th (B) and 5th (A).

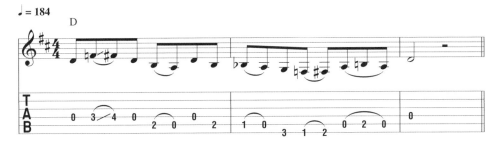

LICK 4

Although technically not a bass note, this example begins on the open G string. From there, the phrase, derived from a hybrid of the G major pentatonic (G–A–B–D–E) and G minor pentatonic (G–B♭–C–D–F) scales, incorporates several hammer-ons and pull-offs to flow across the bass strings to its destination, the sixth-string root (G) note.

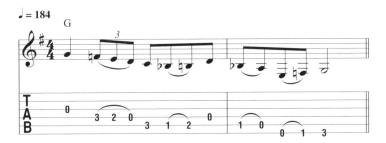

LICK 5

Commencing with a pair of pull-offs, this bass-string lick effectively outlines the C major harmony via notes from the C country composite scale (C–D–E♭–E–G–A), with heavy emphasis on chord tones (C–E–G). Experiment with this example's phrasing, moving the hammer-ons and pull-offs to different notes/beats—or not using them at all!

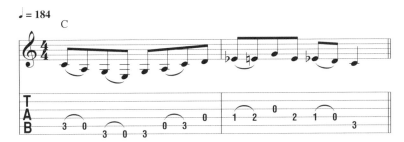

LESSON #42: COMBINING DOUBLE STOPS AND SINGLE-NOTE LINES

With the exception of pedal steel bends, nothing imparts a country sound to guitar licks more than double stops. A double stop is simply two notes played simultaneously—a technique that has become a staple of country guitar playing. While double stops can be articulated with a pick, country guitarists typically favor hybrid picking (a combination of pick and fingers), which enables greater speed, precision, and efficiency.

Common Double-Stop Shapes

In this lesson, we'll take a look at five licks that seamlessly combine double stops and single-note lines. Before we get started, the following are a few common double-stop shapes, or intervals—the distance between two notes.

STRING PAIRS 1–2, 3–4, 4–5 & 5–6

Note: These intervals, shown here on strings 1–2, can be transferred to every other string pair except strings 2–3.

STRINGS 2–3

Examples

LICK 1

This lick is played over a C major chord and consists of a double-stop passage that requires holding a note on string 1 while a G–Gb–F sequence descends string 2. Fret the initial double stop with your ring and pinky fingers, performing the pull-off with your middle and index fingers and repositioning your ring finger so as to fret the third-string Eb note. The figure is repeated in measure 2.

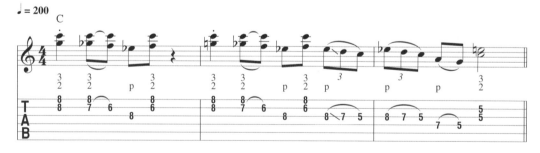

LICK 2

Several interval shapes (minor 3rd, major 3rd, perfect 4th, etc.) are incorporated into the next descending phrase, which derives its notes from a hybrid of the C major pentatonic (C–D–E–G–A) and C blues (C–Eb–F–Gb–G–Bb) scales. Perform the initial double-stop slide with your fret-hand's ring and pinky fingers, thereby freeing up your index finger for the subsequent 8th-fret double stop.

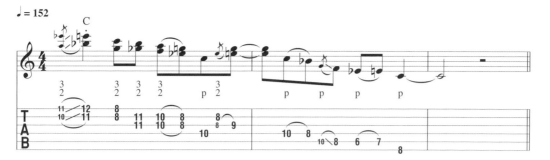

LICK 3

The sound of this lick lies somewhere between country and R&B. While the opening pedal steel-style bend is distinctly country, the double stops are influenced by R&B and soul. Notice that the hammer-ons and slide are ghost notes; therefore, they should be played swiftly, with no rhythmic value.

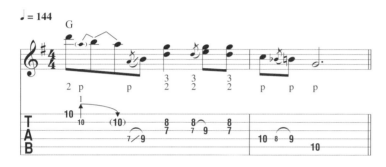

LICK 4

In measure 1 of this example, an oblique-bend double stop emphasizes the 3rd (B) and 5th (D) tones of the G major chord before giving way to double stops that are based on perfect 4th and perfect 5th intervals. In measure 2, a single-note line derived from the G major pentatonic scale (G–A–B–D–E) loosely mimics the double-stop motif from measure 1.

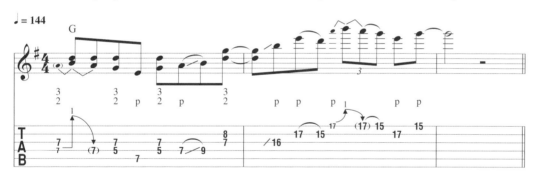

LICK 5

This example features a classic country double-stop riff. The pattern is first established over the E (V) chord, and then shifted down the fretboard to outline the D (IV) chord. In measure 3, the double-stop shape (minor 3rd) moves chromatically down strings 2–3 before giving way to a descending single-note line that resolves to the open A string.

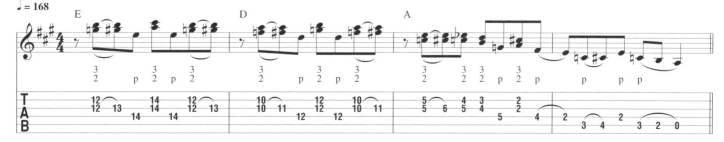

LESSON #43: COMBINING 3RDS AND SINGLE-NOTE LINES

One of the most commonly used intervals in country solos is the 3rd. An interval is the distance between two notes, labeled with its quality (minor, major, perfect, etc.) and a number that represents the distance (scale degrees) between the two pitches (3rd, 5th, 7th, etc.). The two notes that comprise an interval can be played either sequentially or simultaneously. The most common application of the 3rd interval in country music is to play the two notes simultaneously—that is, as a double stop. When major and minor 3rd shapes are combined with single notes, long, elaborate lines can be constructed to outline chord changes.

In this lesson, major 3rd and minor 3rd interval shapes are integrated with single notes to create five licks that demonstrate how the two elements can effectively outline static chords, as well as common chord progressions.

Minor 3rd and Major 3rd Interval Shapes

First, let's take a look at how the shapes are voiced on each string pair.

STRING PAIRS 1–2, 3–4, 4–5 & 5–6

Note: These shapes, shown here on strings 1–2, can be transferred to every other string pair except strings 2–3.

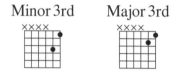

STRINGS 2–3

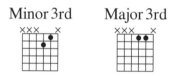

Examples

LICK 1

This example employs major and minor 3rd shapes to create a double-stop phrase that ascends strings 2–3. In measure 2, single-note minor 3rds lead into an oblique-bend passage that resolves to the root note (A) at fret 10 of the second string.

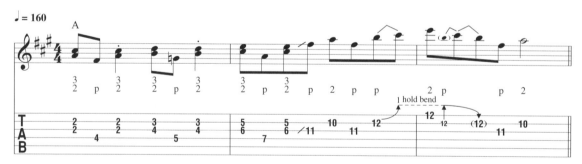

LICK 2

The following E major lick features double-stop 3rds that are executed with "chicken pickin'"—a combination of hybrid picking and string mutes. After the double stops are plucked with a combination of your pick-hand's middle and ring fingers—and, as is the case with the first double stop, slid—simply release finger pressure and mute string 2 with your ring finger, plucking the mute with your pick.

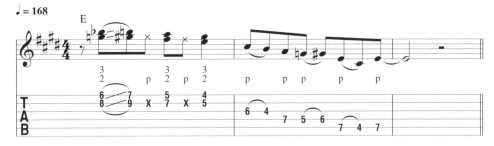

LICK 3

As this lick kicks off, double-stop 3rds are offset with the open G string to emphasize the phrase's G7 tonality. In measure 2, more double stops are employed—this time, along strings 2 and 3—to create a phrase that is quite common in country lead playing.

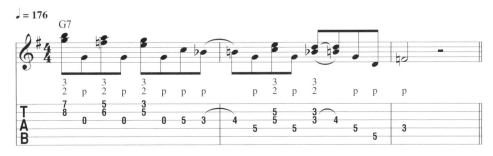

LICK 4

In this example, major and minor 3rd shapes are played along strings 1–2 as single notes, effectively outlining the C7 harmony. The phrase commences with a C/E dyad that is comprised of the chord's root and major 3rd and ends with a G/B♭ shape (the 5th and ♭7th). In measure 3, the lick concludes with a pair of major 3rd double stops that are played on strings 2–3.

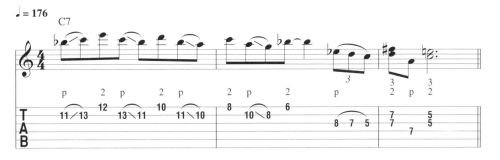

LICK 5

Played over a D7–G7–D7 (I7–IV7–I7) progression, this example incorporates elements from Licks 2 and 3 to create a line that crosses over all six strings before resolving to the root of the D7 chord. After a chicken-pickin' double-stop phrase, the lick shifts down a string set for major and minor 3rd shapes that outline the G7 chord—a phrase that is simulated in the next measure for the return of the D7 chord.

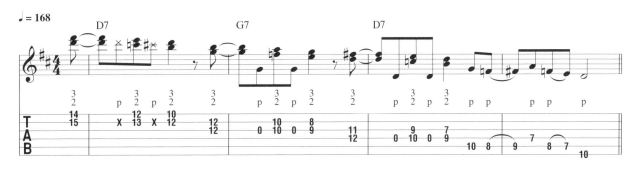

COMBINING 6THS AND SINGLE-NOTE LINES

If major and minor 3rds are the most popular intervals among country guitarists, then 6ths are a close second. By definition, an interval is the distance between two notes. An interval is labeled both with its quality (minor, major, perfect, etc.) and with a number that represents the distance (scale degrees) between the two pitches (3rd, 5th, 7th, etc.).

On the guitar, intervals can be played either sequentially or simultaneously. Although major and minor 3rds are typically played as double stops in country music, the ratio of single notes to double stops among major and minor 6ths tends to be fairly equal. When 6ths are combined with single-note lines, the results are licks with an inherently country sound.

In this lesson, major and minor 6th interval shapes are combined with scale tones to create countrified licks that effectively outline static chords, as well as common chord progressions.

Minor 6th and Major 6th Interval Shapes

Before we get started, here is how the shapes are voiced on each string pair:

STRINGS 1 & 3 AND 2 & 4

Note: These shapes, shown here on strings 1 and 3, can be transferred to strings 2 and 4.

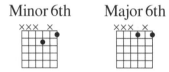

STRINGS 3 & 5 AND 4 & 6

Note: These shapes, shown here on strings 3 and 5, can be transferred to strings 4 and 6.

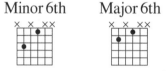

Examples

LICK 1

This example begins with a simple, descending 6ths passage that is heavy on D major (D–F#–A) chord tones, starting with an A/F# dyad (the 5th and 3rd, respectively) on beat 1 and ending on an F#/D shape (3rd and root) that is played as single notes. Pluck the 6ths with a combination of your pick (string 3) and your middle finger (string 1) and reposition your hand for the pre-bend, which should be executed with your fret-hand's ring finger.

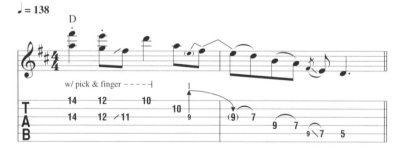

LICK 2

The minor 6th shape, played in the next lick along strings 2 and 4, provides the framework for a common approach to soloing over dominant seventh chords. Here, the top note of the first minor 6th shape, G, shifts down to F, the ♭7th of the G7 chord. In addition to country, this root-to-♭7th movement is commonly found in jazz and blues music as well.

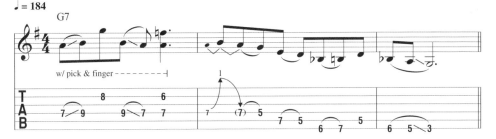

LICK 3

In this example, major and minor 6ths descend strings 3 and 5, leading to a whole-step bend/release, which also happens to be the top note of the final double stop. This bend should be performed by pulling the string downward (toward the floor) for two reasons: 1) to ease its execution, and 2) to avoid interfering with the lower, fifth-string note.

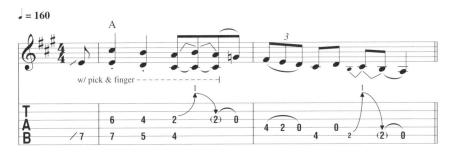

LICK 4

This lick exemplifies how 6ths can be arranged to seamlessly transition from one chord to the next. Here, the I–IV–I progression is effectively outlined with 6ths that are diatonic to their respective chords, particularly the A/F (3rd and root) and D/B♭ (3rd and root) shapes that lead into the F and B♭ chords, respectively. The lick concludes with a short single-note line that would feel right at home in a blues tune.

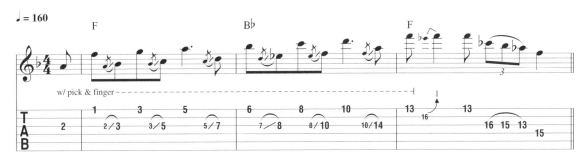

LICK 5

In this example, major and minor 6th shapes are used to create a melodic motif that is played over the F (IV) chord and then shifted down the neck and restated over the C (I) chord. The fretboard shift puts your fret hand in position to play the open-chord lick that resolves the phrase. Notice that the last 6th shape is also part of the voicing to an open C chord.

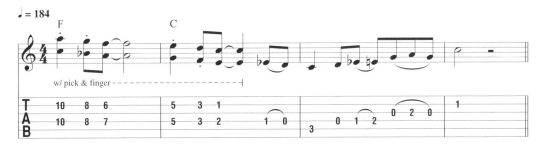

LESSON #45: CONSTRUCTING A GUITAR SOLO: KEY OF C MAJOR

Learning licks is important for any aspiring lead guitarist. After all, one cannot become an effective lead player without some melodic ideas at his disposal. At the same time, players often get preoccupied with learning new phrases that work over a particular chord or are derived from a specific scale, failing to properly apply those licks to an actual solo. It's one thing to know how to play a bunch of licks, but it's quite another to know how to connect those ideas and play them over moving chord changes.

In this lesson, we'll deconstruct a 12-bar country solo in the key of C major to examine how several licks can be strung together to effectively solo over a standard arrangement of I (C), IV (F), and V (G) chords. This solo is played exclusively in open position and is modeled after bluegrass lead playing. Let's get started.

MEASURES 1–4 (I CHORD)

The solo kicks off with a ubiquitous bluegrass-style run that is based on the open C major chord, with notes that are derived from the C country composite scale (C–D–Eb–E–G–A)—the C major pentatonic scale with a minor 3rd (Eb) passing tone. In measure 3, the lick is restated, lending continuity to the four-measure phrase. In measure 4, the phrase continues up the scale before reversing course to makes its way down to the root note of the F major chord. Notice that, before the chord changes a Bb note makes an appearance on beat 4 of the fourth measure, briefly imparting a dominant tonality (Bb is the b7th of C major) to the line.

MEASURES 5–6 (IV CHORD)

Measure 5 features a restatement of the melodic motif that was established in measure 1, transposed here for the F major chord. Again, a reprise of the motif lends continuity to the solo and grabs your audience's attention. In measure 6, a stream of 8th notes is played along strings 1–2, setting up a return to the I (C) chord. Like the C-chord lines, the scale of choice in these two measures is the F country composite scale (F–G–Ab–A–C–D).

MEASURES 7–8 (I CHORD)

As with every chord change in this sample solo, the root note is stated on beat 1. Following the root, the line works its way down to string 4, where it reverses course for a jump back up to the second-string root. Note the inclusion of a passing tone, Ab, on beat 2, which creates a chromatic passage (A–Ab–G). In measure 8, the line skips over string 3 to the chord's 3rd, E, where it continues down the scale, setting up a change to the V (G) chord.

MEASURES 9–10 (V CHORD)

The change to the V chord is emphasized with the root note, G, on beat 1. Once again, the melodic motif from measure 1 is restated to lend continuity to the solo. Here, the motif is simply shifted down one string, without the need to alter your fingering. All of the notes that comprise these two measures are derived from the G country composite scale (G–A–Bb–B–D–E).

MEASURES 11–12 (I CHORD)

The solo concludes with—what else?—a reprise of the melodic bluegrass motif from measure 1, effectively signaling a return to the I (C) chord.

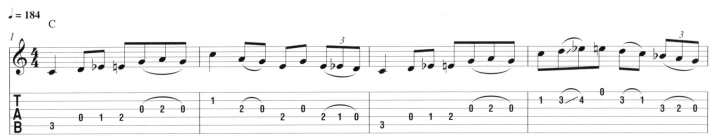

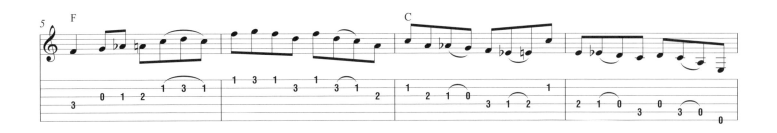

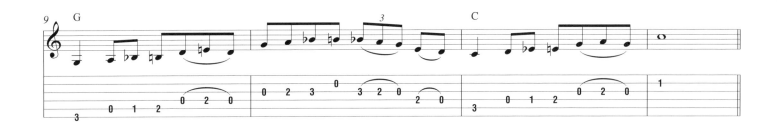

CONSTRUCTING A GUITAR SOLO: KEY OF G MAJOR

If your goal is to become an effective country lead guitarist (and I'm sure it is), one of your first assignments should be to become well-acquainted with one of country's most common keys, G major. In addition to learning the basic chord changes of the key center—G, C, and D (I, IV, and V)—you should become well-versed in melodic ideas that are diatonic to the key. That said, aimlessly learning licks isn't enough—you must be able to string together several melodic ideas to effectively navigate the chord changes. Fortunately for you, that's precisely the focus of this lesson.

The following is a 12-bar solo that juxtaposes banjo rolls and open-string scale licks to create a cohesive solo that emphasizes the I (G), IV (C), and V (D) chords in the key of G major. For best results, follow the hybrid-picking pattern that is indicated between the notation and tab staves.

MEASURES 1–4 (I CHORD)

The solo commences with a "forward roll" that is comprised of a basic G major triad shape and the open high-E string. Notice the three-against-four feel that is created by playing three-note groupings against the 4/4 time signature. In measure 3, open strings and fretted notes are combined for a two-octave run up the G Mixolydian mode (G–A–B–C–D–E–F). Let the notes ring out as long as possible, especially the open strings.

MEASURES 5–6 (IV CHORD)

Similar to measures 1–2, this forward roll consists of a common C major triad shape and the open high-E string. Again, note the three-against-four feel, taking care not to play the groupings as triplets. Instead, all of the notes should be performed as straight 8ths. The phrase ends on the fourth-string root note, C, which leads efficiently (i.e., by a half step) to the first note of the next measure, B.

MEASURES 7–8 (I CHORD)

With a return to the I (G) chord, a first-inversion G major triad (B–D–G) is employed to prolong the forward roll. Notice the retention of the open high-E string, which lends melodic continuity to the solo.

MEASURES 9–10 (V CHORD)

The line in measure 9 is a bit of a departure from the banjo rolls and ascending open-string lick of the previous eight measures. Here, open strings and fretted pitches are juxtaposed to create a descending run down the D Mixolydian mode (D–E–F♯–G–A–B–C). Notice how the open high-E string on beat 2 enables you enough time to switch your fret hand from seventh position to third position. To assist with this lick's execution, follow the hybrid-picking pattern that is indicated between the notation and tab staves.

MEASURES 11–12 (I CHORD)

A half-step slide from F♯ to G commences the final segment of the solo. The slide represents a classic approach to voice leading, as F♯ is the 3rd of D major, and G of course is the root of G major. After the slide, open strings and fretted pitches are combined for a one-octave run up the G Mixolydian mode, resolving to the open G string.

♩ = 168

let ring throughout

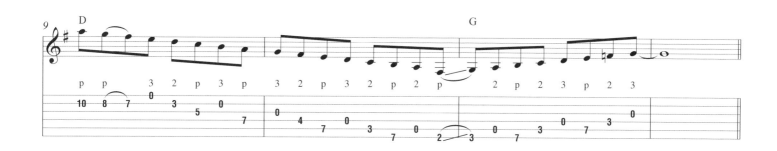

LESSON #47: CONSTRUCTING A GUITAR SOLO: KEY OF F MAJOR

Any country guitarist worth his salt should be well versed in double stops. After all, double stops are, along with string bending, the lifeblood of country lead guitar. But aimlessly learning a bunch of double-stop phrases to increase one's lick vocabulary is a flawed approach. Instead, one must learn how to properly apply the musical phrases to a solo—that is, connect multiple melodic ideas to effectively outline a song's chord changes. To get you started, this lesson will teach you how to construct a basic guitar solo, with special emphasis on double stops.

The following is a 12-bar solo in F major, one of country music's most popular keys. Common double-stop licks are linked together to form a cohesive solo that effectively outlines the I (F), IV (B♭), and V7 (C7) chord changes of the F major key. After learning this complete solo, you will have a greater understanding of how to navigate basic chord changes, as well as a more robust lick vocabulary.

MEASURES 1–4 (I CHORD)

The solo commences with an oblique-bend double stop that is comprised of the F chord's root (F) and 3rd (A). Fret the first-string note with your pinky, bending the second string with your middle finger (reinforcing it with your index finger). After a slide down to first position, a common country riff featuring alternating double stops and a fourth-string pedal tone (F) kicks off. At the tail end of measure 4, a slide into a B♭ note (fourth string, fret 8) anticipates the impending chord change.

MEASURE 5–6 (IV CHORD)

In measure 5, the F-chord riff is moved up to sixth position where it is used to outline the IV (B♭) chord, followed by another oblique-bend double stop. Here, the double stop is comprised of the B♭ chord's 5th (F) and ♭7th (A♭), imparting a dominant tonality to the otherwise major proceedings. Following the double-stop bend, a single-note line effectively transitions back to the I (F) chord.

MEASURES 7–8 (I CHORD)

Notice how effective voice leading connects measure 6 to measure 7. Here, a B♭ note (the root of B♭) leads to an A note (the 3rd of F) by moving down just one half step (one fret). The notes that comprise these two measures are derived exclusively from the F major pentatonic scale (F–G–A–C–D). After an ascending single-note line, an oblique-bend double stop outlines the 3rd (A) and 5th (C) tones of the F chord. At the end of measure 8, a G-note slide anticipates the chord change (G is the 5th of C7).

MEASURES 9–10 (V CHORD)

The C7 chord is outlined exclusively with major and minor 6th interval shapes, played both as single notes and as double stops. In measure 10, an E/C dyad (the 3rd and root of C7) is slid down to a D/B♭ dyad (the 9th and ♭7th) to imply a dominant ninth tonality—a common trick in country and blues music.

MEASURES 11–12 (I CHORD)

The solo concludes with descending double stops on strings 1–2 that alternate with single notes on string 4. Collectively, the three-note shapes spell out major triads with 3rds in the bass (F/A and E♭/G). The double stops are followed by a short reprise of the riff from the F chord's first appearance, lending continuity to the solo.

TRACK 47
0:00
CD 1   ♩ = 144

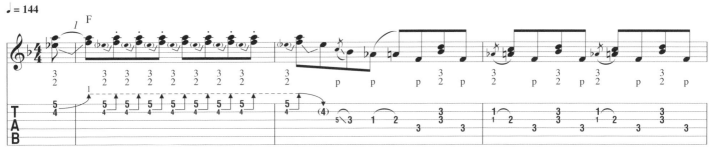

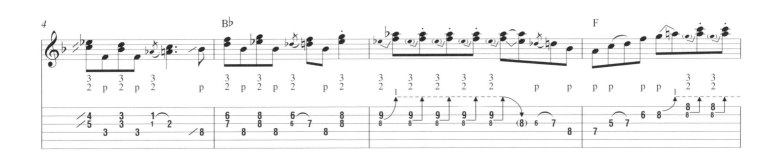

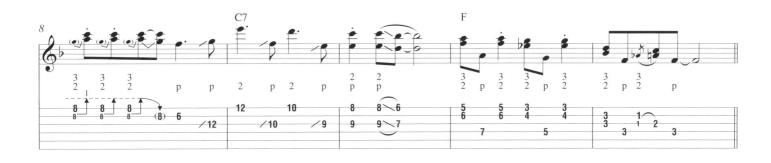

LESSON #48: CONSTRUCTING A GUITAR SOLO: KEY OF D MAJOR

String bending is a staple of country lead guitar. One of its most common applications is to pair a bent string with one or more stationary notes to emulate a pedal steel guitar. These types of bends (i.e., oblique) enable guitarists to create chord melody-style lines that outline the chord changes during a solo, with the bends mimicking the pitch-altering effect of a pedal steel's four levers, which can raise or lower the pitches of its strings by a half or whole step.

In this lesson, we'll use pedal steel-style string bending to solo over a common I–vi–IV–I–V–I (D–Bm–G–D–A–D) progression in the key of D major—a popular key in country music. After learning this solo, you will be equipped with a more robust pedal steel lick vocabulary and have a greater understanding of how several phrases can be strung together to create a cohesive, melodic solo.

MEASURES 1–2 (I CHORD)

The solo begins with a pair of non-adjacent string oblique bends, which lead to a pair of triple-stop bends in measure 2. The first triple stop is comprised of the notes of a first-inversion D major triad (F#–A–D); meanwhile, the notes of the second triple stop (E, F#, and C) imply a D9 (D–F#–A–C–E) tonality.

MEASURES 3–4 (VI CHORD)

Although the triple-stop bend used here is comprised of the same shape as the preceding major-triad (D) shape, the half-step bend results in a much different sound. That's because the half-step bend's target note, D, is the *minor* 3rd, resulting in a first-inversion B minor triad (D–F#–B). The minor shape is rearticulated and manipulated throughout the two measures. Notice, however, that on beat 4 of the fourth measure, the open G string is played, giving your fret hand some time to get repositioned for the impending G chord and offering a sonic preview of the harmony that's to come.

MEASURES 5–6 (IV CHORD)

To outline the IV (G) chord, the bottom string of a common G major triad voicing is manipulated by a half step, raising the pitch of the major 3rd from B to C. The result is a Gsus4 chord, which returns to G major in measure 6. Again, notice the inclusion of the open G string to assist with fret-hand repositioning.

MEASURES 7–8 (I CHORD)

This triple-stop voicing is simply an open-position D major triad (D–F#–A), sans the open D string. Here, the chord's 5th, A, is bent and released a whole step from A to B and back, briefly implying a D6 (D–F#–A–B) chord.

MEASURES 9–10 (V CHORD)

To outline the V (A) chord, a common open-position Am chord is voiced. However, rather than allowing the minor tonality to ring out over an A *major* chord, the chord's minor 3rd, C, is bent a half step to the major 3rd, C#. To perform this bend, pull the string downward (toward the floor), which will prevent the string from interfering with the other chord tones. On beats 3 and 4 of measure 10, major and minor 6th double stops climb up strings 2 and 4 in anticipation of the change to the I (D) chord.

MEASURES 11–12 (I CHORD)

In measure 11, the 6th shapes from the previous measure continue an ascent of the fretboard. Notice that, to emphasize the return of the D chord (D–F#–A), the first double stop is comprised of the pitches A and F# (the D chord's 5th and 3rd). Meanwhile, measure 12 marks the return of the D major triple-stop bend from measure 2, which lends some continuity to the solo.

TRACK 48
0:00
CD 1

♩ = 132

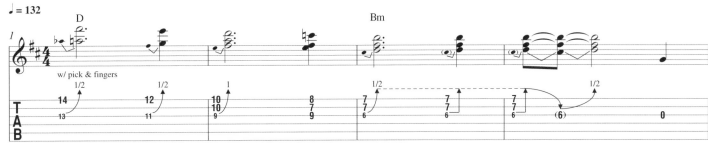

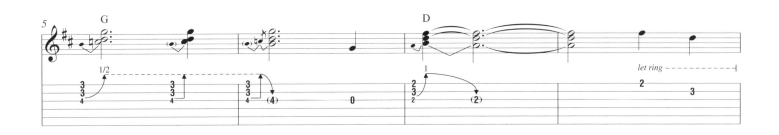

LESSON #49: CONSTRUCTING A GUITAR SOLO: KEY OF A MAJOR

The string bending favored by country guitarists differs from that found in blues and rock music in a couple of ways. First, blues and rock players tend to incorporate bends into their lead lines as a way to enhance the minor-against-major conflict that is so essential to both musical genres. Second, country guitarists favor precise half- and whole-step bends that target chord tones; whereas rock and blues players frequently implement microtonal (i.e., quarter-step) bends whose objective is to create a tonal "feel," rather than complete harmonies.

Of all the various bending techniques, oblique bends are the most popular with country players. A typical oblique bend involves bending one string to a chord tone and, while the bend is held in place, playing single notes on a higher string, adjacent and non-adjacent alike. Once the single notes have been played, the bend is returned to its original pitch and resolved to the root note of the chord over which the phrase is played.

In this lesson, we'll explore how oblique bends can be used to construct a guitar solo in the key of A major, one of country's most popular key centers. In addition to learning each of the licks that comprise the 12-bar solo, pay close attention to how the phrases are linked together to efficiently and effectively outline the key center's I7 (A7), IV7 (D7), and V (E7) chords.

MEASURES 1–4 (I7 CHORD)

Two separate oblique bends outline the first I (A) chord. In measure 1, a third-string bend holds the chord's 3rd, C♯, while a single-note line is played along string 2. In the second measure, the single notes are shifted to string 1, where the chord's ♭7th, G, is emphasized via a half note. In measure 3, a second-string bend holds the chord's root note, A, while single notes are articulated along string 1. To conclude the four-measure phrase, a short, single-note line derived from a hybrid of the A major (A–B–C♯–E–F♯) and A minor (A–C–D–E–G) pentatonic scales resolves to the chord's root, A.

MEASURES 5–6 (IV7 CHORD)

Here, the melodic motif that was developed in measures 1–2 is transposed to fit over the IV (D7) chord. However, notice that, due to the inclusion of an 8th rest and a quarter note, the phrase is played over the bar line and the ♭7th tone, C, is held for only a quarter note (rather than a half note, as was the case in measure 2).

MEASURES 7–8 (I7 CHORD)

To emphasize the return of the I7 (A7) chord, a second-string bend holds the chord's 3rd, C♯, while single notes are played along string 1. Perform this bend with your fret-hand's middle finger (reinforcing it with your index finger), fretting the first-string notes with your pinky and ring fingers.

MEASURES 9–10 (V7 CHORD)

As the solo moves to the V7 chord, oblique-bend double stops outline the chord's 3rd and 5th (G♯ and B, respectively). The two-note phrase resolves to an E/B dyad whose top note, B, is a holdover from the bend.

MEASURES 11–12 (I7 CHORD)

Similar to the previous two measures, an oblique-bend double-stop figure is used to signal a return to the I7 (A7) chord. Here, double stops emphasize the chord's 3rd and 5th (C♯ and E, respectively) and are followed by an A/E dyad, commonly known as an A5 chord.

TRACK 49
0:00
CD 1   ♩ = 144

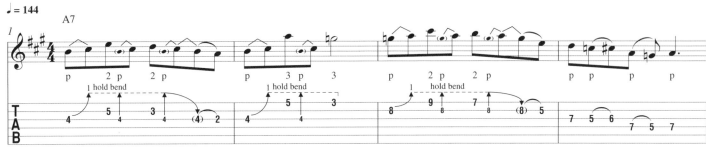

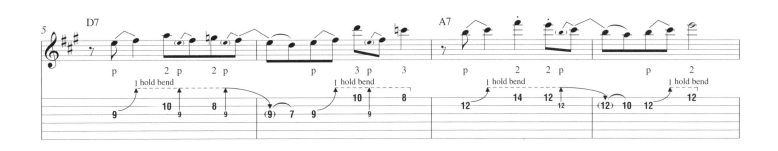

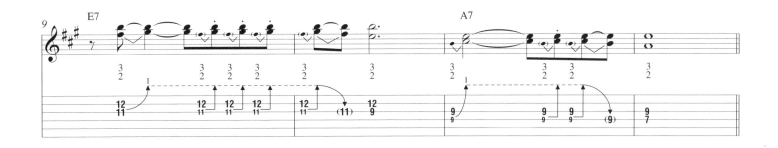

LESSON #50: CONSTRUCTING A GUITAR SOLO:KEY OF E MAJOR

Over the past few decades, technically skilled guitarists have taken country lead playing to new heights. Often affixed with the adjective "hot," the lead guitar styles of players such as Brent Mason, Brad Paisley, Scotty Anderson, Albert Lee, Johnny Hiland, and Ray Flacke, among many others, not only have elevated the role of the guitar in contemporary country music, but brought increased attention to the genre as well, particularly from the guitar playing community.

Equally impressive as their technical chops is the lick vocabulary of these hot country guitarists. In this lesson, we'll link together several licks played in the style of the aforementioned players to create a 12-bar solo that is played over the I7 (E7), IV7 (A7), and V7 (B7) chords in the key of E major, one of country music's most common keys. In true "hot country" fashion, the solo is played at a brisk (176 bpm) tempo and contains a healthy dose of single notes. Let's take a look.

MEASURES 1–4 (I7 CHORD)

The solo commences with a triplet-based legato figure that is mostly derived from the E major pentatonic scale (E–F#–G#–B–C#), with the open A string being the only non-major pentatonic tone. In measure 2, the single-note line continues up the scale, leading to a second-string oblique bend. At this point, the scale choice leans towards the E Mixolydian mode (E–F#–G#–A–B–C#–D), particularly with the addition of the notes A and D. Notice the minor 3rd shapes that descend strings 1–2 at the midway point of measure 4. This chromatic movement effectively leads to the A note at fret 5 of the first string (the root of A7).

MEASURES 5–6 (IV7 CHORD)

A hybrid of the A major pentatonic (A–B–C#–E–F#) and A blues (A–C–D–Eb–E–G) scales provide the pitches for this descending single-note line. Notice how the inclusion in measure 6 of both the minor 3rd (C) and major 3rd (C#) lends a bluesy quality to the line.

MEASURES 7–8 (I7 CHORD)

The return of the I7 (E7) chord brings with it a common bluegrass run. Here, the phrase is derived from the E country composite scale (E–F#–G–G#–B–C#)—the E major pentatonic scale with a minor 3rd (G) passing tone—to outline the E7 harmony. This is followed by a repetitive single-note figure that alternates between second-string root (E) notes and C#-to-B pull-offs, leading to the V7 (B7) chord.

MEASURES 9–10 (V7 CHORD)

To outline the V7 (B7) chord, a third-string oblique bend holds the chord's 3rd (D#) while its 5th (F#) is struck on the second string. After several repetitions of the held D# note, the bend is released to its original pitch, C#, before returning to the chord tone (D#).

MEASURES 11–12 (I7 CHORD)

The solo concludes with a reprise of the bluegrass run from measure 7. Restating melodic motifs at random points in your solo lends continuity to your lead lines and will pique the interest of audience members.

TRACK 50
0:00

CD 1

♩ = 176

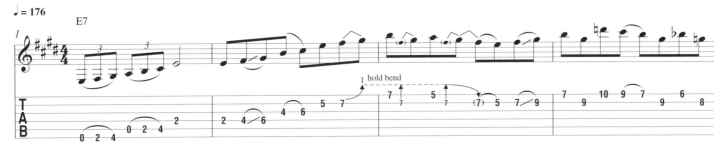

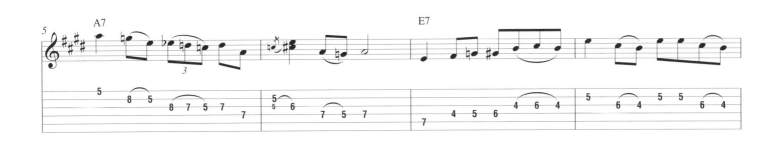

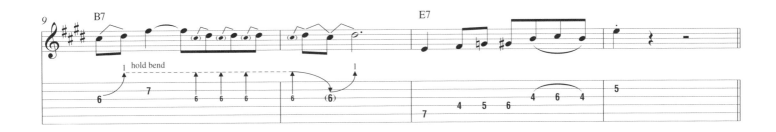

LESSON #51: USING HYBRID PICKING FOR DOUBLE STOPS

Like many styles, country guitar is as much about the sound as it is the notes you play. Obviously, this includes a Telecaster (usually) and a bright, twangy Fender tone, but it also has to do with technique—specifically, pick-hand technique. In country, most players use what's called hybrid picking to pluck the strings. This means that we'll use both the pick and our fingers on the pick hand. Why? It's all about the sound!

Country guitar sounds snappy, clucky, bright, and twangy, and there's a good reason. With hybrid picking, you're able to pluck both notes of a double stop, for instance, simultaneously, creating a snappier sound than when played with the pick alone. A good starting point for the technique is to place your pick on string 4 and use your middle and ring fingers on strings 3 and 2, respectively. Lots of country licks are played with this string group.

EXERCISE 1

Here's a basic exercise in the A Mixolydian mode to get you comfortable with the hybrid picking technique. Use your pick for all the notes on string 4 and your middle and ring fingers for the notes on strings 3 and 2.

EXERCISE 2

And here's another exercise in A that repeats a common double-stop move with this technique. Barre your first finger for the D chords at the 7th fret.

LICK 1

Now let's take a look at a few licks in A that make use of these double stops. This first one adds a few grace-note slides and hammer-ons to spice it up.

LICK 2

Here's a nice variation on Lick 1 that resolves instead to the V chord, E7.

 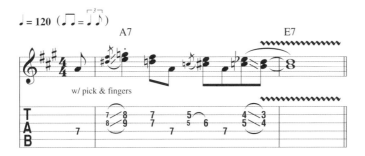

LICK 3

In this last lick, we're sliding into the C#/E dyad from a half step below repeatedly for a three-against-four rhythmic effect. Sliding into double stops from a half step below is another common country move.

Hybrid picking plays a big part in that classic country guitar sound. Though we only stayed on strings 2, 3, and 4 for these examples, be sure to apply the technique to licks on other string sets as well. You'll find it works just as well. Before you know it, the technique will be second nature, and you'll be using it without even realizing it!

LESSON #52: USING HYBRID PICKING FOR SINGLE-NOTE LINES

A Telecaster and a bright Fender amp are only half the sound of country guitar. The other half is in your fingers. And if you want to get that snappy, clucky country sound, you need to use hybrid picking, which involves the use of both the pick and your pick-hand fingers to pluck the strings. The technique is useful on chords, double-stops, and single-note playing. In this lesson, we'll look at how it's used with single-note lines.

With hybrid picking, we'll use our pick, but we'll also use our fingers to pluck notes—often times pulling up on the string and allowing it to snap down forcefully, creating a bright, accented note that really lends some country flair.

EXERCISE 1

Let's start with a simple exercise in G to get a feel for it. We'll be playing melodic 3rds from the G Mixolydian mode. Use your pick for all the notes on string 3, and use your middle finger for all the notes on string 2.

EXERCISE 2

In practical application, of course, we don't always stay on the same strings through every lick. So let's look at two exercises that move down through the strings. This first one moves down the G minor pentatonic scale with a four-note sequence that's moved down through several string sets. Each four-note group uses the same pick-hand fingering: second finger–pick–pull-off–pick.

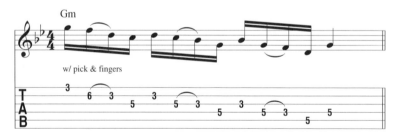

EXERCISE 3

Here's the same thing with a G major pentatonic scale, which is a bit more country-sounding. The plucking pattern is the same: second finger–pick–pull-off–pick. I've including a left-hand fingering (LH) for this one that works nicely for me.

LICK 1

With practice, you can really fly through these patterns with hybrid picking. Let's take a look at a few licks using this technique. Here's one in G that uses the G Mixolydian mode to blend the ideas from all three exercises. The pick-hand fingering is labeled: P = pick, 2 = second finger. The only note that's not in the G Mixolydian mode is the B♭ at the end, which we use to hammer into the major 3rd, B—a typical country sound. For the final high G note, pop that string with your finger to make it really snap!

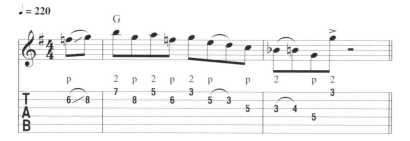

LICK 2

Here's a lick to use over a G7 chord that's resolving to C. It works out of the G Mixolydian mode in tenth position and resolves to an E note, which is the 3rd of C. Notice that we're using hybrid picking for three notes in a row on the high E string (F–E–D) with a finger–pick–pull-off pattern. After that, we're applying our four-note sequence of finger–pick–pull-off–pick from Exercises 2 and 3.

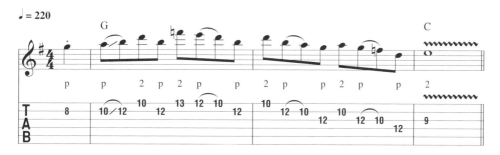

LICK 3

For our final lick, we're playing through a I–IV–V–I progression in G major (G–C–D7–G). We're also incorporating some legato slides and a typical whole-step bend from the 2nd (A) to the 3rd (B).

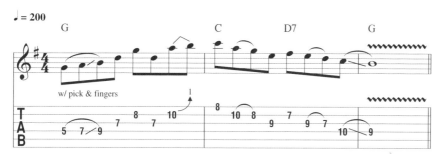

Try this technique on the lower strings as well, where it's equally effective. It may take some getting used to, but once you've got it under your fingers, in combination with the pick and some pull-offs, you can create some lightning fast lines without much effort.

LESSON #53: THE COMPOSITE BLUES SCALE

Country guitar solos are some of the most colorful of all. They can sound bluesy, bright, sassy, jazzy, and sophisticated. One of the elements that lends complexity to country guitar is the use of the composite blues scale. This is a somewhat elusive scale to teach, but it's simply a must-know concept in the world of the country guitar solo.

The composite blues scale is often described as the combined notes of a major pentatonic and a blues scale that share the same root. For example, the C composite blues scale would contain the notes of C major pentatonic (C–D–E–G–A) and the C blues scale (C–E♭–F–F♯–G–B♭). When you put them together, you end up with this nine-note super-scale:

C–D–E♭–E–F–F♯–G–A–B♭

Sixth-String Root Form

Here's a fingering for this beast in seventh and eighth position. It's kind of framed around the E-form C barre chord with its root on the sixth string.

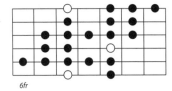

6fr

So how does it work? Well, when soloing in a C major or C dominant setting, pretty much any of these notes are fair game. However, it's not quite that simple. It helps if you use your ear and some common sense to resolve your licks properly. For example, even though the ♭3rd, E♭, is listed here, you probably wouldn't want to end your line on that note and just sustain it over a C chord, which has a major 3rd (E). The same could be said for the 4th (F) or ♯4th (F♯). With practice, you'll get the hang of it and will learn how to make it sound musical.

Here are a few licks to demonstrate what I mean. Notice that both lines end with a strong resolution to a chord tone: the root note, C, in this instance.

LICK 1

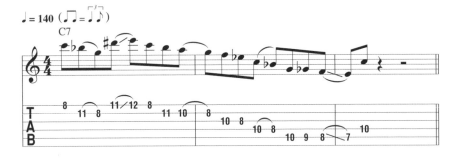

LICK 2

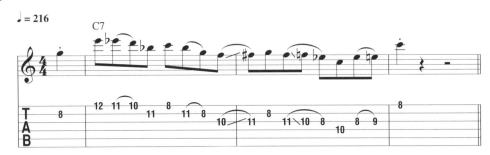

Fifth-String Root Form

Here's another fingering for the C composite blues scale around second and third position. This scale form is centered around the A-form C barre chord.

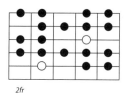

And here are a few lines from that scale form.

LICK 3

We're ending this first lick with a half-step bend from the minor 3rd (E♭) to the major 3rd (E). I like to play this one fingerstyle.

LICK 4

This final lick is in the key of A, and we're sliding into chord tones from a half step below in a one-octave ascending phrase.

If you've been getting tired of the same old major, minor, or Mixolydian scales, give the composite blues scale a try. You can really get some colorful things going.

LESSON #54: COMBINING PARALLEL MAJOR AND MINOR (THE "THREE FRETS" TRICK)

One thing that makes country guitar solos so interesting is the melodic complexity. You often hear major 3rds in the same phrase as minor 3rds, and this lends a certain sassiness that plays a huge role in that country sound. One of my favorite ways to get this sound is combining parallel major and minor pentatonic scales. I call this the "three frets" trick. I know what some of y'all may be thinking: "Wait a minute! Three frets down from a note is the *relative* minor—not the parallel minor!" That's correct, but that's not *exactly* what we're talking about here. A little explanation is necessary.

Let's say we're playing in D major. One obvious choice is the D major pentatonic scale. A common fingering for D major pentatonic is in seventh position, which could also be viewed as a B minor pentatonic scale. And yes, this is a relative relationship: B minor is the relative minor of D major. We've indicated the D root notes with an open circle on the diagram.

D MAJOR PENTATONIC (B MINOR PENTATONIC)

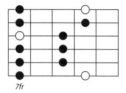

7fr

As the blues teaches us, another common scale of choice over a major chord or (especially) a dominant chord is the *minor* pentatonic. So, if we're playing over a D or a D7 chord, we can also use the D minor pentatonic scale. Here's the common "box" fingering for that in tenth position.

D MINOR PENTATONIC

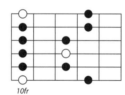

10fr

Now we see the parallel relationship. D minor is the *parallel* minor of D major. It took us a bit to get here, but now we can state it plainly:

Over a D or D7 chord, we can use either the D major pentatonic or D minor pentatonic scale.

We can also state it this way:

Over a D or D7 chord, we can use the B minor pentatonic or D minor pentatonic scale. This is because B minor pentatonic and D major pentatonic are the same scale.

We can take this concept one step further and say this:

Over a D or D7 chord, we can use either the B blues scale or D blues scale.

Remember: the only difference between a minor pentatonic and a blues scale is that the blues scale adds the ♭5th note; the two scales are virtually interchangeable.

Knowing this, we can take the same exact lick and transpose it up (or down) three frets to get a fresh sound.

LICK 1

This lick shows how it sounds when we transpose a D blues lick down three frets to B blues.

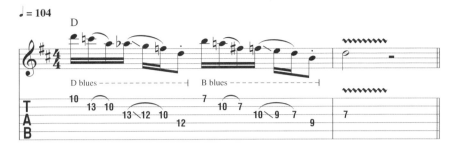

LICK 2

Here's the opposite effect—moving from the country-sounding B blues up three frets to the tougher, bluesy sounding D blues.

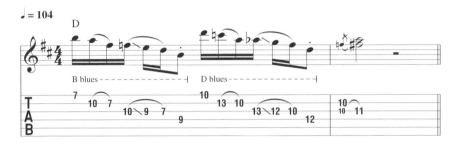

Notice that, when we ended that last phrase on the downbeat of measure 2, we resorted back to D major (or B minor). This is because, though a ♭3rd (F♮ in this case) can be used in passing without offending the ear, it's generally not common to sustain the note over a major or dominant chord, which of course contains a major 3rd (F♯ in this case).

LICK 3

Let's look at another example that moves from B blues to D blues. After transposing the exact same lick, we tack on a few more notes from the D blues scale to finish it off.

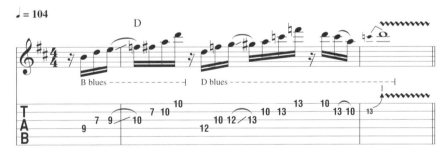

LICK 4

In this last lick, we're moving back and forth between D minor pentatonic and B minor pentatonic on every beat, transposing the same four-note lick each time.

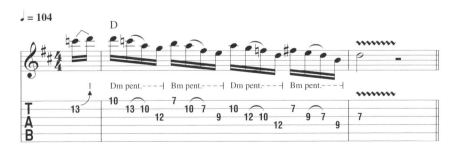

Play around with this idea and you'll begin to incorporate it without thinking about it. It's a great way to throw a melodic surprise into a solo and keep the listener on their toes!

BLENDING PARALLEL MAJOR AND MINOR PENTATONIC/ BLUES SCALE FORMS

A great way to spice up your solo lines is by thinking outside the box—or in this case, combining two different boxes. Most players are well versed with the box position minor pentatonic scale based off the E barre chord form, with its root on the sixth string. It looks like this:

MINOR PENTATONIC SCALE - E BARRE CHORD FORM

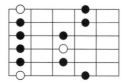

And many players have also learned another common pentatonic scale form based off the A barre chord form, with its root on the fifth string. That looks like this:

MINOR PENTATONIC SCALE - A BARRE CHORD FORM

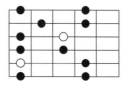

I'd like to show you a creative way of combining these scale forms that mixes parallel tonalities for a fresh sound.

The Major Pentatonic Sound

Let's say you're playing in the key of E major and you want to use the major pentatonic scale. Lots of people are familiar with the relative minor concept with regards to this. That is, if you have a root note on string 6, you move three frets down to find the root of the relative minor pentatonic scale.

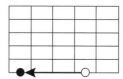

12–3 = 9. The 9th fret on the sixth string is C♯. So, to get an E *major* pentatonic sound, you can play C♯ *minor* pentatonic. They are the same scale. So far, so good.

The Minor Pentatonic Sound

However, country players also include lots of bluesy phrases in their solos. And if you've played much blues, you know that a common choice over a major or dominant chord is the tonic minor pentatonic. In other words, if you're playing a blues in E, you can play the E minor pentatonic scale.

Combining the Two

Now let's bring this together. We're going to combine these two scales, but we won't be shifting the same scale form up and down the neck (though you certainly can do that). Refer to the scale forms above. We'll use them as follows:

C♯ MINOR PENTATONIC (*E MAJOR PENTATONIC) IN NINTH POSITION: *E BARRE CHORD FORM*

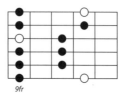

9fr

*Notice that the E notes are circled as the root here because we're thinking in the key of E major.

E MINOR PENTATONIC IN SEVENTH POSITION: *A BARRE CHORD FORM*

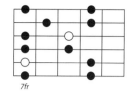

This is a nice way to combine the tonalities because the scale forms are in close proximity to each other and can be easily accessed at any time with a quick position shift.

LICK 1

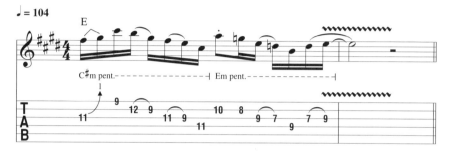

LICK 2

Notice in Lick 2 that, though we end on the G♮ note, we don't sustain it, because the underlying chord is E major, over which the G would clash. If I were going to sustain that note, I would likely bend it a half step up to G♯.

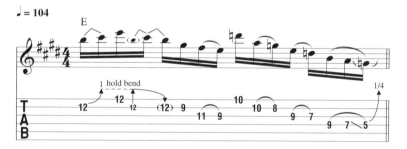

LICK 3

This concept also works with the minor pentatonic's first cousin—the blues scale. So we can play blues versions of each scale form as well, as demonstrated in these last two licks.

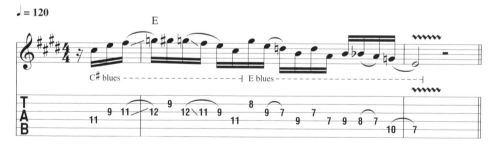

LICK 4

In this last lick, we cheat a little bit by including the B♯ note, which is not in the C♯ blues scale, but is used to maintain the half-step lower-neighbor figure sequence.

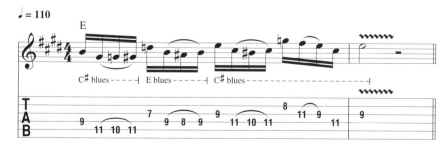

As you can hear, this is a great way to add some tartness to your standard relative minor pentatonic lines. Experiment with it and have fun. You'll find all kinds of creative ways to slip between these two neighboring scale forms.

SCOOPED CHORDS FOR A PEDAL STEEL EFFECT

The pedal steel guitar is one of the most expressive instruments of all, regardless of genre. Therefore, it only makes sense that we, as guitar players, have been trying to emulate it for decades. There are many useful ways to do this, and in this lesson, I'd like to talk about one of my favorites. I call it the scooped chord.

The concept is simpler to describe than it is to execute, but that's par for the course when trying to emulate the pedal steel. To execute a scooped chord, you simply play the notes one fret down and bend them all up a half step into pitch. When executed properly, it'll sound very steel-like.

Dyads

Let's start with some dyads, or two-note chords, as they are by far the easiest. Yes, theoretically chords have three or more notes, but you can easily suggest a harmony with only two notes, and, combined with context, that's all that's usually necessary.

LICK 1

Here's an E major pentatonic lick in which we're bending into a major 3rd dyad of E/G♯—the root and 3rd of an E chord. You'll most likely need to fret each note of the bend with a different finger in order to get the varying degrees of pitch bend necessary to hit both target notes. (Note: Target notes shown on fretboard map.)

9fr

LICK 2

In this C Mixolydian line, we're capping it off with a bend into a minor 3rd dyad of E/G—the 3rd and 5th of a C chord. Notice that these pitches aren't on the same fret, so it will feel a bit different than the first lick.

8fr

LICK 3

And here's an ascending A Mixolydian line that uses chromatic lower neighbor tones and finishes off with a tritone of G/C♯—the ♭7th and 3rd of A7.

Triads

Scooping a three-note chord, or triad, is much more difficult, but it can be done. However, a simpler yet still very effective method is to only bend one or two notes and fret the other(s) normally.

LICK 4

In this lick in A, we're running though a bluesy phrase and capping it off with this partial A7 voicing: E/G/C♯, which is the 5th, ♭7th, and 3rd of A7. Even though we're fretting the G and C♯ notes normally and only bending into the E note from a half step below, it still has that pedal steel sound.

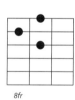

With all of these bends, play the unbent target pitches first and then try to match them with the bends. It will take a good bit of practice, but the resulting sound is well worth the effort.

LESSON #57: USING PRE-BENDS TO SIMULATE A PEDAL STEEL ON SINGLE-NOTE LINES

Have you ever wondered what gives some country solo phrases that slinky, slithery, pedal steel sound? Well, they're not greasing up their fretboard! It's most likely due to the use of pre-bends (and releases).

A pre-bend is executed by bending a string before picking it. So you only hear the target pitch; you don't hear the scoop up into it. When you release a pre-bend back to its unbent state, it sounds convincingly like a pedal steel guitar manipulating its levers. Here's a simple exercise to get used to the idea.

EXERCISE 1

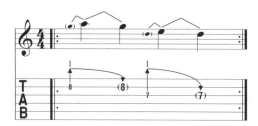

EXERCISE 2

Of course, you can execute pre-bends of different values as well. Half-step pre-bends are also very common, as illustrated in this exercise.

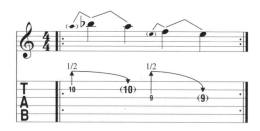

PRECISION

Since a pedal steel executes its bends via mechanical means, it's very precise. And in order to sound convincing, we guitar players need to be very precise with our pre-bends as well. So be sure to go back and forth with your target pitches to make sure you're executing clean and well-intonated bends.

Building Licks

Now that you have a grasp on the basic idea, let's look at how to incorporate them. The basic idea is to play a lick you would normally play, but find a spot or two where you can replace two notes with a pre-bent note and its release.

LICK 1

Here's a C Mixolydian line in which we're using a pre-bent A note up to Bb and releasing it. You should fret and pre-bend the A note even before picking the first C note.

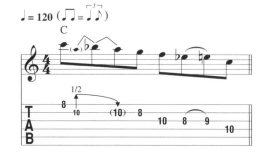

LICK 2

Here's an open-position line in A that uses a pre-bent D up to E♭ with a release to create a chromatic E–E♭–D line.

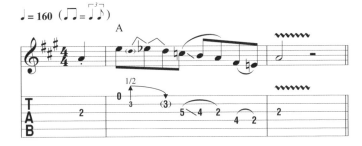

LICK 3

This line in G uses a whole-step pre-bend from A up to B and a half-step pre-bend from E up to F. Notice that we've built in an 8th rest before the second pre-bend, giving us adequate time to prepare for it.

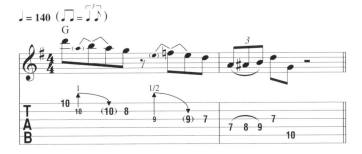

LICK 4

In this final lick in D, we're again making use of both whole- and half-step pre-bends. For the final pre-bend, however, we're bending back up again after the release. Try to get a clean ending by cutting off the third-string bend just before you pluck the high D note. I find this easiest by playing the lick with my fingers. You can use the thumb to quiet the third string just before you pick the last D note. You should hear that bend reach back up to the F♯ and stop—no drooping at the last minute.

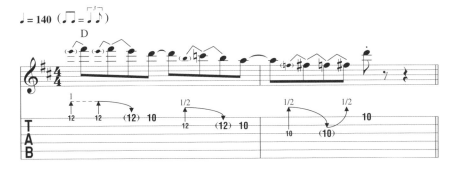

Pre-bends aren't easy to do, but they really can add to the pedal steel quality of a line. With time, you'll begin creating lines with pre-bends in mind, which will aid in the ease of execution.

LESSON #58: PEDAL STEEL PRECISION

It's no easy task trying to emulate the expressive sound of a pedal steel guitar. That's because pedal steel bends are precise, and in order to sound convincing, we guitar players need to be very precise as well. Many times, this precision (or lack thereof) is the only thing separating a mediocre faux country lick from a professional-sounding one.

Single Notes

With all of the bends in this lesson, try to visualize each one stretching right to pitch cleanly and smoothly. A wavering bend can destroy the pedal steel quality instantly.

LICK 1

In this first lick in C, we're using all half-step bends, including a pre-bend-and-release at the beginning and one in the middle. The latter will be much more difficult because you won't have much time to prepare. Play the line without any bends (fretting every note) and then play it with the bends to check your accuracy. (Hint: For the pre-bend at the beginning, fret and pre-bend the F♯ note before you even pick the first C note.)

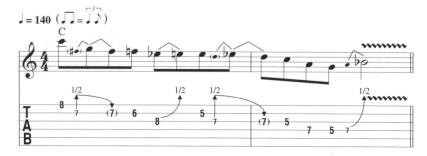

LICK 2

Here's one in D major that uses the same bend and release repeatedly against different notes on top. Bending one note against another pitch that's stationary is called an oblique bend. Try to make that bend-and-release move sound the same each time.

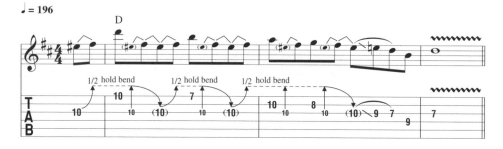

LICK 3

This lick in C uses two more oblique bends—one a half step and the other a whole step. Again, precision is the name of the game here.

Double Stops

Next, let's try incorporating some double-stop bends. Some of these will involve bending both notes, while others will involve bending only one. Use hybrid picking on the double stops for an authentic country sound.

LICK 4

This first one outlines a V–IV–I progression in E (B7–A7–E) and uses three different double-stop bends. The first two are oblique bends (one bent note and one stationary), and the last one involves two bent notes.

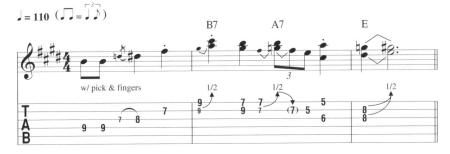

LICK 5

Here's one in E that mixes major and blues sounds throughout. The first set of bends keeps the same bent note, but changes the unbent note on top before allowing the bend to fall. The second set is a nifty move that outlines a D chord by holding a C♯ bent a half step to D while pivoting with A, F♯, and E on top.

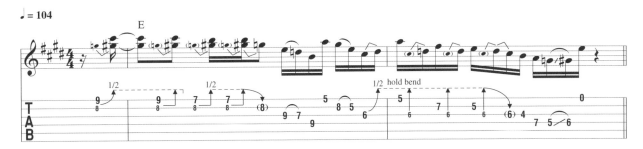

Triple Stops

And let's close off with a few triple-stop bend licks. These are considerably more difficult, because you'll often end up bending without any support for the bending finger.

LICK 6

Here's an easy one (relatively speaking) in G outlining a ii–V–I progression. We're creating a sus4 sound on the V chord with a half-step bend from the 3rd to the 4th.

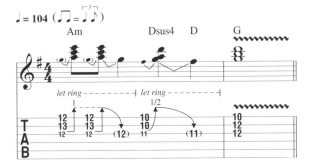

LICK 7

This final lick is a tough one, as it incorporates some pre-bends and a few awkward fingerings. Take it slowly at first.

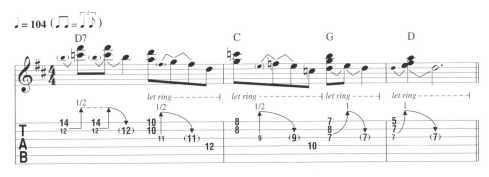

Remember that the key to making these licks sound great—instead of just passable—is precision. Make those bends crisp and clean!

LESSON #59: THE THREE-NOTE CHROMATIC TRICK

Country solos are often laced with jazzy chromatics, lending a sophisticated and complex sound. This can be the result of numerous strategies: different scale combinations, chromatic approach tones, and so on. In this lesson, I'd like to share a specific trick that I like to use. It's a simple, versatile, little tool that can open the door to jazzier-sounding country phrases. I call it the three-note chromatic trick.

Three Notes in a Row on One String: Pick–Pick–Pull

The concept is simple. We're going to start a line with three descending chromatic notes on one string; this is most often the high E, but it can certainly be others as well. Articulate these notes like this: pick the first two notes and pull-off to the third one. The reason for this is two-fold: 1) I like the jazzy sound it gives, and 2) it makes it easier at faster tempos.

Now, we obviously don't want to just pick three random notes for this. We'll start on specific notes of the key in order to produce different-sounding lines. There's no hard and fast rule, but for this lesson the first note and the last note will both be diatonic to the scale, whereas the middle note will be a chromatic passing tone. We'll work in the key of G throughout for simplicity's sake.

Starting from the 5th: D

If we start from the 5th, the three-note fragment would look like this:

Seems harmless enough, right? But it makes a great little beginning to a lick which colors the whole phrase.

LICK 1

I like to follow this three-note fragment with a note on the second string, and one of my favorites is the A note. Check out how this little G major pentatonic line sounds when it begins with this trick.

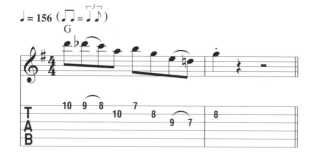

LICK 2

Here's another variation that you might follow with. This one's from the G Mixolydian mode but contains one other chromatic note, D♯, which acts as a lower neighbor note to the 6th, E.

Starting from the 3rd: B

When starting from the 3rd, I like to follow with the ♭7th (F♮) as the fourth note.

LICK 3

TRACK 9 0:17 CD 2

LICK 4

In this variation, we're using two three-note chromatic tricks: first starting from the 3rd on string 1, and then starting from the 5th on string 3. It lays under the fingers very well and sounds great over a dominant chord.

TRACK 9 0:26 CD 2

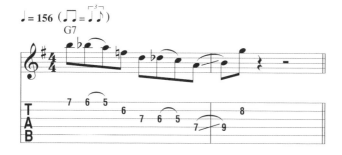

Starting from the 2nd: A

When starting from the 2nd, which could also be thought of as the 9th, the ♭7th or 6th is a nice note with which to follow.

LICK 5

We use the 6th in this lick and also include a classic ascending chromatic phrase on string 3.

TRACK 9 0:34 CD 2

Starting from the Root: G

Another excellent choice is starting from the root. This really suggests a dominant sound, as the first two notes heard on the downbeats are the root and ♭7th.

LICK 6

We'll start this line on the second string and follow with the 5th on string 3. In beats 3 and 4 of measure 1, roll your first finger back and forth, shifting down on beat 4, to play all of the notes.

TRACK 9 0:42 CD 2

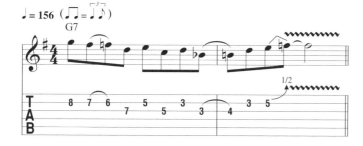

This trick is a great way to add some jazziness to your country lines. The more you fool with it, the more variations and ideas you'll come up with. Have fun and remember to pick–pick–pull!

LESSON #60: ENCLOSING THE MAJOR 3RD

In this lesson, we're going to talk about something that you hear in literally thousands of country solos. You'll even hear it several times in some solos. It's a melodic device that helps resolve a line with clarity and finality, and it does so in style. I call it enclosing the major 3rd.

Enclosure is a musical device that means we'll surround a target pitch with notes above and below. Enclosures can be diatonic, which means all three notes (higher, lower, and target pitches) are all within the key, or chromatic, meaning one (or both) of the surround pitches (higher or lower) is not found within the key. In this lesson, we'll focus primarily on the latter.

The Basic Idea

Let's work in the key of A for this lesson. The basic idea is to play the 4th (D), the ♭3rd (C), and then the major 3rd (C♯), like this:

By itself, it already suggests an A major or dominant tonality. There are a few guidelines that we usually follow with this little device:

▶ The target pitch, C♯ in our case, usually lands on a downbeat—many times beat 1 of a measure.

▶ The target pitch is often followed by the root of the scale, A in our case—either a major 3rd below or a minor 6th above.

▶ The target pitch is often articulated with a slur—either a hammer-on or a slide.

Again, these are only guidelines, and you'll certainly find plenty of exceptions. But this is a good place to start.

Examples

Let's take a look at how this sounds in some licks. Note that we won't always play this enclosure in fifth position on string 3; we'll move around as is necessary with the licks.

LICK 1

Here's a nice starter phrase in A Mixolydian.

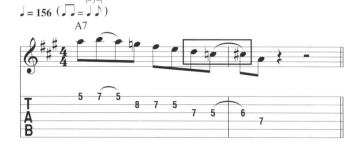

LICK 2

This one makes use of chromatic passing tones on the way down. Note that the enclosure is articulated on two different strings this time.

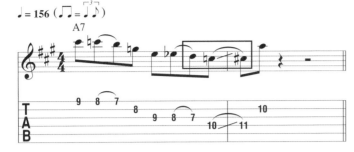

LICK 3

Though the enclosure commonly concludes a phrase, it doesn't always have to, as demonstrated here.

LICK 4

In this lick, we're playing over a I–IV–I progression (A–D–A) and using the enclosure trick for each chord. Over the D chord, we enclose its 3rd, F♯, and we finish by enclosing A's 3rd, C♯.

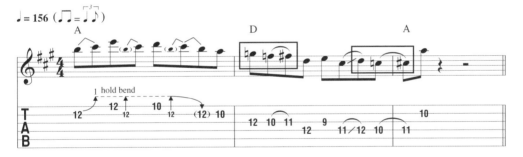

LICK 5

We'll finish with a lick that spans from tenth to fifth position and makes use of the D–C–C♯ enclosure twice along the way. Be sure to use hybrid picking for this one—especially on the descending 3rds on strings 2 and 1.

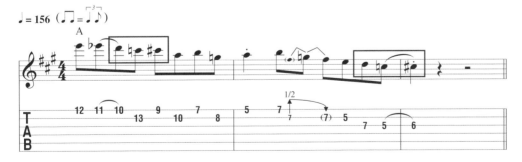

The enclosure technique is a lot of fun to mess around with, and once you're tuned in to it, you'll hear it all over the place in your favorite solos. Before you know it, you'll find yourself incorporating it into your lines without even thinking about it. Remember also that you can enclose any chord tone—root, 5th, etc.—so experiment with that as well. Good luck!

LESSON #61: THE 6TH-TO-♭3RD MOVE

Most guitarists have little favorite melodic fragments that they often include in their lines. In this lesson, I'd like to talk about one of mine: the 6th-to-♭3rd move. This is a great, sassy, country-sounding device that aims to please every time. We'll look at several things you can do with it and how you can implement it into lots of different lick ideas.

The Notes

We'll go ahead and work in D for this lesson. The notes we'll be talking about then are the 6th, B, and the ♭3rd, F. Here are several places on the neck that these occur in the key of D:

6fr

10fr

3fr

8fr

These notes form a tritone relationship, which is the same as a diminished 5th or augmented 4th interval. This is an unstable sound that's a cornerstone in blues, jazz, and country.

Examples

In these examples, we'll look at how the 6th-to-♭3rd move can be included in your lines for an ear-catching effect.

LICK 1

This first one begins with some chromatics and ends with a nice use of the 6th-to-♭3rd move, after which we continue down the scale through the 2nd to the root.

LICK 2

Here's a bluesy-sounding lick in the tenth position that finishes with a classic 6th-to-♭3rd move. We bend the ♭3rd a quarter step for a nice bit of sass.

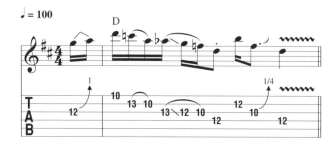

LICK 3

This lick includes another classic finish: 6th–♭3rd–major 3rd–root.

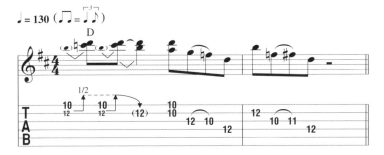

LICK 4

Here's a fun one that uses a syncopated 6–♭3–1–3 pattern and some sliding double stops for a slightly Western swing feel.

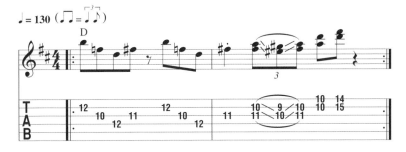

LICK 5

In this final lick, we're taking an original four-note sequence of 6–♭3–2–1 in fifth position and transposing it up the neck where it functions at different intervallic groups: first at eighth position for 1–♭5–4–♭3, and then in twelfth position for 3–♭7–6–5. Be sure to use hybrid picking on this one.

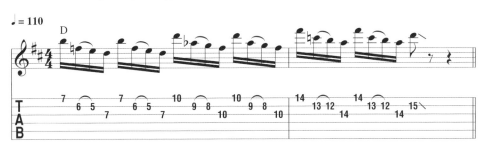

Listen for the 6th-to-♭3rd move in the recordings of some of your favorite players, and I'll bet you find it sprinkled in there. It's a great sound that always gets the listener's attention.

LESSON #62: THE PIVOT-NOTE OBLIQUE BEND

String bending has long been a mainstay in country guitar, and oblique bends are often the bends of choice when creating pedal steel-sounding licks. An oblique bend is one in which one bent note is played against one unbent note. In this lesson, we're going to take that concept, which is fairly common in rock, country, and blues, and expand it with what I call the pivot-note oblique bend.

What's a Pivot Note?

A pivot note is one that sounds repeatedly against which other notes "pivot." For example, in this line the G note on string 2 is the pivot note.

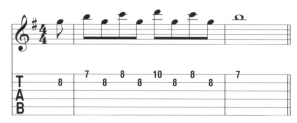

To make this idea sound more country, we'll bend up to a note and hold that as a pivot note, against which we'll play notes on higher strings, eventually releasing the bend (usually) and completing the lick.

Examples

We'll work in the key of G for this lesson, but remember that you can transpose these licks into any key you want to.

LICK 1

This first lick takes place in tenth position and uses half-step bends. The B note (bent up from the B♭) is the pivot note. Use hybrid picking, plucking the notes on string 1 with your fingers.

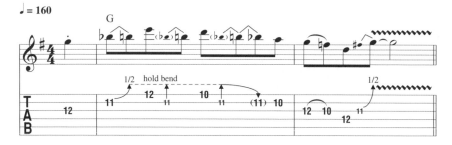

LICK 2

This lick features a pivot note of the ♭7th (F) bent up a whole step to the root (G). The 3rd (B) and 2nd (A) are played against it on top. Though it's not easy, it's most comfortable to play the bend with your second finger.

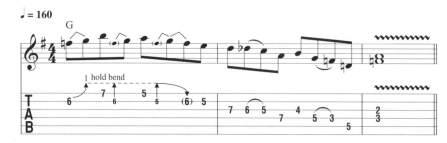

LICK 3

In this one, we're using three different pivot-note oblique bends—the first two are whole-step bends and the last one is a half-step bend. The bends are from A (2nd) up to B (3rd), from F (♭7th) up to G (tonic), and from E (6th) up to F (♭7th).

TRACK 12
0:18
CD 2

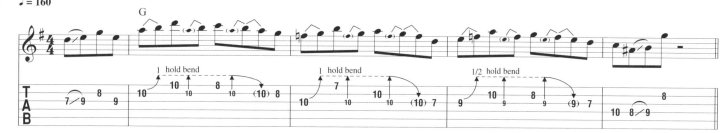

LICK 4

Here's a nice, old country-sounding lick that holds the same bent pivot note (A bent up to B) against three different higher notes.

TRACK 12
0:29
CD 2

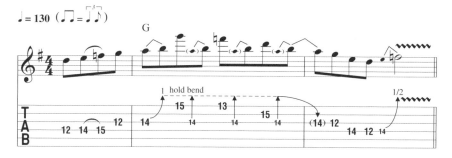

LICK 5

In our final lick, we're again using three different pivot-note bends, but we're pivoting against them with double stops this time. Make sure you're getting those bends in tune and holding them steady until you release them. I find it most comfortable to use the second finger for all three bends.

TRACK 12
0:38
CD 2

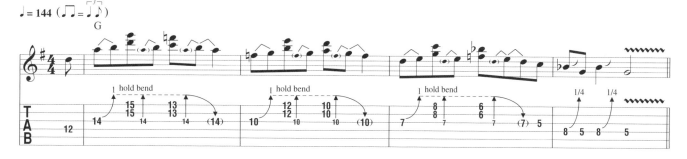

There are infinite variations on this type of thing, so have fun experimenting with it. The most important thing to achieving an authentic pedal steel sound is to be extremely accurate with your bends. Try to visualize stretching up to the exact pitch with a mechanical lever, and then hold it there steadily until you release.

CHROMATIC APPROACH TONES

From Chet Atkins and Jerry Reed to Brent Mason and Scotty Anderson, country soloists have relied on chromatic notes to dress up their lines for decades. One favorite device in this regard is the chromatic approach tone.

An approach tone is a note that leads into a chord tone from below. These can be diatonic (in the key), but here we'll mostly be dealing with chromatic ones. All of the approach tones we'll use in this lesson will be one half step below the chord tone.

How It Works

It's really quite simple in theory. You simply have a target pitch in mind that's a chord tone, such as the root, 3rd, 5th, or maybe 7th, and slide or hammer-on to it from a half step below. Here's a very basic exercise in C:

EXERCISE 1

In this example, the 3rd, E, is the target pitch, and we use a chromatic approach tone, Eb, to precede it. That's the basic idea.

EXERCISE 2

This is also commonly used on double stops. Here's how the previous example could be adjusted for double stops. Notice that we've replaced the hammer-on with a slide.

Examples

Let's take a look at how we can apply these to some licks. In the previous exercises, only the target note fell on the downbeat, but you'll see in the following examples that either the approach tone or the target pitch can fall on the downbeat.

LICK 1

This first one in C is an example of what you can do with the idea presented in Exercise 2. Hybrid picking is a must here.

TRACK 13
0:00
CD 2

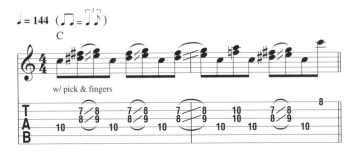

LICK 2

Here's an idea in D where we're working down a D7 chord with double stops on the top two strings. Pick all the double stops with your fingers and pick the dead notes with the pick.

LICK 3

Here's a nice ascending idea that moves double stops up through A7 and resolves to D. Use hybrid picking, again playing the double stops with the fingers and the dead notes with the pick.

LICK 4

Our final lick is in G and returns to single notes. After approaching each tone of a G7 chord, we end with a surprise E note (6th).

You can use this technique to spice up even the simplest of phrases. Although it's not nearly as common, you can also try approaching notes from above for a different sound. Experiment with it!

LESSON #64: LOWER NEIGHBOR TONES

Sometimes, the note you need to liven up a line is only a fret away. A case in point is the use of lower neighbor tones, a favorite in the Western swing sound and a staple in the pedal steel player's bag of licks. A lower neighbor tone is one that lies just below a target pitch—often a chord tone—and it can be diatonic (within the key) or chromatic. In this lesson, we're going to focus on neighbor tones that are a half step below. Consequently, most of these will be chromatic.

The Basic Idea

The most common application of this idea is to play a single note, double stop, or sometimes a triple stop, slide down a half step, and then slide back up. Usually, the first note is the only one picked. Here's how it would look with a G note on string 5.

Now we take same idea and apply it to all the notes of, say, a G chord. Let's work through a few exercises to get the basic concept under our fingers.

EXERCISE 1

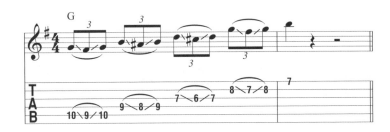

EXERCISE 2

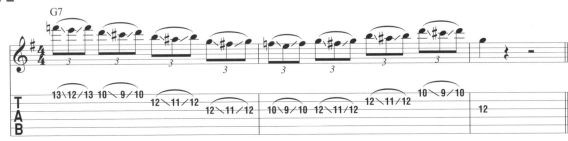

You'll find that the fingering can be a bit tricky at times, and you may need to experiment with a few different options to find the smoothest execution. This is especially true when dealing with double stops and triple stops, as we'll soon see.

Examples

Now let's see this idea in action with five slinky licks.

LICK 1

Though the exercises were triplet-based, 8th notes are commonly used to generate an on-the-beat, off-the-beat syncopation. That's the thought behind this single-note lick in A.

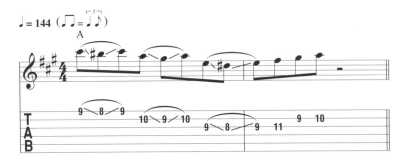

LICK 2

Here's a slinky phrase in G that moves 6th intervals down with lower neighbor tones on each note. Take this one slowly at first and let the muscle memory set in before you try to speed it up. There's a lot of precise sliding going on.

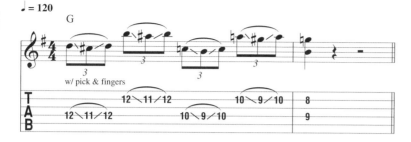

LICK 3

Here's a double-stop example in E that moves up some dyads suggesting an E9 harmony. Again, learn the lick slowly and correctly first before turning up the speed. With licks like this, the proper fingering can make or break a smooth execution. I've included the one that makes the most sense to me.

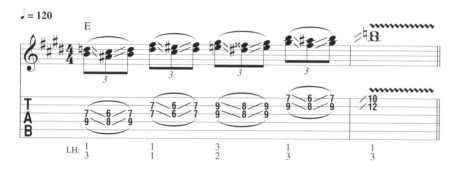

LICK 4

This lick in A moves up A and Bm chords in double stops with lower neighbor tones and caps off with a chromatically descending 3rds line.

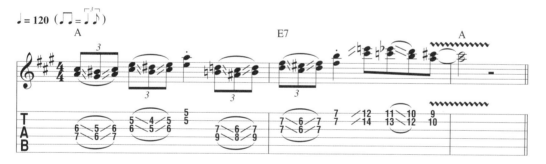

LICK 5

We'll finish off with a triple stop lick in G that's not too difficult due to the fact that it doesn't stray too far from third position.

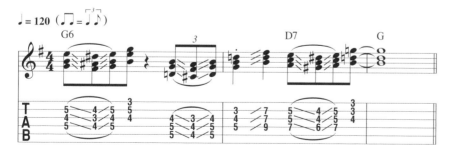

Remember to experiment with the fingering for these licks to find the smoothest way to play them. Strive for a smooth, slippery sound and have fun!

LESSON #65: 6TH CHORDS

Western swing has a distinctive sound. It's part jazz, part country, and a whole lot of fun. One harmony that's often played by its practitioners is the 6th chord. This bright, sunny chord only differs from a major triad by one note, but it makes quite a big difference.

What Is a 6th Chord?

As you may know, a major triad, or major chord, is built from a root, major 3rd, and perfect 5th. The 6th chord adds a major 6th to this.

In actual practice, the 5th is not always present in a 6th chord, so you may only see it as a three-note chord with the root, major 3rd, and 6th.

Common 6th Chord Voicings

Below are some 6th chord voicings commonly used in country guitar. They're shown here with a G root.

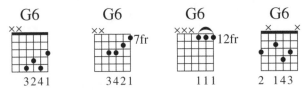

Note that partial versions of these voicings are also used. Some of these voicings could actually be called Em voicings, because they don't contain a D note. However, when played in context, especially with a bass or secondary rhythm instrument, the 6th chord sound can be inferred.

Examples

LICK 1

These chords are often used as rhythmic punctuation at the beginning or ending of a line, as demonstrated here.

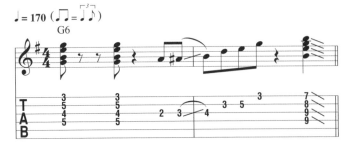

LICK 2

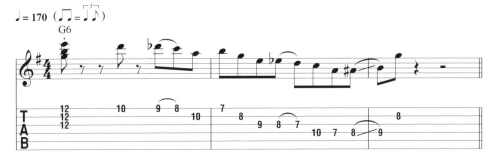

LICK 3

It's also common to outline 6th harmonies by using double stops or triple stops decorated with chromatic lower neighbor tones.

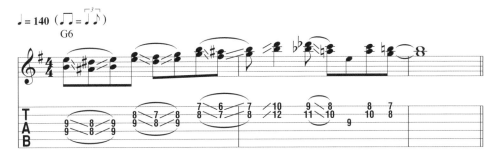

LICK 4

Be sure to fool around with this great sounding chord. It's a nice way to interject a jazzy, Western swing flavor into your country lines. Check out Chet Atkins for a prime example of this type of thing.

LESSON #66: DIATONIC 3RDS

Double stops are a common thread throughout country guitar, and two intervals are among the most widely used in this regard: 3rds and 6ths. This immediately recognizable sound can add a bit of flair to your lines and help outline the harmony, especially when playing in a three-piece band with only a bass guitar as your backup.

In this lesson, we'll be dealing with diatonic 3rds. This simply means that all the notes we play will be within a certain key or scale.

Harmonizing the Major Scale

We'll work in the key of G here. First we'll harmonize the G major scale in 3rds. We'll do this by playing the scale horizontally along the neck on strings 3 and 2 in parallel 3rds. It'll look like this:

EXERCISE 1: G MAJOR SCALE IN 3RDS

So that's the basic idea. If we analyze the above exercise, we see that we have two shapes of 3rds: major 3rds and minor 3rds. However, we won't always be playing 3rds on strings 3 and 2, so we need to learn how to finger those intervals on each string set. Here are the shapes for each interval on every string set.

3RD SHAPES ON THE GUITAR

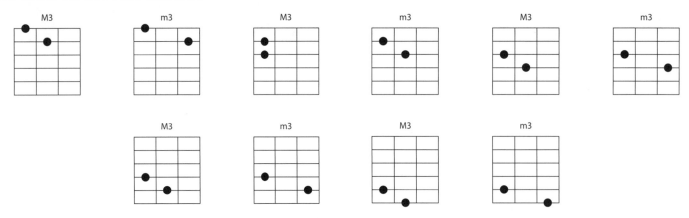

You should practice harmonizing the major scale on each string set in every key until you're familiar with it inside and out.

Examples

Now let's see how we can implement these sounds with some licks.

LICK 1

This first lick works well over a I–V–I progression (G–D7–G) and accesses 3rds via bends in the beginning and fretted versions in the second half.

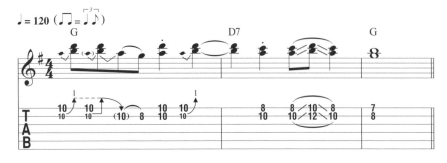

LICK 2

Here's one to use over a V–I progression. We're just starting from a D/F♯ double stop and walking our way down to the tonic G/B with a little syncopation to give it some life.

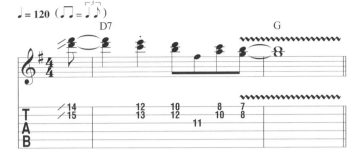

LICK 3

You don't always have to sound the 3rd intervals simultaneously. Here's an idea using slides to travel down in 3rds melodically.

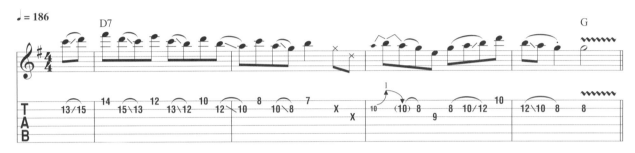

LICK 4

And here's a neat trick for sliding 3rds even when you're moving between the minor and major version. If you use a fingering of middle finger on string 3 and first finger on string 2 throughout, you can slide to all the double stops just by cramming your fingers together for the major 3rd shapes.

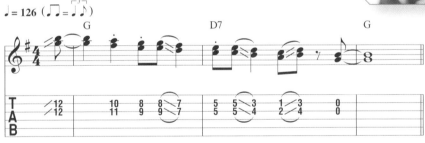

LICK 5

And here's another great way to incorporate these 3rds. In this final lick, we're working out of the D Mixolydian mode, which contains the same exact notes as G major, but it just treats D as the tonic. We're moving up in 3rds on strings 4 and 3 melodically and pulling off each note on string 3 to the open string. We're partially palm muting on the fourth string throughout to give it a little oomph.

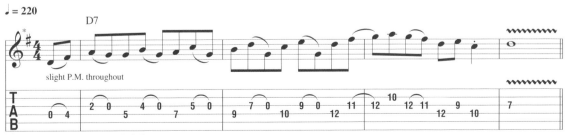

*Key signature denotes D Mixolydian.

LESSON #67: DIATONIC 6THS

Double stops have always been common in country guitar, and two intervals are among the most widely used in this regard: 3rds and 6ths. These devices can add a bit of flair to your lines and help outline the harmony, especially when playing in a three-piece band with only a bass guitar as your backup.

In this lesson, we'll be dealing with diatonic 6ths. This simply means that all the notes we play will be within a certain key or scale.

Harmonizing the Major Scale

We'll work in the key of G here. First, we'll harmonize the scale in 6ths with strings 3 and 1. That looks like this:

EXERCISE 1: G MAJOR SCALE IN 6THS

So that's the basic idea. If we analyze the above exercise, we see that we have two shapes of 6ths: major 6ths and minor 6ths. However, we won't always be playing 6ths on strings 3 and 1, so we need to learn how to finger those intervals on each string set. Here are the shapes for each interval on every string set.

6TH SHAPES ON THE GUITAR

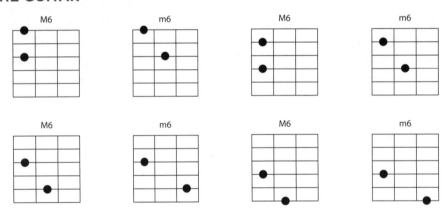

You should practice harmonizing the major scale on each string set in every key until you're familiar with it inside and out.

Examples

Ok, now let's see what these things can do.

LICK 1

This first lick is a nice one to use on a classic country shuffle.

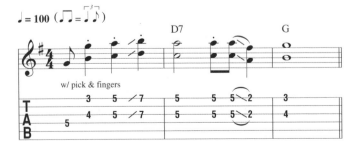

LICK 2

And here's a similar idea that includes a bend. Notice that the note on string 3 is bent a whole step, while the note on string 1 is bent a half step. This actually looks a bit harder than it is. The trick is to try to keep the strings parallel as you bend them. That will automatically bend the strings the different amounts they need to be.

Be sure to check your target pitches (fret 9, string 3 and fret 8, string 1) though to make sure you're accurate.

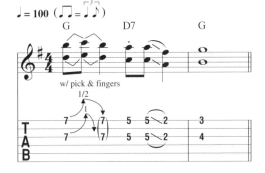

LICK 3

Another possibility is to play melodic 6ths, as demonstrated here. We're sliding up 6th shapes on strings 4 and 2 with a three-against-four rhythmic feel.

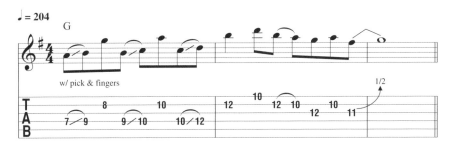

LICK 4

This lick will give you practice sliding between different interval shapes. You can use your index finger on string 3 and ring finger on string 5 throughout, but you'll need to adjust the spacing to accommodate the different distances.

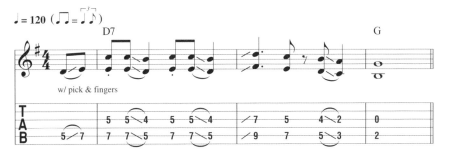

LICK 5

This final lick takes the idea from our previous lick to more of an extreme, sliding continuously between various interval shapes. This type of idea is more forgiving the lower you are on the fretboard.

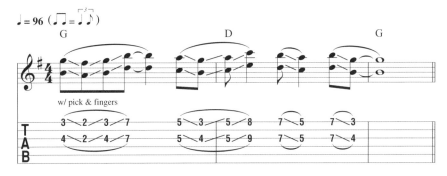

Have fun playing with these intervals. You can certainly do some colorful things with them. And remember that you can interject short phrases of 6ths; you don't have to play an entire solo or even an entire phrase with them. Sometimes only a few notes are all that's needed to turn the listener's ear.

LESSON #68: CHROMATIC 3RDS

With the hybrid picking technique so commonly used in country guitar, certain sounds come naturally and can therefore be exploited easily. One such sound is the double-stop 3rd interval. With hybrid picking, these can be picked out harmonically (both notes played together) or melodically (notes played one at a time) with equal deftness. Country guitarists, as well as pedal steel players, often dress up their lines even more with chromatic 3rds, and that's the focus of this lesson.

By chromatic 3rds, I mean we'll be including some 3rds (major or minor) that are not normally found in a scale. These are very often used in passing between two 3rds that are in key.

3rd Shapes on the Guitar

Before we get to the licks, let's make sure you're familiar with how 3rds look on the fretboard.

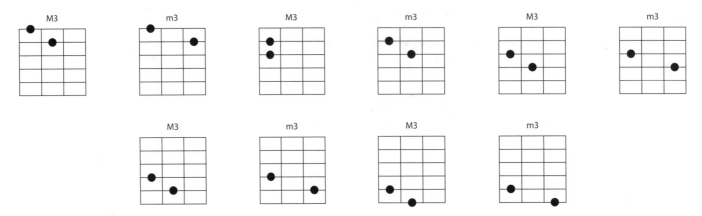

Examples

Ok, now let's take a look at how these shapes can be used.

LICK 1

This first lick is in the key of A and uses the same chromatic 3rd (major 3rds) descent in two octaves. The key to this lick is the articulation. Make those 3rds sharp and staccato! Hybrid picking will help with this.

LICK 2

And here's another one in A that's got a Western swing flavor to it, with its allusion to the 6th sound (F#) in the beginning. We end by moving a minor 3rd down chromatically to connect the 3rd and the 5th (C#/E) to the 2nd and 4th (B/D).

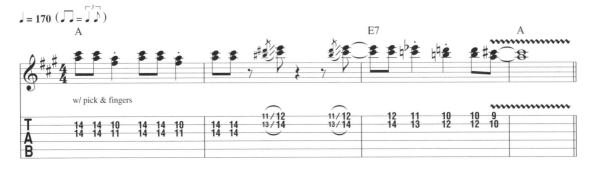

LICK 3

This is a slightly jazzy line in D that begins with a pedal steel-sounding oblique bend in twelfth position. In the middle of the line, we descend through chromatic 3rds in melodic style using hybrid picking before enclosing the major 3rd and resolving to the root to wrap it up.

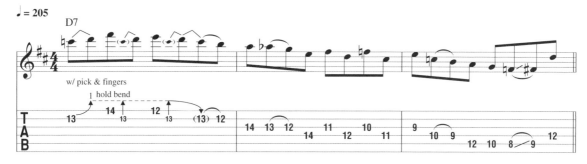

LICK 4

In this line, we're using two different sets of descending chromatic 3rds—major 3rds in measure 1 and minor 3rds in measure 3. Note, however, that we abandon the 3rds pattern in measure 3 on beat 3, as we finish off with an F7 arpeggio.

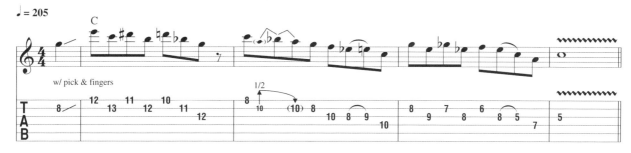

LICK 5

Although descending 3rds are probably more common, ascending 3rds are a possibility too, as this final lick demonstrates. We move up through the ♭7/9, 7/♯9, and root/3rd of A before we finish off with an A Mixolydian line implementing a pedal steel pre-bend and release.

These chromatic 3rds can be a great way to add a bit of fire and flair to your solos. With hybrid picking, it's relatively easy to blur through them quickly, and they'll help lead to other ideas that may be new to you. Experiment with them and try to spot them in solos from your favorite players.

With the hybrid picking technique so commonly used in country guitar, certain sounds come naturally and can therefore be exploited easily. One such sound is the double-stop 6th interval. With hybrid picking, these can be played harmonically (both notes played together) or melodically (notes played one at a time) with equal deftness. Country guitarists, as well as pedal steel players, often dress up their lines even more with chromatic 6ths, and that's the focus of this lesson.

By chromatic 6ths, I mean we'll be including some 6ths (major or minor) that are not normally found in a scale. These are very often used in passing between two 6ths that are in key.

6th Shapes on the Guitar

Before we get to the licks, let's make sure you're familiar with how 6ths look on the fretboard.

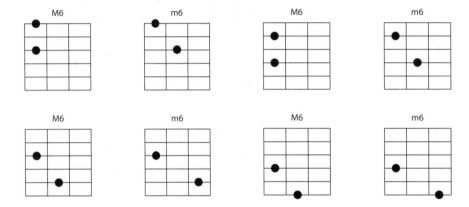

Examples

Now let's see what we can do with these 6ths.

LICK 1

In this first lick in C, we're sliding down chromatically from G/E to F/D and then approaching the tonic E/C 6th via a half-step slide from below. Use hybrid picking for this one.

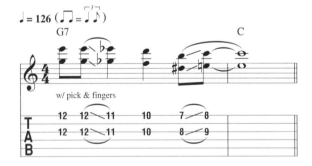

LICK 2

Here's a common hybrid picking approach with 6ths. We're playing melodic 6ths and pulling off each lower note to the open G string. Apply a slight palm mute to the G string to help keep it lean and clean.

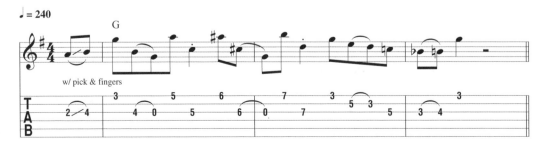

LICK 3

Here's a variation on the previous idea using triplets and playing on the 4/2 string set. Although this lick sounds as if it's in G at the beginning, we discover at the end that it's actually been a long G7 lick resolving to C. Again, use hybrid picking and apply a slight palm mute to the fourth string.

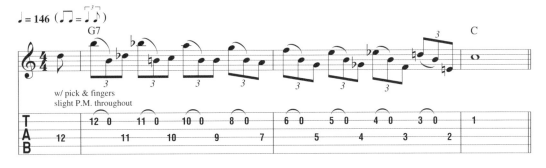

LICK 4

This lick takes that idea to the extreme, using sets of chromatic 6ths on two different string sets. Start slowly and make sure you have the timing clean and accurate before bringing it up to speed.

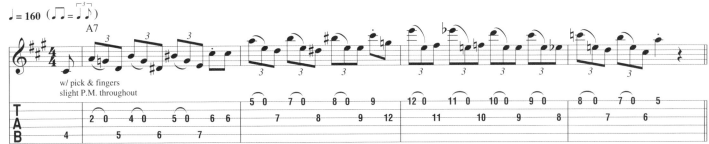

Listen to Pete Anderson and Brent Mason for some jaw-dropping examples of this kind of thing. It's a great way to add some flash with relative ease, and it always gets the listener's attention.

LESSON #70: OPEN-STRING PULL-OFFS

Country music often appears in the sharp keys of G, D, A, and E, as well as C, and country guitarists have not let this fact go unnoticed. It just so happens that most of the open strings on the guitar can work well in those keys. What does this mean? It means we can implement them in our runs to shake things up and create some scary twang. This lesson is all about open-string pull-offs.

Bluegrass-Style Licks

When you remain in open position, you can use open-string pull-offs to play bluegrass-sounding runs with relative ease.

LICK 1

Here's a classic lick in the key of G.

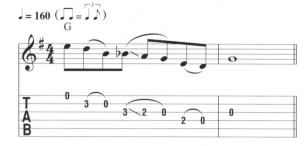

LICK 2

And here's a nice one in the key of C that adds a hammer-on into the mix.

Rockabilly-Style Licks

Open position can also generate some barn-burning rockabilly style licks. Chet was a master at this.

LICK 3

There are a few out-of-key notes in this lick, but the flash wins out. It's much easier to blaze through this line when the fingering is the same for each string.

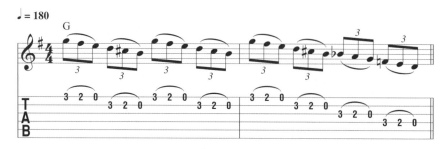

LICK 4

Here's one in G that uses hybrid picking to roll through some arpeggios and create a faux banjo roll sound. Try to let the notes ring as much as possible.

Neck-Climbing Licks

We can also climb up the neck while still pulling off to open strings to get a great, clucky country sound.

LICK 5

Here's a lick in D Mixolydian that moves up into third position before ending with a cascading run barred at the 5th fret and a pedal steel bend.

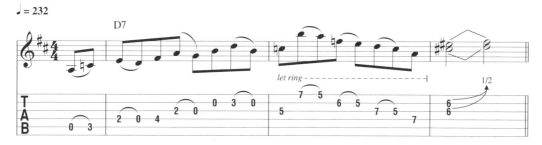

LICK 6

This one in the key of E pulls off to the open D and G strings. Though the D string is within the E Mixolydian mode and therefore could be considered in key, the open G string is blatantly not. However, the lick moves by quickly enough that the tonal mismatch doesn't offend the ear. In fact, it creates a tartness that's desirable.

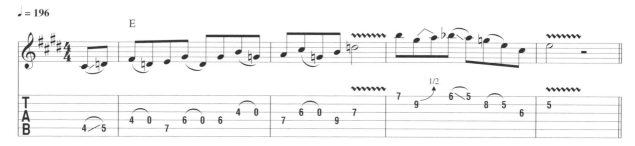

The next time you find yourself playing in one of the sharp keys, try working a few open-string pull-off lines in. You'll often be surprised at what you can come up with, and nothing twangs like an open string!

LESSON #71: THE MINOR V SOUND OVER THE I CHORD

Country guitar has borrowed equally from not only blues and rock, but also jazz throughout the years. In fact, many of the genre's best pickers are also quite competent jazzers (an understatement in some cases). If you don't believe me, just check out Brent Mason, Scotty Anderson, and the late, great Chet Atkins. When you analyze the chord progressions of (especially) older country songs, this isn't all that hard to believe. Many popular country songs of the thirties, forties, and fifties used chord progressions that have much in common with jazz standards, such as ii–V–I progressions and cycle of 5ths movement.

This jazziness has crept its way into the solos of some of the finest country pickers, and it helps lend the country sound a sophisticated side. In this lesson, we're going to look at a melodic device that's popular in jazz and see how it can sound perfectly at home in a country lick. I'm talking about the minor v sound over the I chord.

A Little Chord Theory

Normally in a major key, the V chord is major (or dominant, which adds the 7th). This helps provide the leading tone relationship (the major 3rd of the V chord is the 7th scale step of the key) that defines the key. However, as is common in blues and jazz, country music often makes use of a dominant tonic chord. In actuality, its practitioners often treat the tonic chord as a dominant chord, whether the rhythm section plays a triad or a dominant chord.

Playing a minor v sound over the I chord is a melodic strategy that helps you get a dominant 9th or 11th sound. This is illustrated below, as the tones of a G minor triad and Gm7 chord are analyzed in comparison to a C root.

As you can see, playing through the notes of a Gm triad over a C chord automatically highlights the 5th, ♭7th, and the first extension, the 9th. A Gm7 over C stretches that to include the next extension, the 11th.

Generally speaking, it's most often used to create a brief bit of tension that's resolved to a tone (or tones) of the I chord.

Examples

Let's take a look at what I'm talking about with some licks. We'll work in the key of C in this lesson for simplicity.

LICK 1

This first lick begins with C major pentatonic and finishes off by arpeggiating through Gm before landing on the final C note. You can get these notes by simply playing the C Mixolydian mode, but by thinking in G minor for a moment, it's easier to target the specific pitches you want.

TRACK 21
0:00
CD 2

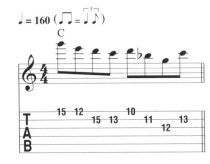

LICK 2

Here's another basic line that begins with a Gm7 arpeggio and resolves to a C major pentatonic line.

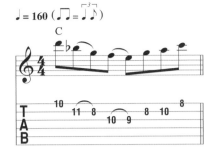

LICK 3

In this line, we play up a C7 arpeggio and then slide down to descend through a Gm7 arpeggio, resolving to the 3rd (E) of C at the end, followed by a leap up to the root, C. This is a classic ending in both country and jazz lines.

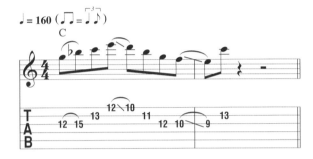

LICK 4

Now let's look at a few more advanced examples. This line begins with a three-note chromatic descent from the major 3rd (E) to the 2nd, or 9th (D). At that point, we run down the Gm triad before pulling off another three-note chromatic descent—this time from the 5th (G) to the 4th (F).

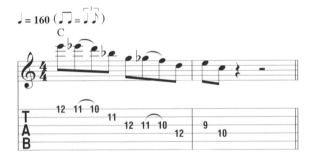

LICK 5

Let's finish off with a neat line in fifth position that combines slides, pull-offs, and a triple-stop oblique bend. The minor v sound takes place on beats 1 and 2, where we're arpeggiating up through Gm7.

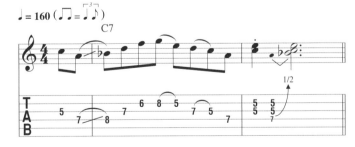

The more familiar you get with this sound, the more you'll begin to pick it out in solos that you hear. It's often only a few beats long, but that's all that's needed to give the line a sophisticated color.

LESSON #72: TRANSPOSING LICKS FOR THE I, IV, AND V CHORDS

One of the great things about the guitar is the ease of transposition. If you're playing something that doesn't involve any open strings, you can transpose it up or down to a different key by sliding the exact same fingering up or down. We can take advantage of this within the same key as well by transposing a lick to fit another chord. In this lesson, we'll deal with transposing licks for the I, IV, and V chords.

In any major key, the pattern of triads in the harmonized scale remains the same:

I: major	ii: minor	iii: minor	IV: major	V: major	vi: minor	vii°: diminished

This means in any key there are three diatonic major chords: the I, IV, and V.

If we have a line over the I chord that's based on the arpeggio or the major pentatonic, we can transpose that *same exact line* to the IV and V chords as well. For example, let's take this simple phrase to start. We'll work in A for this lesson.

Here's a basic phrase from the A major pentatonic scale in second position. (You may think of this as the F♯ minor pentatonic scale, which is the relative minor.)

We can take that same exact fingering and slide it up to seventh position for the IV chord, D, and ninth position for the V chord, E.

And that's the basic idea. It's simple, but effective.

Examples

Let's take a look at a few licks to demonstrate this concept.

LICK 1

This first lick makes use of a pedal steel bend for each chord. This is a very common application of this technique.

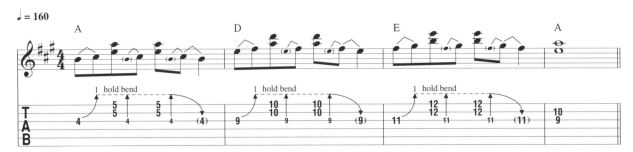

LICK 2

This lick starts on the V chord and moves V–IV–I. We add a few notes on the end to round out the phrase on the I chord.

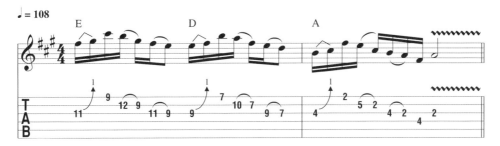

LICK 3

In this A lick, we're using a classic oblique bend phrase for each chord.

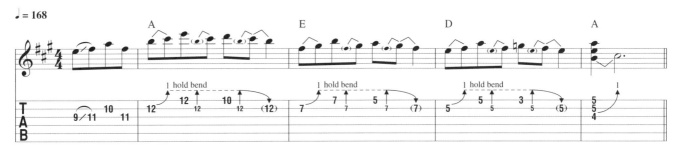

LICK 4

You don't always have to move the same shape around the fretboard on the same string set. With a little fretboard knowledge, you can transpose the idea to a different string set, which will prevent you from having to move all over the fretboard. This is demonstrated in this G lick.

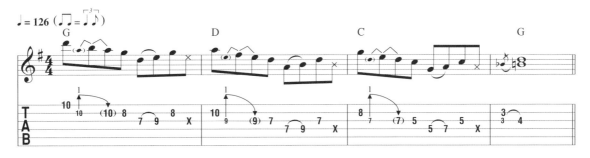

Listen for this kind of idea in your favorite solos. You'll hear it more than you think. Also remember that you don't always have to transpose the same line to the I, IV, and V chords. Sometimes it's nice to only play it for two chords and then follow up with a contrasting idea to wrap it up. Experiment and have fun with it.

Country music has always borrowed heavily from the blues, as has rock, jazz, and just about any other genre, for that matter. The blues influence is ubiquitous in country solos, and sometimes the only thing separating a country lick from a straight up blues lick is tone and articulation. In this lesson, I'd like to talk about a concept that's prevalent in both styles; I call it the blues/Dorian hybrid scale.

The Two Scales

Before we look at a hybrid, let's make sure we know each scale individually. We'll work in A for this lesson. Let's first take a look at the typical A blues scale fingering in fifth position.

A BLUES SCALE

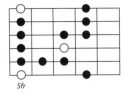

And now let's check out the A Dorian mode in fifth/fourth position.

A DORIAN MODE

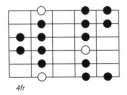

Make sure you're familiar with these scale shapes before moving on.

Combining Them into a Hybrid

What we'll do now is combine the two scales to form a hybrid scale with eight different notes. In reality, we're only adding one note, the ♭5th, to the Dorian mode.

A BLUES/DORIAN HYBRID

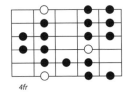

Examples

Now let's see what we can do with this new hybrid.

LICK 1

Lick 1 in A uses a typical move with this form: sliding double stops. Be sure to use hybrid picking.

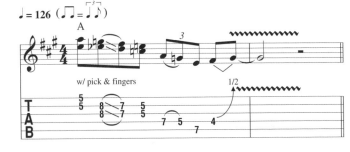

LICK 2

Here's a similar idea in C.

TRACK 23
0:10
CD 2

LICK 3

In this C minor lick, we use a series of pre-bends for a faux pedal steel effect.

TRACK 23
0:18
CD 2

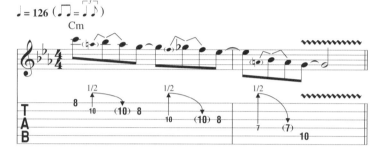

Incorporating the Major 3rd

When we bring the major 3rd into the mix, things open up considerably. We end up with a nine-note scale that some people refer to as the composite blues scale.

A BLUES/DORIAN HYBRID WITH ADDED MAJOR 3RD

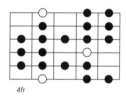

4fr

LICK 4

A nice way to work with this is to use the minor 3rds until the end of the lick and then resolve to the major 3rd.

TRACK 23
0:28
CD 2

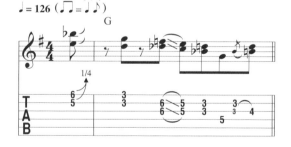

LICK 5

Or you can mix and match them throughout, as in this ascending lick in E.

TRACK 23
0:36
CD 2

Country guitarists love the tone of open strings, and with most country songs written in the sharp keys of C, G, D, A, and E, we get to use them quite often. One device in particular makes the most of this phenomenon. Some people call them "harp licks." I like to call them open-string cascade licks. Pull one of these off in a solo and you can really turn a head or two.

The Basic Idea

So, how does it work? Well, the idea is to play a scale run that combines fretted notes with open strings, allowing as many notes to ring together as possible. The effect is something like a harp or a piano playing a scale with the sustain pedal down. The sharp keys (C, G, D, A, and E especially) will work best because most of the open strings on the guitar will be in key.

Depending on the key and scale you wish to play, you'll need to experiment with fingerings in order to find the right combination of fretted and open-string notes. Many times, especially if you're playing a seven-note scale (as opposed to a pentatonic, for instance), you may end up with some wide stretches for major or minor 2nd intervals on adjacent strings.

EXERCISE 1

For example, let's say we wanted to play this G major scale:

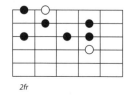

But we wanted to play it as a cascade. After some experimentation, we might come up with this.

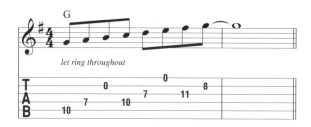

Examples

These licks are normally performed with hybrid picking or fingerstyle. Let's take a look at some more examples to see how it's done.

LICK 1

In this first lick, we're descending a D major scale. Be careful, as the string pattern is a bit tricky.

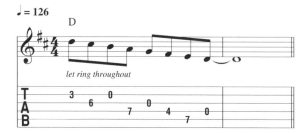

LICK 2

You don't always have to run up or down the major scale. Here's a descending run through the E minor hexatonic scale (E–F♯–G–A–B–D) that sounds nice over either an Em or G chord.

LICK 3

You can also run down and back up a scale as demonstrated with this A major pentatonic lick.

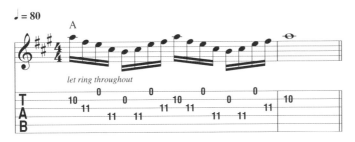

LICK 4

You can get as elaborate with this idea as you want, spanning multiple octaves and adding chromatic passing tones. Here's an idea based off the A Mixolydian mode with an added C♮ passing tone on the second octave of the ascent.

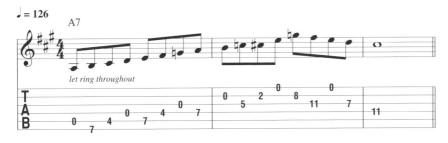

Chet Atkins was a master at this type of thing, so listen to some of his recordings to hear how it can sound. It's a lot of fun to mess around with, and there are so many variations with the combinations of fretted and open notes that you'll never get tired of it.

LESSON #75: UNISON SLIDE TRICK

One of the true joys when soloing is the ability to glide all over the fretboard, shifting between positions effortlessly. This isn't always easy to do, though, and some players get so comfortable in that good ol' box position that they never leave. In this lesson, I'd like to show a neat little trick that can let you smoothly and painlessly change positions at the beginning, end, or in the middle of a lick. I call it the unison slide trick.

The Basic Idea

In this trick, we'll play one note on a higher string followed by a note on the next string down. We'll then slide that lower note up to match the pitch of the higher note, thereby shifting us into the next position. It's basically another approach to alternating x two notes that happens to move us into another region of the neck.

For example, instead of just playing E–D–E
with one of these two fingerings:

EXAMPLE A   EXAMPLE B

We can use the unison slide trick to move us from fifth position up to seventh position.

So, instead of playing this lick all in third position:

We can use the unison slide trick to play it like this:

EXAMPLE C   EXAMPLE D   EXAMPLE E

What are the benefits? Well, there are a few:

▶ It sounds interesting and provides a unique tone.

▶ It puts you in a different part of the neck, which can lead to phrases that you normally might not play and/or connect you to a phrase that you like to play in a certain spot on the neck.

▶ It helps you comfortably move up the neck without requiring abrupt shifts or wide stretches.

Licks

LICK 1

Now let's see this idea in action. This first lick in E expands the idea from the examples and shows what can be done.

LICK 2

Here's a Western swing type lick that works well over a G dominant chord.

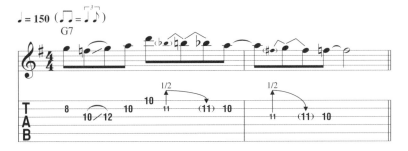

LICK 3

This lick is an example of just where this idea can lead. After starting with the first few notes, I stumbled upon the rest of the phrase, which was completely new to me.

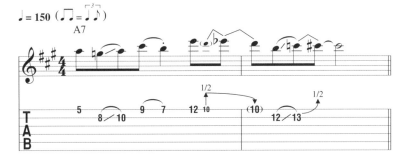

LICK 4

And here's an idea in G minor that strings a few unison slides together and finishes off with a blues lick.

Of course, this trick isn't limited only to country licks. It works equally well in rock, jazz, blues, etc. It lays particularly well in the country style though because it's so compatible with hybrid picking. The next time you find yourself running through a lick you've played a thousand times the same way, try using this trick and see where it takes you!

LESSON #76: HYBRID PICKING PIVOT LICKS

Hybrid picking is an integral part of country guitar. Its snappy sound, though, is only half the benefit. It also allows the alternating of notes on different strings to be executed with ease. This fact affects much of what we play as country guitarists, just as the tuning of the guitar itself affects the licks that are idiomatic to it, as opposed to those idiomatic to a piano or saxophone.

One of the ways we can use the hybrid picking technique to our advantage is with pivot licks. This is a nifty little melodic device that has roots in classical music—and neo-classical shredders, such as Yngwie Malmsteen, play their share of pivot licks—but it's been adopted by many other genres, including country.

What's a Pivot Note?

A pivot note is one that sounds repeatedly against which other notes "pivot." For example, in this line, the B note on string 3 is the pivot note.

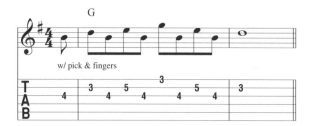

A pivot note can be higher in pitch than the notes pivoting against it, but more often than not, especially in country guitar, it's lower in pitch.

As mentioned earlier, the use of hybrid picking is essential here. When the pivot note is lower in pitch than the notes pivoting against it, the pick will play the pivot note and the fingers will play the notes above. It's also common to apply a slight palm mute to the lower note to keep things nice and clean sounding.

Examples

Let's take a look to see how this works.

LICK 1

Here's a lick in G that uses the same B pedal tone from our example above.

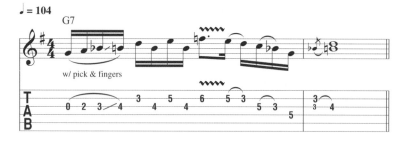

LICK 2

Here's another one in G that uses a tonic G pedal.

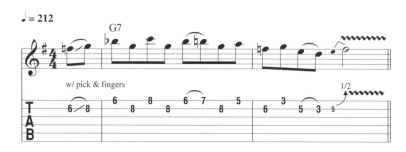

LICK 3

Here's an idea in A based off an A6 chord.

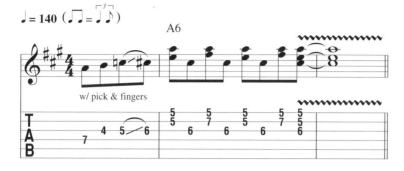

LICK 4

You can also make the pivot note a held bent note for a nice pedal steel effect. Here's an example of that in C. I bend the A note with my middle finger in order to reach the high E note easier.

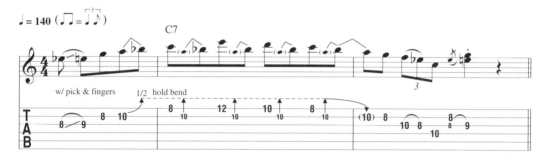

LICK 5

Double stops are also common with this type of thing. Here's a typical example in A. You'll have to learn this one slowly to get the position shifts smooth. Until the very end (and save the pickup notes), the only time I'm in fifth position is for the C/E double stop and the A note immediately following it. I play everything else in seventh position.

LICK 6

Let's round things out with one more bent-and-held pivot note in C. This one is a classic.

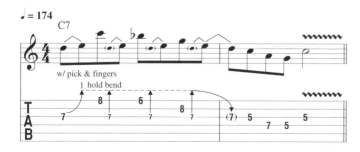

Have fun messing around with this idea. It can be incorporated many different ways, and it's a great-sounding trick that can be flashy too.

LESSON #77: BEHIND-THE-NUT BENDS

If you've ever listened to Jerry Donahue, then you've no doubt heard his mastery of one of country guitar's most beloved tricks: the behind-the-nut bend. This trademark of the Tele will turn heads every time, and it will add a whole new array of possibilities to your bag of pedal steel licks.

The Logistics

Behind-the-nut bends can't be executed on every guitar. For starters, if you have a locking nut, they won't work at all. They won't work well on a Les Paul-style guitar because of the headstock design. You need an inline tuner design to provide enough room to manipulate the string. They're somewhat possible on a Strat, but you're limited with what you can do. The Tele is far and away the axe of choice for this trick.

It should be noted that you may have tuning problems with this trick. Often times, after a bend the string will get bound in the nut slot and not fall all the way back into place, resulting in the string being a bit sharp. Applying graphite to the nut slots can work wonders in this regard. There are also other lubricant products available on the market that accomplish the same thing. An alternative is to install a roller nut, which all but eliminates this problem altogether.

The Technique

Though the technique is a bit self-explanatory, it will take some serious getting used to. On a Tele, the most commonly bent strings behind the nut are the fourth, third, and second. You may see the others, but not nearly as often. To execute the bend, use at least two fingers (the first and second or second and third usually) and push down into the headstock behind the nut.

It takes a good amount of finger strength, so don't get discouraged if it's not happening at first. Start off with some half-step bends before moving on to the whole-step variety.

EXERCISE 1

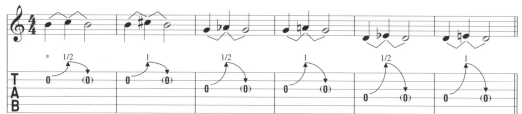

*Bend behind the nut throughout.

EXERCISE 2

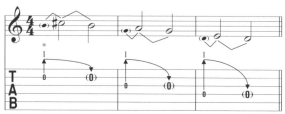

*Bend behind the nut throughout.

Examples

Now let's check out what these sound like in action.

LICK 1

This first lick moves from an A7 chord to a D6 chord. Other than bending the B string up a whole step behind the nut, there's another technical challenge. For the A/C♯ double stop on beat 3, you'll need to fret with fingers 3 and 2, low to high. This will allow you to slide up to the double stop on beat 4 and then be in position to shift down for the D6 chord in measure 2.

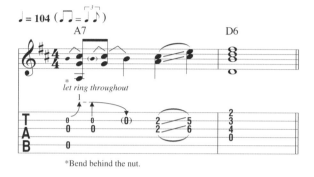

LICK 2

This lick in E moves through two different pedal steel bends on the B and G strings before ending with a half-step behind-the-nut bend on the G string up to G♯. When the open D, B, and E strings are sounded, this G♯ becomes the 3rd of an E7 chord.

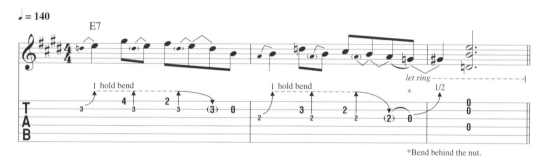

LICK 3

Here's a lick in G that uses two different behind-the-nut bends: a whole-step bend on the D string and a half-step bend on the B string.

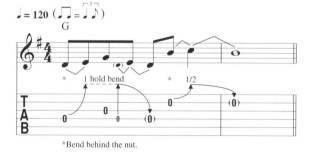

LICK 4

This final lick in E combines a pre-bend and release in the beginning with a half-step bend on the open G string at the end.

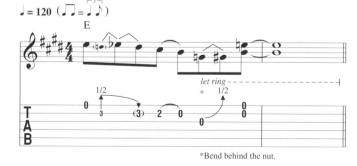

Again, the main man to check out for this kind of thing is Jerry Donahue, but many players implement the technique. It's a lot of fun, and it can really make those open strings sing!

LESSON #78: ENDING ON THE ♭7TH

Most guitar players have their fair share of "go to" licks—those licks you usually play without even thinking about it when you first pick up a guitar. Beyond that, we carry other playing habits with us as well. We tend to favor certain rhythms in our lines, and we may also gravitate toward beginning or ending phrases on certain notes.

These tendencies are often responsible for what makes our style recognizable. But in order to expand ourselves as players and not become bored with the instrument (or worse, boring for others to listen to!), it's important to become conscious of some of these tendencies so we can expand and try out other ideas.

One common trait shared by guitar players is to frequently end a phrase on the tonic note. While this certainly has its place, it can become monotonous if repeated throughout an entire solo. In this lesson, we're going to consciously avoid that tendency; we're going to end on the ♭7th.

All About the Dominant

The ♭7th note of any chord is a whole step below the root. If we have a C chord, for example, the ♭7th will be B♭. It's the note that, when paired with the major 3rd, is responsible for giving a dominant chord its sound.

When we end a phrase on this note, we create a deliberate tension that can really add some zest to your solo. It's not something we'd want to do all the time, for sure. But mixing it up helps keep the listener interested, and that's always a good thing.

Examples

Let's take a look at some licks that make use of this device.

LICK 1

This first line is a descending phrase in A that's fairly straightforward.

LICK 2

Here's a lick in C that begins with a bit of chicken pickin' and ends with a half-step bend up to the ♭7th.

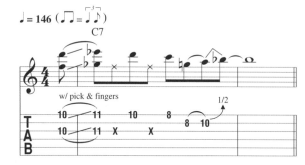

LICK 3

This is another line in C that descends with a pre-bend and release to reach the ♭7th at the end via a half-step bend.

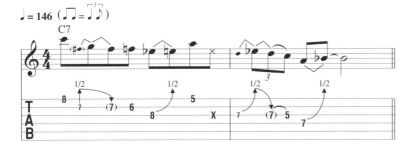

LICK 4

In this D7 lick, we begin with a chicken pickin' bend and come down the D composite blues scale before bending the 6th (B) up a half step to the C.

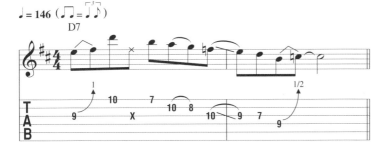

LICK 5

This final lick in E makes use of an interesting pedal steel-type bend in the beginning in which the tonic E is bent up a step to the 2nd and sounded against the 3rd and 5th. We finish off by changing the dyad on top to the 2nd (or 9th) and 5th and bending the 6th (C♯) up to the ♭7th for an E9 sound.

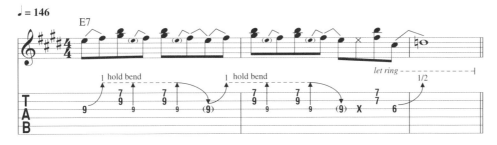

Again, this is not something you'd want to use all the time. Just try to find maybe one or two spots out of a whole solo to throw it in and see where it leads you. If nothing else, it helps you break out of your comfort zone, and that can't be a bad thing.

LESSON #79: USING OPEN STRINGS TO SHIFT POSITIONS

Besides looking impressive, having the freedom to traverse the range of the guitar neck allows you to create long, flowing multi-octave lines that take the listener for a real ride. Guitarists make regular use of several specific techniques to achieve this: slides, stretches, outright shifts, and more. In this lesson, I'd like to talk about another option: using open strings to shift positions.

The Sharp Keys

Most country music is played in the keys of C, G, D, A, and E, and as guitarists we can take advantage of that fact. Almost all of the open strings on the guitar will sound good in these keys. So why not exploit that?

The Basic Idea

So how does it work? Well, it takes some time to shift positions—especially when moving more than just a few frets—so any help we can get in this regard is a good thing. A well-placed open string can give you that extra 16th note or 8th note you need to make a smooth shift up or down into the new position.

For example, let's say we're in A and we want to play this line:

But the speedy tempo is making it difficult to get the line clean, or you just want to add an extra bit of twang to the line. We can replace the B note with the open string, and it makes the shift relatively easy.

You may need to experiment a bit to see where and when you can make use of an open string, but eventually you'll probably find a good option.

Examples

Let's check out how we can put this trick to use.

LICK 1

Here's a descending lick that spans over two full octaves. We use the open G string to shift from sixth to open position.

TRACK 29
0:00
CD 2

LICK 2

This one begins with some F7 arpeggio figures in fifth position and uses the open G string to shift down to open position for the resolution to C.

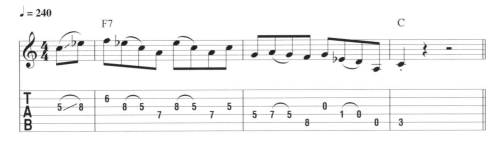

LICK 3

Here's an E lick that begins in seventh position and shifts down to open position via the open B string.

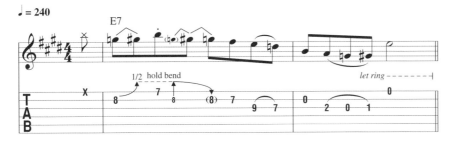

LICK 4

And here's one more in A that actually uses two open strings to shift: the open A string and the open G string.

This trick is not just about facilitating speed, either; it also creates an interesting tone. Mess around with it and I'm sure you'll find plenty of useful ideas.

LESSON #80: PEDAL STEEL TRIPLE-STOP BENDS

Country guitarists have been doing their best to emulate the pedal steel guitar for decades, and we've come a long way. One of the most commonly used tricks in this regard is the triple-stop bend. This is a triple stop (three notes played simultaneously) in which one or more strings are bent. In this lesson, we'll be dealing with the easiest version, which deals with only one bent string.

It's important to remember that accuracy is the key to emulating the pedal steel effectively. It uses mechanical levers to achieve its pitch bends, which means extreme precision. Taking the extra time to make sure your pitches are rock steady will make all the difference here.

The Classics

Let's start with a few classic moves that every country player should know. These are pretty much pedal steel bends 101.

BEND 1

This first one is by far the most famous of all; it's been used by everyone from Keith Richards to Lynyrd Skynyrd to every player in Nashville. It's in D here, and we're bending the 2nd up to the 3rd while holding the 5th and root on top.

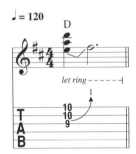

BEND 2

In this variation, the only thing that's changed is that the top two notes, A and D, have been moved down an octave to the fifth and fourth strings. You'll have to bend the E up to F♯ with your first finger, which may take a little practice.

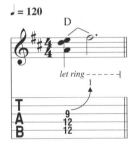

Intermediate Bends

Here are a few bends that are a bit more challenging, but still not all that difficult. (None of these licks are easy, by the way!)

BEND 3

This first one bends the 5th of a C major triad up a whole step to create an Am triad and then resolves it.

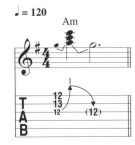

BEND 4

This next bend follows the previous one nicely. We're holding a D7 fragment with the 3rd, ♭7th, and root, low to high, on the top three strings. We bend the 3rd up a half step to create a D7sus4 sound and then release it back to D7.

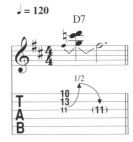

Advanced Bends

Now let's check out a few bends that are a bit more advanced. Remember to check the bends against unbent target pitches to make sure you're in tune.

BEND 5

This first one is in C and uses an open-voiced triad, meaning the notes span more than one octave. The 5th is on bottom, the root is on top, and we're bending the 2nd up to the 3rd on string 4. This one will take a bit of getting used to.

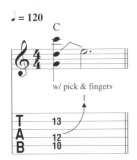

BEND 6

Here's a really pretty one in E that takes a standard root–3rd–5th major triad on the top three strings and bends the root up a whole step to create a sus2 sound. Be sure to keep the notes on strings 2 and 1 absolutely still.

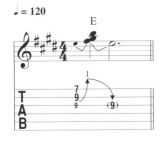

You can hear these types of bends on country records everywhere, but check out the Hellecasters (Jerry Donahue, John Jorgenson, and Will Ray), Brad Paisley, and Albert Lee for starters to hear these things in action.

LESSON #81: EXTREME DOUBLE-STOP BENDS – THE SNAG

Double-stop bends have been a favorite trick that country players can use to emulate a pedal steel, and a repertoire of standard double-stop bends has evolved. In this lesson, however, we're not going to address those standard double-stop bends. We're going to be focusing on what I call extreme double-stop bends.

Two Notes, One Finger: The Snag

I haven't heard a universal term for this specific technique, so I call it "the snag." Along with country players, many blues players, including Stevie Ray Vaughan, make regular use of this technique. However, country guitarists are the only ones I've heard who refined the technique to pitch-perfect accuracy.

The basic idea is to bend one string up and then "snag" the adjacent lower string under the same bending finger. For example, you may bend the 10th fret on the high E string up a whole step with your third finger and then snag the 10th fret on the B string under it as well.

Blues players use this device to get a visceral, grinding sound, in which the sound itself is more important than the actual pitches. But, with careful attention to detail, we can achieve different pitches with these bends and create some colorful licks in the process.

Examples

With all of these examples, you'll need to constantly check your bent notes against unbent target pitches, to ensure accuracy. A chain is only as strong as its weakest link, and one botched bend can destroy the effect.

LICK 1

This first lick is in the key of C and begins with the extreme bend. First, bend the D on string 1 up a whole step to E. Allow the second string to move under your finger so that it's right up against the first string. Play those two strings. You should have an E note on string 1, and string 2 should be sounding a B♭ note. (You're bending string 1 up a whole step and string 2 up a half step.) We continue with a more standard double-stop bend and some chromatic sliding 3rds before wrapping up with a nice C13 voicing.

TRACK 31
0:00
CD 2

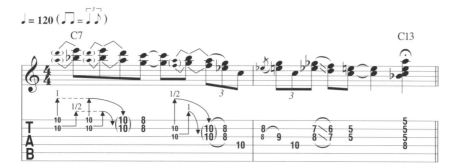

LICK 2

This bizarre lick finishes with an extreme bend. Bend the E note up a whole step to F♯ with your ring finger and snag the G string under that finger. Pick both notes and release the bend. You'll need to apply a decent amount of pressure to keep the G string from slipping; I find it helps to pull down on the string with the second finger behind the third. In doing so, you should be releasing the F♯ back down to E and also bending the G note on string 3 up a half step to G♯.

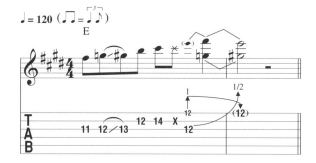

LICK 3

Here's a difficult one I stole from the Jerry Donahue playbook. For the extreme bend, first bend string 3 up a whole step. Allow string 2 to snag beneath your bending finger and release the bend while maintaining pressure on string 2. If you do it correctly, as you're releasing the whole-step bend back down, you'll also be bending string 2 up a half step. It creates a beautiful V–I sound in A.

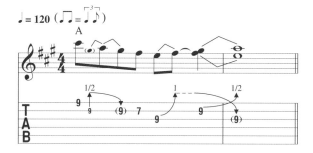

LICK 4

I got the idea for this last one from the previous Jerry Donahue lick. This one takes place on the first and second strings and uses different intervals, but it's the same concept. Bend the E note on string 1 up a half step to F and snag string 2 beneath your finger. Then release that bend, which in turn bends string 2 up a half step. The notes you have are B and F (low to high) during the bend and C and E (low to high) at the release.

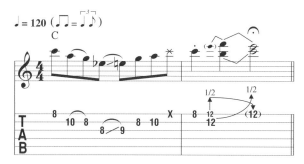

Take your time, adjust your fingers when you need to, and get the pitches right. This is not something that will fall under the fingers in five minutes! It may take months before you're able to even approach the fluidity that Jerry Donahue displays with this type of thing. The rewards are well worth the effort though, so practice, practice, practice!

Double-stop and triple-stop bends have been a favorite of country players for years. Besides doing a great job at emulating a pedal steel, they sound great and are lots of fun. A repertoire of standard bends has been established over the years, and they're considered prerequisites for every aspiring country player. In this lesson, however, we're not going to be addressing many of those standard bends. We're going to be focusing on what I call extreme bends.

Value Your Independence

In this lesson, we're going to be bending two strings with two different fingers, and each one is going to be bent a different amount. In other words, one string may be bent a half step, while the other is bent a whole step, etc. In addition, we may be performing this while holding a third string unbent, significantly complicating things.

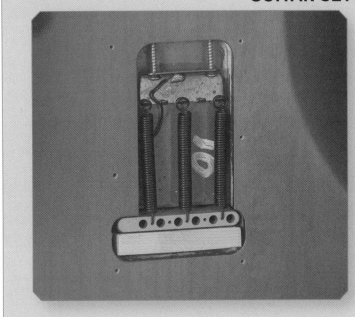

GUITAR SETUP TIP

If you have your guitar set up with a tremolo system, such as a Strat or an Ibanez "Super Strat" type, and you don't have all the springs installed, you may have problems with these bends. This is because, when the bridge is not locked down, it will move slightly when a string is bent. So if you bend a note on the G string, for instance, all of the other strings will go slightly flat. It's not noticeable when it's just a single note, but you can definitely hear it when you perform an oblique bend (one bent string and one unbent).

If you don't want to put all the springs in, you can temporarily "block off" the system by shoving a small piece of wood between the spring block and the wall of the cavity, preventing it from moving.

Double-Stop Bends

Let's first take a look at some double-stop bends.

LICK 1

Here's one that moves from a C7 chord to G7. We're bending A on string 2 up a half step and F on string 3 up a whole step. This is about as tame as these extreme bends get.

TRACK 32
0:00
CD 2

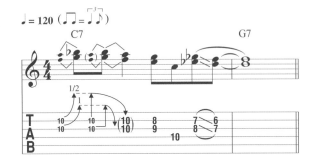

LICK 2

This one is in C and uses a bend on non-adjacent strings. At the end, we're bending string 3 up a whole step from D to E and bending string 1 up a half step from B to C.

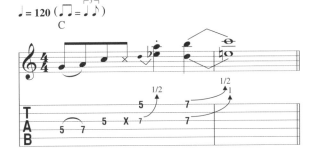

LICK 3

Here's one that's quite difficult. For the extreme bend at the end, we'll be bending the C# on string 4 up (toward the ceiling) a half step to D and bending the E (down toward the floor) up a whole step to F#. This will feel pretty weird at first!

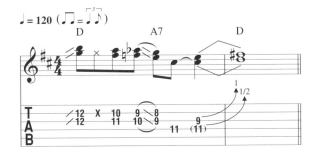

Triple-Stop Bends

Now we'll check out some triple-stop bends. We're still only bending two notes, but having to hold another one stationary significantly adds to the difficulty level.

LICK 4

This first one in C ends with the extreme bend. While holding the G on string 5 with your first finger, you'll need to bend the D on string 4 a whole step and the B on string 2 up a half step. I prefer to do this with the third and fourth fingers, respectively, but you should experiment to see if the second and third feels better.

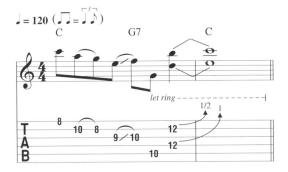

LICK 5

This one's just cruel. While holding the A on string 5 down, you'll need to bend the C# on string 4 up a half step while bending the E on string 3 up a whole step. This is one I nicked from Jerry Donahue.

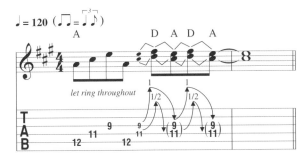

Experiment with this idea and see if you can come up with some of your own licks. These things aren't easy, but they're a lot of fun, and when executed well, they sound great. Good luck!

LESSON #83: COMPOUND BENDS

Country players are known for their expert bending chops. It's a huge part of the country sound, and the intonation of a bend can make or break an entire phrase. Accuracy of pitch is paramount in many bending licks, and that's certainly the case with compound bends, which are the subject of this lesson.

A compound bend is one in which a note (or notes) is first bent up to one pitch and then bent up farther to another. Bent notes can be released in compound fashion as well. This is an excellent device for emulating a pedal steel guitar, as we'll soon see.

The Basic Idea

We'll start simple. Let's say you have an A note at the 10th fret of the second string. To execute a compound bend, we'll first bend it up one half step to A♯ and then one more half step to B.

EXERCISE 1

Here are the target pitches we're going for:

And here's what it sounds like with the compound bend.

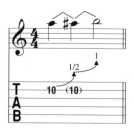

EXERCISE 2

Now let's do the same thing, but we'll release the bend in the same fashion. Here are the target pitches.

And here it is with the compound bend and release.

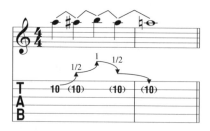

EXERCISE 3

When we add a pre-bend into the mix and just release it in a compound fashion, it gets a little more difficult.

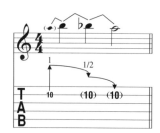

Examples

Now let's take a look at how we can use this concept in some actual licks.

LICK 1

This first lick in A uses a bend from the 5th to the 6th and nicks the ♭6th as you release the bend on the way back down to the 5th.

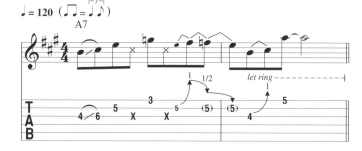

LICK 2

Here's a common application in the key of C. We pre-bend the ♭7th, B♭, up a whole step to C, pick it twice, and then release it a half step at a time back down to B♭. Watch for the quick position shift at the end, where you'll need to move from eighth position down to fifth position in the space of an 8th note.

LICK 3

This type of thing is used with double stops as well. This lick in A features a G bent up a whole step to A against a C♯ on top. It's released in half steps and followed by a half-step slide up into the 3rd and root of the D chord.

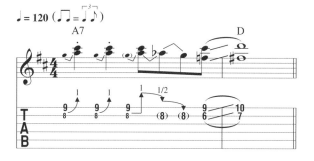

LICK 4

Here's a classic pedal steel-style intro in the key of G. This one is the toughest by far, because we're using compound bends on both notes of the double stop. You'll have to mess around with it until you find the right pressure needed to get the pitches right. Be sure to check your target pitches on this one.

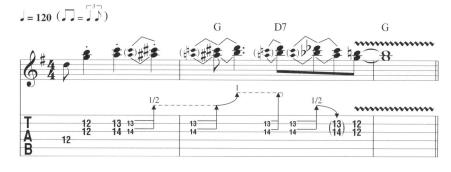

Try to create your own lines with this technique. You can start by simply replacing a few notes in a standard line with a compound bend or release to get a different sound. Before you know it, you'll find all kinds of ways to work them in.

LESSON #84: CHICKEN PICKIN' 101

The sound of country guitar is one of the most recognizable of all genres. From the tone to the technique, everything stands out on a good country guitar track. And one of the most country of all techniques is chicken pickin'—that melodic concoction of squawks and clucks that brings to mind a chicken struttin' across a barnyard. Hybrid picking is a must with this technique.

What exactly is chicken pickin'? There's actually not a straightforward answer to that question. Different players achieve a similar squawky tone with different techniques. It's kind of like the fact that all squares are rectangles, but not all rectangles are squares. Some people refer to just using hybrid picking for country licks as chicken pickin', while others make more of a distinction. However, there's a technique that involves muted, dead notes that's generally always agreed on as chicken pickin', so that's what we'll focus on in this lesson.

The Basic Idea

Chicken pickin' is so named because it sounds like… well, a chicken. Chickens have their short, little "bock" clucky noises as well as their louder squawks. The chicken pickin' technique is similar to this with muted, clucky dead notes and sharp, accented notes.

There are a few different ways to get the muted dead sound, so let's check those out first.

MUTED METHOD A: FRET HAND MUTE

The first is to simply lay your finger on a fret, but don't press the string down to the fretboard. You'll get a percussive, click sound. Be sure to try this with both the pick (using a downstroke) and your finger.

MUTED METHOD B: PICK HAND MUTE

Another way is to fret a note normally, but use your pick hand's second finger to touch the string while you pluck it with the pick. When using this method, the technique is almost always alternated with an accented, un-muted note plucked by the second finger.

A variation on this technique involves using the palm of your right hand to deaden the string while you pluck downward with the pick. It's kind of like a palm mute, but your palm is well in from the bridge, so only a dead note is produced.

So, the idea is to alternate a muted note, produced by one of the two previous methods, with an accented note that's most often plucked or snapped by a finger. By "snap," I mean the string is lifted up and allowed to snap back down to create a loud, accented note. (It's actually very similar to the "pop" in the slap and pop technique used by bassists.)

Examples

So let's check it out with some licks.

LICK 1

This first one is a classic in C. We're using the pick hand mute here—the first time with the finger and the second time (while holding the bend) with the palm.

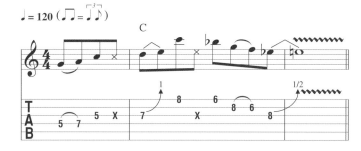

LICK 2

Here's another classic idea in A. This time we're using the fret hand mute. Be sure to make those double stops nice and staccato!

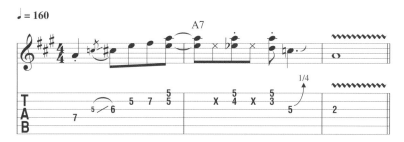

LICK 3

Here's a quicker one in D that chicken picks notes on the high E string before settling into a classic bending move on the G string.

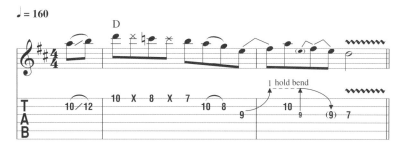

LICK 4

We'll end with another classic use that involves chicken pickin' double stops in more of a riff style. These kinds of parts are a blast to play. In this type of line, the fingers are plucking all the double stops, and the pick is plucking all the dead notes.

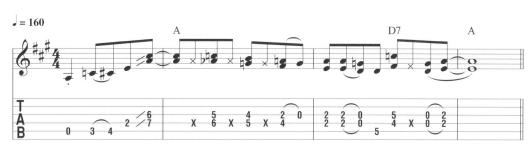

Have fun playing with this technique; it's one of the most charming sounds you can produce on a Tele. Remember to start slowly and make sure your tempo is solid. It's easy to sound lopsided with this sort of thing if you're not aware of the time. Once you get a feel for it though, it's a whole lot of fun.

TAKIN' THE JAZZ TO THE BARNYARD

Many rock and blues players tend to use one scale to play over an entire chord progression, but country players often use an approach similar to jazz musicians, changing scales to match the individual chords or a group of chords. In the Western swing style, this approach is even more apparent, and indeed many of the genre's phrases could hold up quite well as jazz lines.

In this lesson, we're going to talk about how to play through some common jazzy chord progressions while still sounding country. We'll do this by applying a few specific techniques here and there that will color the whole line.

The Pre-Bend

The pre-bend is one our greatest assets as guitarists when trying to create a sound similar to a pedal steel guitar—perhaps the most country-sounding instrument of all. Therefore, by simply interjecting a carefully placed pre-bend into a line, we can automatically create a more country sound.

LICK 1

For example, let's say you're playing through a I–VI–ii–V progression in A: A6–F#7♭9–Bm7–E7. Here's a line that a jazz player might play over it.

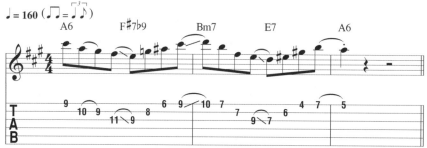

Now, here's the same exact line, but with a pre-bend used for the second note. We're pre-bending the G# up to A and releasing it. Notice how it colors the entire phrase.

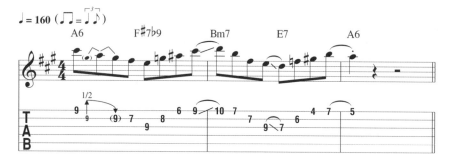

LICK 2

Let's take a look at a few more licks using this device. Here's one that moves from E7 to A and uses two pre-bends. The first is used to create a three-note chromatic descent from E to D, and the final one falls from the 4th, D, to the 3rd, C#.

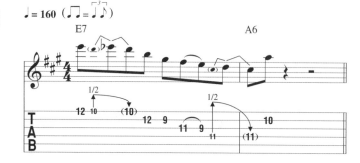

LICK 3

Here's a line in C that weaves through a C6–D7–G7–C progression. It's slightly reminiscent of Charlie Christian (save for the bend) and uses a pre-bent B♭ up to C with a release.

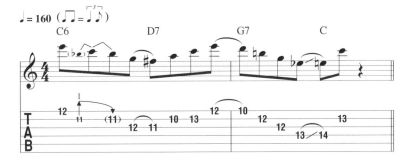

Chicken Pickin'

Another great way to lend a country sound to jazzier lines is with some chicken pickin'. This involves adding some muted notes alternated with some accented finger-popped ones. You can achieve the muted dead-note sound one of two ways:

▶ Touch a string with your fret hand, but don't push it down to the fretboard, and then pick (or fingerpick) it.

▶ Fret a note normally, but use your pick hand's second finger or palm to touch the string while you pluck it with the pick.

LICK 4

Let's see how this technique can countrify a jazzy-sounding line. Here's an A7 line that uses chicken pickin' in between a chromatic descent of C♯–C♮–B at first and once more at the end. It doesn't take much to make it sound country!

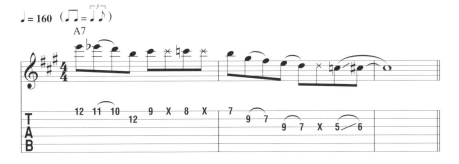

LICK 5

And here's a ii–V–I in D that runs through a few arpeggios before it gets to clucking at the very end. Notice that we chicken picked only once in this entire lick!

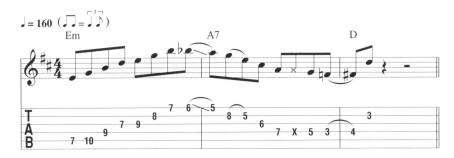

It's a whole lot of fun to blend styles this way and jazzy lines can fit incredibly well in most country settings—especially when treated with the techniques presented in this lesson. Experiment with other ideas like this when you're feeling in a rut; it's a great way to break out of it.

BANJO ROLLS

Besides the pedal steel, there are other country instruments we guitarists like to emulate. Enter the banjo roll. This fancy bit of fingerpicking seeks to simulate the way a banjo player sounds as he or she rolls through arpeggios fluidly (and often quickly). We don't have the open high G string to use as banjoists do, but we make do by usually including an open string of our own.

When performing banjo rolls, players either use hybrid picking or a thumbpick and fingers. Chet Atkins and Brent Mason are ones to check out with regards to the latter. If you've never used a thumbpick before, it'll be awkward at first. But some players swear by them, and the obvious benefit is that you have one more free finger to pluck with.

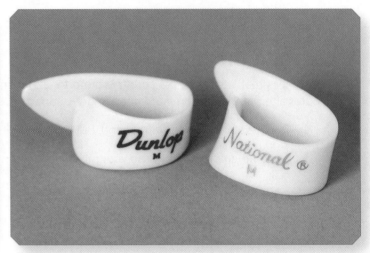

The Basic Idea

On guitar, as on the banjo, rolls are usually performed in continuous 8th notes, but they're grouped in sets of three. So you end up with a syncopated three-against-four effect. The pattern usually lasts for one or two measures and then starts again. Let's look at a few exercises with open strings to get a feel for it.

EXERCISE 1

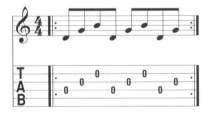

EXERCISE 2

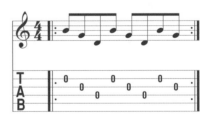

EXERCISE 3

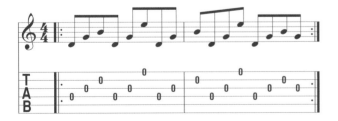

EXERCISE 4

Examples

Now let's check out a few rolls in action. As mentioned earlier, the usual practice is to make use of one or more open strings throughout, altering the fretted notes to fit the changing harmony. The open strings normally result in some colorful extended harmony for one or more of the chords.

LICK 1

This first one is a classic banjo roll in C that runs through a VI–II–V–I progression and uses the open high-E string as a common tone throughout. For the first A7 chord, you'll need to fret both the A and C♯ notes with the first finger while allowing the high-E string to ring open. This will take a bit of practice if you're not used to this type of thing.

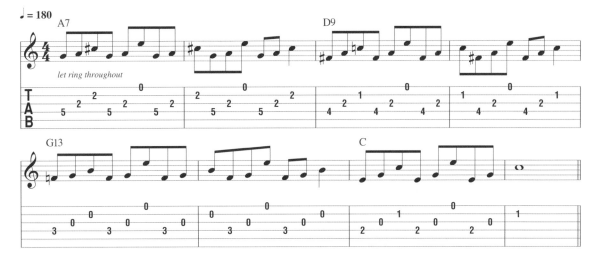

LICK 2

There's no rule that says you can't pair two of the notes together at times to create some syncopation. Here's a beautiful roll in the style of Mr. Guitar himself that swings like crazy.

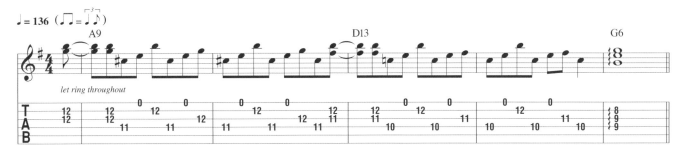

LICK 3

Here's a great little lick that, although not the syncopated type of roll we've talked about, is a classic intro lick and a great one to be able to pull out. It's in C here.

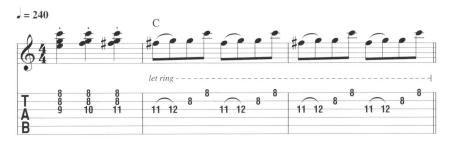

LICK 4

This last one is a nice roll in G that's got a bit more of a modern country sound to it. It sounds nice with a half dirty tone too.

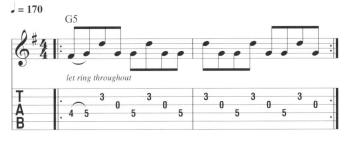

Be sure to listen to some Chet to hear complete mastery of this style. Also check out Albert Lee, Jerry Donahue, and Brent Mason. Have fun!

LESSON #87: CHORD VOICINGS THAT MIX OPEN AND FRETTED NOTES

If you listen to some truly classic country pickers, such as Chet Atkins, Jerry Reed, and the like, you'll hear some creatively voiced chords that are quite intelligent in terms of economy on the fretboard. These voicings use a mixture of open strings and fretted notes, but they're not played in open position. In this lesson, we'll take a look at some of those voicings and learn what makes them so appealing.

The Basic Idea

Since most country music takes place in sharp keys, such as C, G, D, A, and E, we often have the benefit of using open strings in our licks or chords. When you mix fretted notes and open strings in open position, you're normally dealing with intervals of 3rds, 4ths, or 5ths, with the occasional exception. But when you move the fretted notes up the neck a bit, we're able to access colorful intervals like 2nds rather easily, thereby making certain voicings playable that would otherwise be impossible.

Seventh Chords

Let's take a look at an E7 chord voiced in first inversion—i.e., with the 3rd, G♯, on the bottom.

This type of closed voicing (i.e., one in which all four notes are within one octave) is normally not possible—or certainly not practical—on the guitar because of the way the instrument is tuned. However, since at least one of the notes is an open string, it becomes a simple matter of using that and finding the other three notes in a playable configuration.

For example, here's how we might play this first-inversion E7 chord using the open E string with the other three notes fretted.

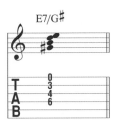

Sounds nice, huh? However, E is not the only note in this chord that matches an open string; we also have a B note in the chord. We can therefore replace that note with the open B string. That leaves us with G♯ and D, which we can fret here in sixth position. This fingering is even easier than the previous one.

Let's try the same thing with this A7 voicing in first inversion. Here are the notes:

We do have an open A string, but that's in a lower octave, and we want the voicing to be closed. But we also have an open E string, and we can use that one. Therefore, we can come up with this voicing.

TRACK 37
0:11
CD 2

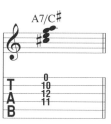

SEVENTH VOICINGS

Here are several other seventh voicings of various roots in different inversions using this concept. This is hardly a comprehensive list. You can find these kinds of things all over the place if you look for them.

TRACK 37
0:16
CD 2

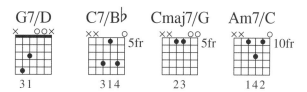

Extended Chords

When we deal with extended chords, such as 9ths, 11ths, or 13ths, the opportunities expand. This is because more of the open strings will be usable as extensions. Here then are some extended voicings using this concept.

TRACK 37
0:34
CD 2

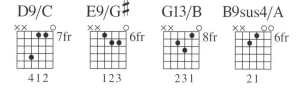

You can really take this idea as far as you'd like. It's unlikely that you'll run out of options anytime soon. They sound great, and they're easy on the fret hand, which is always nice. Happy hunting!

LESSON #88: THE ♭VII SOUND OVER THE I CHORD

When soloing over dominant chords, many players use certain strategies in order to create different sounds. In this lesson, I'd like to talk about one of my favorites: the ♭VII sound over the I chord. This trick is equally suited to jazz or country lines, and many times the only thing that colors the line one way or the other would be the tone and articulation used. With a dark, mellow hollowbody tone, these ideas will sound jazzy. But with a bright, spankin' Tele tone and maybe a few bends here and there, it's all country.

A Little Chord Theory

Normally in a major key there is no ♭VII chord at all; that is to say, it's not diatonic. (It is often borrowed from the parallel minor, though.) However, in blues, jazz, and country, the tonic chord is often a dominant chord, which suggests the Mixolydian mode. Therefore, we can look at a harmonized Mixolydian mode for superimposition ideas. Here's the C Mixolydian mode, harmonized in triads.

As we can see, we have a B♭ chord, which is the ♭VII chord. Let's analyze the tones of this chord against the root note C.

We have the ♭7th (B♭), the 9th (D), and the 11th (F). These are all very colorful notes against a C or C7 chord when used sparingly. Many times, players will hint at this sound with a ♭VII arpeggio of only a few notes before resolving back into chord tones. In other words, I wouldn't make a habit of landing on the 11th (F) over C or C7. But grazing through it can create some beautiful tension in your lines.

Examples

LICK 1

Let's check out how this works. This first line in C runs down the B♭ arpeggio after beginning with a classic pre-bent pedal steel move. It resolves immediately after the ♭VII sound with a minor-to-major 3rd move.

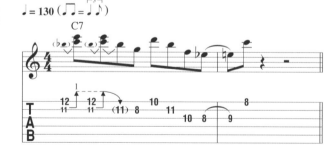

LICK 2

Here's a triple-stop idea in A that applies some pedal steel bends to a tonic I triad (A) and the ♭VII chord (G).

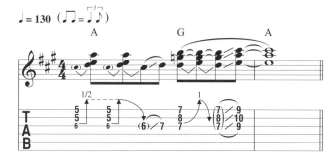

LICK 3

Here's a classic use of this device. We're ascending up the neck through alternating F and G triads in different inversions. We end this one with a really nice move where the F note is bent up a whole step against an A and C on top, creating a colorful G9sus4 type of sound.

LICK 4

Here's a tricky little line in E that ascends up an E7 chord with chromatic lower neighbor tones before arpeggiating the ♭VII chord, D, and resolving back to E via a three-note chromatic climb of F♯–G–G♯ followed by the high tonic note.

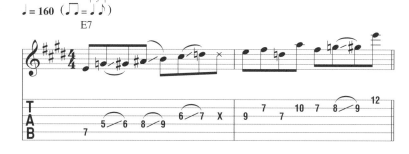

Again, treat these tones with care. While they can really spice up a line and add a new dimension to your phrases, they can easily overstay their welcome if you linger on them too long. Experiment with this and have fun!

LESSON #89: THE MAJOR OR DOMINANT II CHORD

While country music shares many elements with other styles, it has certain idiosyncrasies that make it unique. One of these lies in the harmony. The ii–V–I progression in jazz is ubiquitous, and the progression often shows up in country songs as well. However, when it does, the ii chord is normally not minor, as in jazz. It's much more often major or dominant, making it a secondary dominant.

In this lesson, we're going to look at how we handle this specific instance when it comes time to solo. While a key center approach—i.e., one scale for all the chords—can work most of the time, the major or dominant II chord demands some special treatment.

A Little Background Theory

We'll work in the key of C for this lesson for simplicity. When we look at a harmonized major scale, such as the C major scale below, we can see all the diatonic triads in the key.

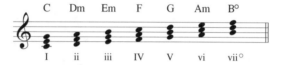

Notice that the ii chord is Dm. In many classic country songs, this chord appears immediately before the V chord. However, the chord is often changed into a major or dominant chord, which leads even more strongly to the V, because its 3rd (normally F) has been raised a half step (F♯) to become the leading tone of the V chord. We say the II chord is temporarily tonicizing a chord other than the tonic, which is why it's called a secondary dominant.

Here's how a typical progression in C using the II chord might go:

Soloing over the II

Ok, so how do we handle that pesky II chord when we solo? Well, we need to remember how it's functioning. The II chord, D (or D7), is temporarily tonicizing the V chord, G. Another way to look at that is to say, when the D chord arrives, we temporarily change keys to G. The only difference between the C major scale and the G major scale is that the F note becomes F♯.

G MAJOR SCALE

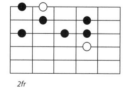

2fr

Since we'll want to target chord tones of that D chord, it may be more helpful to think of the G major scale in its fifth mode, which is D Mixolydian. This is simply a G major scale that treats D as its home base.

D MIXOLYDIAN MODE

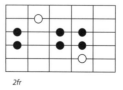

2fr

Therefore, we can use the D Mixolydian mode over that D chord and that D chord only. Remember that, once we reach the G chord, it will be functioning as the V chord in the original key of C major, so we'll want to revert back to the C major scale (or G Mixolydian, if you prefer) once the G7 arrives.

Examples

Note that we'll be moving to different areas on the neck here, so if you're not familiar with these scales all over the neck, you may want to consult some scale diagrams for reference.

LICK 1

This first one in C plays through the changes with a jazz sensibility, similar to the way Charlie Christian did. Over the D7 chord, we're using the D Mixolydian mode with a run up a D9 arpeggio: F♯–A–C–E. We include a few chromatics for the G7 chord to decorate it further.

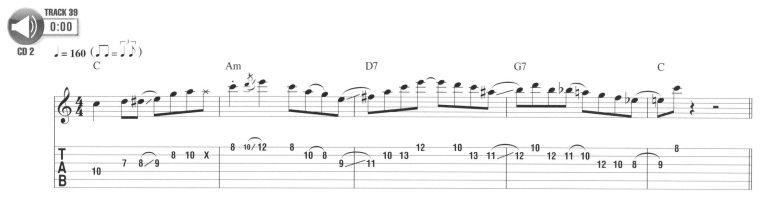

LICK 2

Here's one in A that moves through a I–II–V–I progression. After some pedal steel bend maneuvers for the A chord, we use a similar motif over the II and V chords, sliding into both chord's 3rd from a half step below. The B Mixolydian mode is played over the II chord, B7.

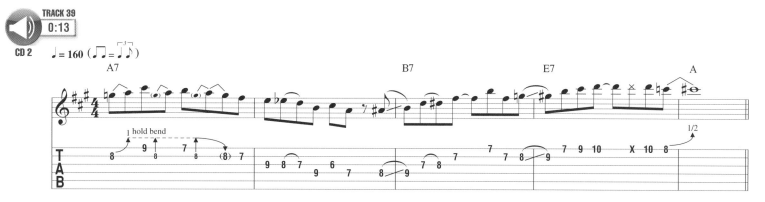

LICK 3

We'll finish with a snazzy little line in G that again takes place over a I–II–V–I progression. This one makes use of a similar line over the II and V chords, altering the tones slightly to fit the changing harmony. Though it's only four notes long, the line played over the A7 chord is from the A Mixolydian mode.

Remember that you will occasionally see or hear minor ii chords in country, so don't go blindly soloing over every II chord with its matching Mixolydian mode! When it is dominant though, you'll be ready. Have fun!

There's an old joke about being a studio musician in Nashville:

Being as good of a player as the session players in Nashville isn't your first problem. Your first problem is being as good as the janitors who sweep up after the session.

This probably dates back to the fact that, until recently, country music remained largely separated into two categories: songwriters and performers. Thus, the performers (such as Brent Mason, etc.) were able to devote almost all of their time to their craft. The end result is that you have exceptionally talented players who are often well-versed in many styles and musical strategies.

Perhaps because of this, country guitar players often treat soloing differently than the typical rock or blues player. They tend to take it one chord at a time, targeting certain notes and perhaps even changing scales altogether for each chord. In this lesson, we're going to look at one musical strategy in this regard: resolving to the 3rd.

The Basic Idea

A chord is built with three (in the case of a triad) or four (in the case of a seventh chord) different notes. A triad contains a root, 3rd, and 5th, while a seventh chord contains those as well as a 7th.

The 3rd is perhaps the most important tone of a chord, because it defines whether its sound is major or minor. Therefore, if you make it a habit of resolving to 3rds often, your solo will tend to flow with the harmony. There are three basic methods we're going to look at here for resolving to the 3rd:

▶ From a half step below

▶ From a half step above

▶ Enclosing it by playing the 4th and ♭3rd before it*

*Note that this enclosure move will end by leading into the 3rd from a half step below, but since it's a unique sound, we're treating it as its own method.

From a Half Step Below

LICK 1

In this first lick, we're moving from C to F. After a chicken pickin' pedal steel bend over the C chord, we slide from G♯ up to A, the 3rd of F. I'm using my pinky for the G, G♯, and A notes here.

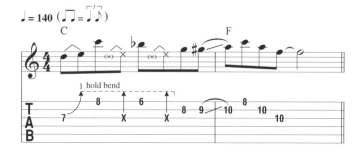

LICK 2

Next is a nice line in A that moves from A7 to D7. After a unison pre-bend, we finish off the A7 measure with a descending A9 arpeggio, B–G–E, and then lead into the F♯ (3rd of D7) by sliding into it from the E♯.

TRACK 40
0:10
CD 2

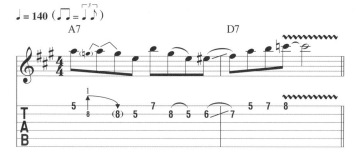

From a Half Step Above

LICK 3

This lick moves from a G7 to a C chord and begins with a nifty pre-bend of B♭ up to B. At the end of measure 1, we slide down into E, the 3rd of C, from the 7th of G7, F.

TRACK 40
0:19
CD 2

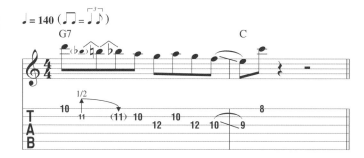

LICK 4

This one moves from a V chord (D7) to a I chord (G) and makes use of lots of chromatic passing tones.

TRACK 40
0:26
CD 2

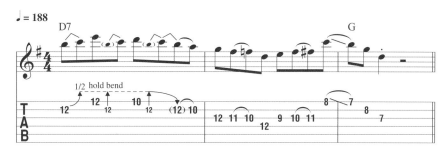

Enclosure

Let's finish off with a few licks that use the enclosure technique.

LICK 5

TRACK 40
0:34
CD 2

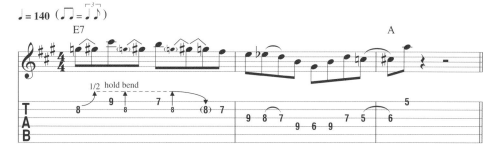

LICK 6

TRACK 40
0:44
CD 2

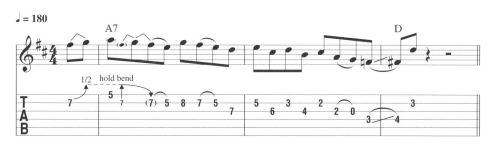

This strategy is equally useful in other styles as well, including blues, rock, and jazz. The more familiar you become with this concept, the more tuned in you'll be to the changing harmony in general, which can only be a good thing.

COUNTRIFYIN' THE BLUES BOX

Country solos certainly have their fair share of blues licks, but they also have distinctive country licks that don't fall as easily under the fingers as standard pentatonic ones do. Although most country solos are performed by seasoned studio musicians that know the instrument inside and out, there's still quite a bit you can do to countrify some licks without straying from the good ol' basic pentatonic box shape. Some of the fingerings may feel a bit awkward at first, but with a little time, these ideas will become as natural as your first blues lick. So get ready to start bendin'; this lesson is about countrifyin' the blues box.

Home Base

The minor pentatonic box shape and/or blues scale is one of the most widely known shapes on the guitar fretboard. It's often literally the first thing someone learns with regards to lead guitar, and sadly, it's sometimes the last! Suffice it to say that almost every guitarist who plays lead guitar is at least somewhat familiar with this shape. Here it is in C in the eighth position.

C BLUES SCALE

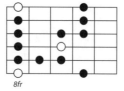

Now, by altering just a few notes at times by a half step, we can stay in this same basic position and churn out some real country gems. We'll do this with a few different methods.

Adding 2nds, 3rds, and 6ths

Country solos often make use of the major pentatonic scale, and our minor pentatonic scale lacks many of those tones. So we'll be adding major 2nds, major 3rds, and major 6ths to our scale. These tones are circled on the diagram.

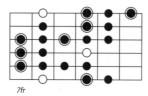

Incorporating Half-Step Slides from Below

Half-step slides are very country sounding. We can use this simple device to country up even the tamest lick. The basic idea is to target a note or notes and slide up into them from a half step below. Here's a basic example.

Tightening Up the Bends to Sound More Country

Most bends in country aim to mimic a pedal steel guitar, which achieves its pitch-bending via mechanical means. This results in extreme precision. Therefore, in order to sound more country, we generally want our bends to be snappy and pitch perfect. Pre-bends play a big role in the country sound, as does hybrid picking for that snappy sound.

Examples

Ok, let's check out some examples. These will all take place in the C box—roughly in eighth position.

LICK 1

This first one uses lots of sliding double stops; be sure to use hybrid picking!

LICK 2

This lick begins with a pre-bend of A up to B♭ against a tonic C note, creating a dissonant 2nd that's resolved to a 3rd as the bend is released. It ends with a nice move of 6–♭3–2–1 (A–E♭–D–C).

LICK 3

Here's a speedy descent that mixes the major and blues sounds throughout. Hybrid picking will help with the snappiness.

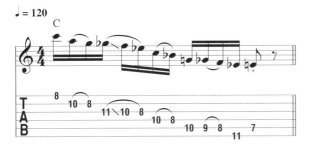

LICK 4

This last one is a bit jazzy, with the three-note chromatic descent in the beginning and the presence of the C9 sound in beat 2.

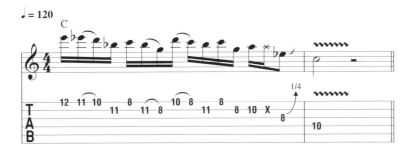

As you can hear, you don't have to make drastic changes to get a country sound. Often, it only takes one or two notes. Have fun messing around with this idea, and remember to incorporate hybrid picking for the most authentic country sound.

LESSON #92: BENDING THE RULES

In country lead guitar, bends are all over the place. Many of them aim to imitate the weeping sound of the pedal steel guitar. Though sometimes we guitarists forget, the pedal steel is played with a bar or slide. (Any "bending" is actually achieved via pedals and levers.) It's quite an easy and natural move for a pedal steel guitarist to grace up into a note with a quick slide. And, since a bend on the guitar is a convincing way to imitate this sound, it only makes sense that we can employ the same idea.

Of course, we do this (bend up into notes) all the time. But we guitarists tend to have a repertoire of common bends from which we don't normally stray. In this lesson, we're going to start employing some maneuvers that aren't quite as common, bending out-of-key notes up into ones that are in key. I call this approach bending the rules.

The Basic Idea

It's a simple concept, but it can make a huge difference. The idea is to occasionally replace a normally fretted note with one that's bent up to that pitch from a half step below. For example, instead of playing this G major pentatonic phrase this way:

We can instead bend up to the 6th, E, from a half step below to get this sound.

You can make these bends grace-note bends (i.e., immediately up to pitch), or for a more exaggerated effect, you can make them more rhythmic, lasting for an 8th or 16th note. The important thing to remember is to be as precise as you can with regards to the target pitch. The more accurate you are, the more effective the idea will be.

Examples

LICK 1

Let's hear this idea in some examples. This first lick in A uses a rhythmic bend of the ♯5th, E♯, up to the 6th, F♯.

TRACK 42
0:00
CD 2

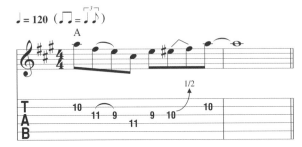

LICK 2

This lick moves from a D chord to a G chord and uses two half-step bends: one from F♮ to F♯, and one from B♭ to B.

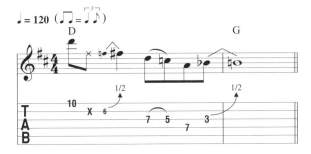

LICK 3

Here's another take on this idea in E. We're pre-bending G up to G♯, releasing and re-bending for a little melody.

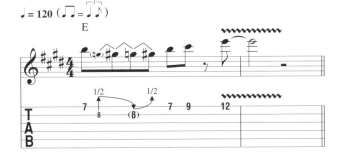

LICK 4

Our final lick in C applies this idea to double stops. After chicken pickin' a few double stops from the C Mixolydian mode, we end with a half-step bend up into the 3rd and 5th.

You can get as far out as you'd like with this idea. Though he's not a country player per se, Jeff Beck makes use of this concept occasionally, and the results are often quite ear-grabbing. Experiment with it and see what you can come up with.

Although many country recordings include a jumbo acoustic playing open "cowboy" chords, they also often feature an electric guitar playing different chord shapes all over the neck. The ability to play the same chord at several different places on the neck is invaluable when it comes to creating a full-bodied sound without stepping all over someone else's sonic feet. In order to do this, you need to be familiar with the concept of inversions. This simply means arranging the notes of a chord so that a note other than the root is on the bottom. In this lesson, we're going to focus on triad inversions.

The Basic Idea

A triad has three different notes: a root, a 3rd, and a 5th. The normal voicing for this chord is root, 3rd, 5th, from low to high. This is referred to as root position, because it has the root on the bottom. Here's a C triad to demonstrate.

C CHORD: ROOT POSITION

If we take the lowest note, the root C, and move it up an octave, we're left with the 3rd, E, on bottom. This is known as first inversion.

C CHORD: FIRST INVERSION

If we continue this process once more and again move the lowest note—the 3rd, E—up an octave, we're left with the 5th, G, on the bottom. This is known as second inversion.

C CHORD: SECOND INVERSION

Repeating the process once more again puts the root on the bottom and returns us to root position (albeit an octave higher than we started).

Learning the Shapes

In order to gain freedom to move anywhere on the neck, we need to be able to venture from our open C chord. We can do this by working through the inversions and remaining on the same string set throughout. In other words, we'll play root position on strings 6–5–4, and then we'll slide up the neck to play first and second inversions on those same strings.

STRING SET 6-5-4

We'll work with a C chord here. Whenever all three notes reach above the 12th fret, we'll transpose them down an octave. Here are the three versions of C on the 6–5–4 string set. The root notes (C) are all open circles.

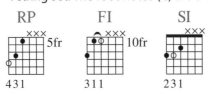

STRING SET 5-4-3

Here are the three versions of C on the 5–4–3 string set.

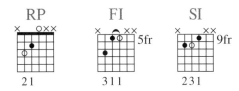

STRING SET 4-3-2

Here are the three versions of C on the 4–3–2 string set.

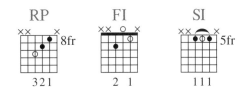

STRING SET 3-2-1

Here are the three versions of C on the 3–2–1 string set.

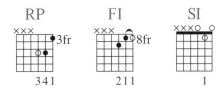

Minor Chords

In order to make these Cm chords, simply find all the E notes and lower them a half step to E♭. For example, here's what the 4–3–2 string group would look like as Cm chords.

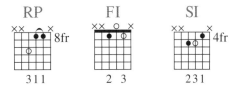

Summary – Moveable Shapes

Remember to work on these in other keys as well. Here are the basic moveable shapes for each string set—i.e., how they would look in keys that don't allow any open strings to be used.

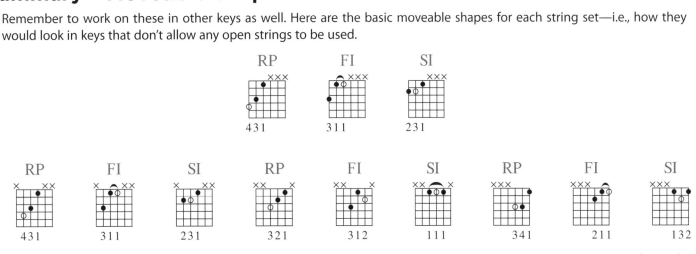

Becoming familiar with these chord shapes will not only allow you the freedom to play any chord anywhere on the neck, but it will also help your lead playing, as you'll be more familiar with chord shapes and chord tones at different areas on the neck. Have fun!

LESSON #94: SEVENTH CHORD INVERSIONS

Many country recordings include a jumbo acoustic playing open "cowboy" chords, while an electric guitar plays different chord shapes all over the neck. The electric guitar creates a full-bodied sound without stepping on the acoustic player's sonic toes. In order to do this, you need to be familiar with the concept of inversions. This simply means arranging the notes of a chord so that a note other than the root is on the bottom. In this lesson, we're going to focus on seventh chord inversions.

The Basic Idea

A seventh chord has four different notes: a root, a 3rd, a 5th, and a 7th. The "normal" voicing for this chord is root, 3rd, 5th, 7th, from low to high. This is referred to as root position because it has the root on the bottom. Here's a C7 to demonstrate.

C7 CHORD: ROOT POSITION

If we take the lowest note, the root C, and move it up an octave, we're left with the 3rd, E, on bottom. This is known as first inversion.

C7 CHORD: FIRST INVERSION

If we continue this process once more and again move the lowest note—the 3rd, E—up an octave, we're left with the 5th, G, on the bottom. This is known as second inversion.

C7 CHORD: SECOND INVERSION

Repeating this process once more leaves us with the 7th, B♭, on the bottom. This is known as third inversion.

C7 CHORD: THIRD INVERSION

CLOSED VS. OPEN VOICINGS

Due to the way the guitar is tuned, we rarely, if ever, play seventh chords with these voicings. These are closed voicings, meaning that all the notes are within one octave. Attempting to play these on the guitar results in some extremely impractical fingerings, if not outright impossible. So we use open voicings on the guitar, in which the notes are spread out a bit and span more than an octave.

Learning the Shapes

In order to gain freedom to move anywhere on the neck, we'll work through the inversions by remaining on the same string set throughout. In other words, we'll play root position on strings 6–5–4–3, and then we'll slide up the neck to play the inversions on those same strings. We'll work with a C7 chord here. Whenever all four notes reach above the 12th fret, we'll transpose them down an octave. The root notes (C) are all open circles.

STRING SET 6–5–4–3

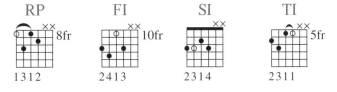

STRING SET 5–4–3–2

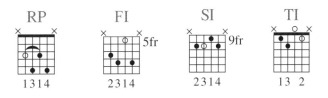

STRING SET 4–3–2–1

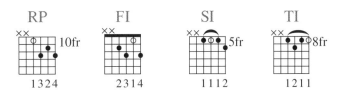

MINOR AND MAJOR SEVENTH SHAPES

In order to make these Cm7 chords, you'd just simply find all the E notes and lower them a half step to Eb. To make Cmaj7 chords, you'd take the C7 shapes and raise the b7th, Bb, a half step to B.

Believe it or not, learning these shapes will also help your lead playing, as you'll be more familiar with chord shapes and chord tones at different areas on the neck. A great exercise is to try to play through a whole song by using inversions and staying in one position on the neck as much as possible. Have fun!

Many country solos are incredibly colorful outings, filled with all kinds of chromatics and fancy maneuvers. Most of them are performed by professional studio musicians who are usually adept at many styles, such as Brent Mason. These players are paid extremely well to make the records stand out and measure up with their sonic contribution, so it makes sense that they're generally not going to play the types of things that beginners do. In this lesson, we're going to talk about something that nearly all professional country pickers make use of on a regular basis: the almighty passing tone.

The Basic Idea

A passing tone in the classical sense is usually a scale tone connecting two chord tones. For example, if you had a C triad with a melody that went E–D–C, the D note would be the passing tone.

However, it can also mean a chromatic tone that lies between two scale tones. For example, if you had a line over a C chord that went D–D♯–E, the D♯ would be the passing tone.

It's the latter that we're going to concern ourselves with here. As shown in the example, these passing tones are usually brief, lasting only an 8th or 16th note in most cases.

Basically, you can insert a chromatic passing tone between any two scale tones to add a bit of spice to your line. The passing tone *usually* falls on a weak beat (upbeat), but there are exceptions to this.

Examples

LICK 1

Let's check out how this sounds. This first lick in C is a classic example based off the Lester Flatt "G run." We're using a passing tone between the 2nd (D) and 3rd (E).

LICK 2

And here's kind of the opposite of lick 1, this time in A. Here we're descending and using a passing tone between the 3rd (C♯) and the 2nd (B).

LICK 3

This line in G uses two different passing tones during the descent: one in between the 3rd (B) and 2nd (A), and one in between the 5th (D) and the 4th (C).

LICK 4

This final lick in C again uses two different passing tones. The first is a colorful one in between the 6th (A) and the 5th (G), while the second one is the common tie between the 2nd (D) and 3rd (E).

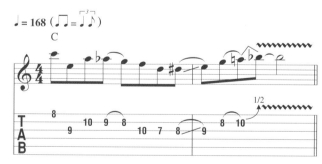

As you can hear, these passing tones can really add another dimension to otherwise stock phrases. Many times, all it takes is one passing tone to color an entire measure. Experiment and have fun with this idea; before you know it, you'll find yourself slipping them in unconsciously.

THE "PLUCK–PLUCK–RELEASE" MOVE

There are certain phrases idiomatic to any style that are instantly recognizable. That three-note Chuck Berry guitar intro immediately brings to mind the sliding double stops that follow. Country music is no different, and it has its own library of stock country licks and maneuvers that keep turning up everywhere without becoming tired or outdated. This lesson is about one of those country maneuvers I like to call the "pluck–pluck–release move."

The Basic Idea

This idea always starts with a pre-bend, which can be a single note or part of a double stop (or triple stop occasionally). If part of a double or triple stop, one or more of the notes may be pre-bent.

Let's take a look at the bare bones idea here. We're pre-bending a B♭ up a whole step to C on string 2 while holding an E note on string 1. We pluck the resulting C/E double stop twice (pluck–pluck) and then let the pre-bent note fall back down to the original pitch (release). It sounds like this:

So that's all there is to it. It's simple enough, but you'd be surprised at how it colors an entire phrase. You can start a lick with this idea, and it'll sound country almost regardless of what follows.

Examples

LICK 1

Let's hear this idea in action. This first lick begins with the move from our earlier example.

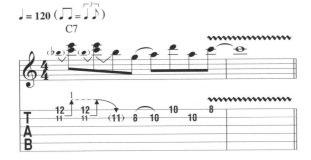

LICK 2

In this G lick, we begin with a dissonant pre-bend of E up to F against a G. This is released and then followed with another nice pre-bend move suggesting a Gsus4 sound resolving to G.

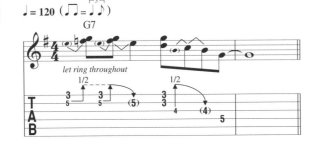

LICK 3

Here's a lick in A that begins with the 5th bent up to the 6th against the high A note on top. We finish off with a few chicken-picked double stops.

LICK 4

Here's a lick in C that's based off the C blues scale, save for the low A note at the very end.

LICK 5

This final lick in D moves from a D7 chord to an A7 chord via sliding double stops. The first bend of G and B up to A and C, respectively, is a classic country move.

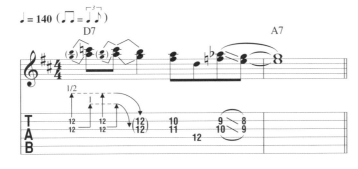

This is a great way to build up a phenomenal repertoire of bending licks. It makes a classic phrase beginning, and if you get in the habit of finding different ones on a regular basis, you'll soon be armed with a whole slew of pedal steel bends. Have fun.

One of the things that makes the pedal steel guitar such an expressive instrument is that the pitch bending of each string is controlled by individual levers. So you can have one string bent a certain length while another is bent and released on its own. The melodic possibilities with this are vast.

In an attempt to emulate the instrument in this regard, I'd like to show you a favorite device I call "the pretzel." It's so named because it tends to make your fingers do things they don't always want to do.

The Basic Idea

With this idea, there are three basic parts that usually happen.

1. A note, usually on string 3 or 4, is bent up and held.

2. A few notes are sounded on the higher strings while the bent note is ringing.

3. The bent note is released, or picked again and released, and the phrase concludes.

The possibilities with this idea are as numerous as the stars that shine bright deep in the heart of Texas. It can involve a half-step bend, a whole-step bend, or more. The notes on top can be two, three, four, or more. The intervals can be whatever you can grab. Here are some basic guidelines that I usually follow. They're certainly not rules, but they sound good to me.

▶ I tend to use a melody on top that descends in pitch.

▶ The melody on top generally involves legato at some point (hammer-on or pull-off).

▶ 2nds against the bent note sound very nice, especially when those are resolved to 3rds after the bend is released back to pitch.

Examples

Without further adieu, let's get to some pretzel licks.

LICK 1

This first one in E is actually the first lick I came up with using this technique. It's made more difficult by the fact that, toward the end, you have to simultaneously release the half-step bend and slide down a half step.

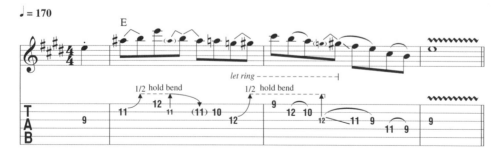

LICK 2

Here's a nice one in D that seems to morph smoothly from a D7 sound to a C chord.

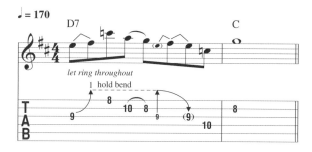

LICK 3

This lick moves smoothly between a C7 chord and a Gm sound. We're using an ascending phrase while we're holding the bend, which, for some reason, requires a bit more effort in my opinion.

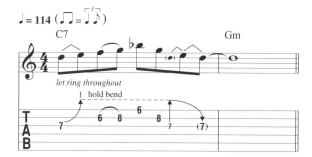

LICK 4

This is one of the easier ones. It only involves notes on the first string while holding a bend on the second string.

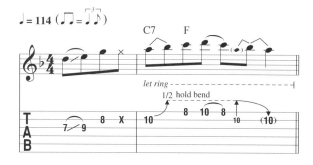

As I mentioned, you can spend years coming up with different licks like this. They're a whole lot of fun, and they'll definitely turn a head or two. Have fun and remember to check your bends for accuracy against fretted target notes. The effectiveness of these licks depends on the intonation of the bend.

LESSON #98: THE THIRTEENTH CHORD

Country music has more in common with jazz than many people think. In fact, if you look back at the classic country songs of the thirties, forties, and fifties, many of the progressions are quite similar to jazz songs of the day. The early music of Chet Atkins, Merle Travis, and Hank Garland, to name a few, was filled with sophisticated harmonies, extensions, and altered chords. One harmony in particular that's often heard in the Western swing genre, as well as some rockabilly, is the thirteenth chord. In this lesson, we'll take a look at this snazzy harmony and how we can use it to dress up our country phrases.

Extended All the Way

Chords are built by stacking 3rd intervals. In a triad, you have a root, 3rd, and 5th: 1–3–5. With seventh chords, you continue this stacking-3rds process and put a 7th on top: 1–3–5–7. Extended chords continue this process past the octave and present three more chord types.

- ▶ **Ninth Chord**: 1–3–5–7–9
- ▶ **Eleventh Chord**: 1–3–5–7–9–11
- ▶ **Thirteenth Chord**: 1–3–5–7–9–11–13

Once you get over 8, you can subtract 7 from the number to find its lower octave equivalent. As you can see, the 13th chord is extended all the way. It technically includes all seven notes within a key. However, besides the fact that it's impossible for us guitarists to play a chord with seven different notes, thirteenth chords rarely appear in music this way. Many notes are usually omitted, and the voicing often only includes three, four, or five notes.

In this lesson, we're going to be looking at the dominant thirteenth chord. This means the 7th tone will be a ♭7th. The tones that are absolutely essential are the 3rd, ♭7th, and 13th. Even the root, though it's commonly included, is omitted occasionally.

Common Voicings

We'll work with a C13 chord for simplicity. Here are some common voicings for country or Western swing guitar. The root, when present, is shown as an open circle.

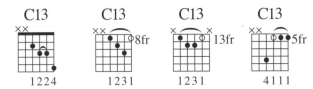

Beginnings and Endings

It's common to use these chords at the beginning or ending of a phrase. When used at the beginning, they're often punched quickly in a rhythmic manner. At endings, they're usually sustained. Let's take a look at some examples.

LICK 1

Here's an example in A that begins with a few A13 chords for rhythmic punctuation.

LICK 2

After some tricky pedal steel bends and chromatically descending 3rds, we cap off this lick in C with a nice C13 voicing in fifth position.

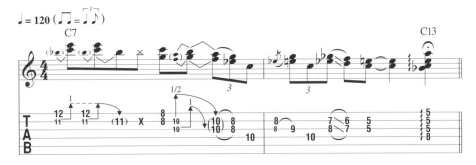

LICK 3

Here's a jazzy flourish in G that begins with some rhythmic G13 and G7 voicings before ending with an understated half-step bend up to the ♭7th.

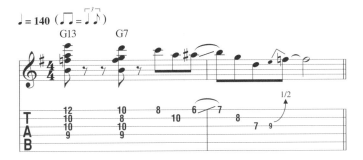

LICK 4

And we'll finish off with a Western swing-style run in A that begins with some chicken-picked double stops and finishes off with a strummed A13 voicing in fifth position.

These are especially nice to use when you're playing with just a bass player and a drummer, and there are no other instruments to provide a harmonic backdrop. Many players become so adept at this idea that they pepper chords throughout their solo. Enjoy!

If you've ever listened to Chet Atkins in his early days, you know that he had a million tricks up his sleeve. One of the most ear-catching was his use of artificial harmonics. An artificial harmonic is basically any one that's not a natural harmonic. In other words, an artificial harmonic deals with a fretted note, thereby requiring the harmonic to be created "artificially."

The Basic Technique

To perform an artificial harmonic, first fret a note normally—preferably around the 5th or 7th fret to start with. Next, with your pick hand's first finger, lightly touch the string twelve frets higher than this fretted note. Remember, as with a natural harmonic, you want to touch directly over the metal fretwire. Then, with either the third finger of the pick hand, or with the pick held between the thumb and second finger, pluck the string.

PLUCKED WITH PICK

You should hear a chiming note that's one octave above the fretted one.

PLUCKED WITH FINGER

After you get the basic idea down, you can use this technique to play entire melodies.

Examples

LICK 1

Let's take a look at what we can do with this idea.

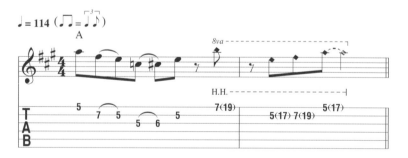

LICK 2

You can also bend the harmonics, which is a nice effect.

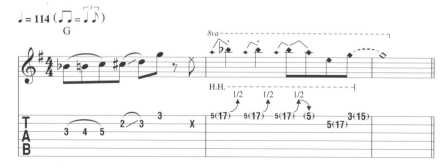

LICK 3

Another thing Chet would do is pair a normal note with an artificial harmonic. When you play 6th intervals, they become 3rds, since the lower note is sounded an octave higher.

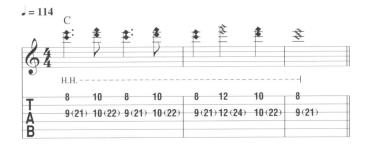

Harp Harmonics

Perhaps the ultimate application of this technique is called the "harp harmonic." Chet Atkins and Lenny Breau were both acknowledged masters of this trick. With this idea, you barre a fret and skip strings with the pick hand, alternating a normal note with a harmonic. In other words, you pluck the fourth string normally and then play an artificial harmonic on the sixth string. Then you pluck the third string normally, followed by an artificial harmonic on the fifth string, etc.

When using this technique, it's normally done without a pick (or with a thumbpick). The artificial harmonic is produced by plucking with the thumb (while the index finger touches the harmonic spot), and the higher strings are normally plucked with the ring finger.

Here's what the basic idea sounds like with a barred 5th fret:

EXERCISE 1

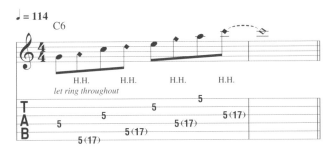

LICK 4

This lick takes it even further. Chet would normally incorporate a few hammer-ons and pull-offs to play seven-note scales with this technique.

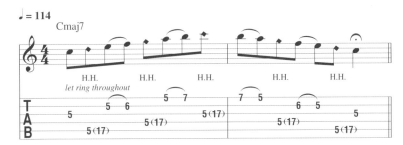

You can really turn some heads by pulling out one of these licks at the right time. Experiment with it and have fun.

Country music has been home to some flashy pickers throughout the years, and guitar players love their flashy tricks. Everyone's got a favorite trick, and this is certainly one of mine. It's something that you use at the very end of a song—or possibly at the end of an unaccompanied intro—and I like to call it the "intentional mistake" final bend.

The Basic Idea

With this trick, the idea is to end with a bit of dissonance that's eventually resolved into consonance. It's meant to sound as though it was almost a mistake before confirmation that you did in fact mean to do it. There's a sense of humor in it.

So how do we do it? It's simple. You take a final chord, which can be any chord you'd like, and you find a way to bend into one of the notes from a half step below. The chord could be a mixture of open strings and fretted notes, all fretted notes, or, when you include behind-the-nut bends, all open strings. The key is to first sound the chord with one of the notes a half step flat and then bend it up to pitch for resolution.

Bending the Bass Note

This is probably my favorite, because it can really sound ugly before coming into resolution.

LICK 1

A classic example is the open G chord. It sounds like this.

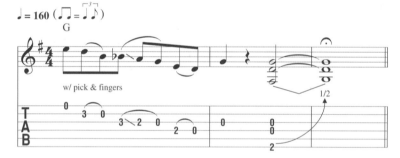

Notice that, unlike many pedal steel bends, this is a bit more deliberate sounding. The dissonance is held a bit longer to really rub it in before bending.

LICK 2

Here's an example in E that features a double disaster. The high E and B strings are sounded against an open G string and a fretted D♯ note on string 5. Mute string 4 with the same finger that's fretting string 5. Then play the chord and simultaneously bend the G string up a half step behind the nut (with your pick hand) while you bend the D♯ up a half step to E.

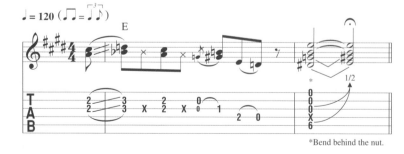

*Bend behind the nut.

LICK 3

Of course, the bass note doesn't necessarily have to be the root. If the chord is inverted, it could be the 3rd or 5th. Here's a lick in A that demonstrates this.

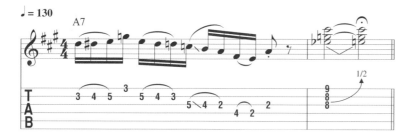

Bending the Top Note

Bending up into the top note can be great as well, because it sounds really sour at first.

LICK 4

One of my favorites is bending from the minor to the major 3rd, as with this lick in A.

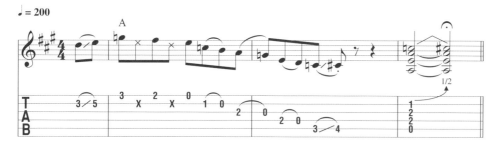

LICK 5

We'll close out with a humorous one in D that ends on a D7 chord with the 5th being bent up to from the ♭5th.

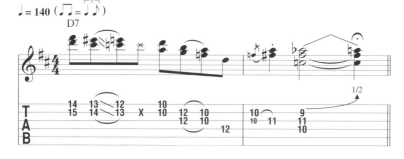

You can have a lot of fun with this idea, so remember to keep a sense of humor about it. It's supposed to throw people for a bit of a loop. It's worth it though when everything comes together at the end. Enjoy!

Get Better at Guitar

...with these Great Guitar Instruction Books from Hal Leonard!

101 GUITAR TIPS
INCLUDES TAB

STUFF ALL THE PROS KNOW AND USE

by Adam St. James

This book contains invaluable guidance on everything from scales and music theory to truss rod adjustments, proper recording studio set-ups, and much more. The book also features snippets of advice from some of the most celebrated guitarists and producers in the music business, including B.B. King, Steve Vai, Joe Satriani, Warren Haynes, Laurence Juber, Pete Anderson, Tom Dowd and others, culled from the author's hundreds of interviews.

00695737 Book/CD Pack..$16.95

AMAZING PHRASING
INCLUDES TAB

50 WAYS TO IMPROVE YOUR IMPROVISATIONAL SKILLS

by Tom Kolb

This book/CD pack explores all the main components necessary for crafting well-balanced rhythmic and melodic phrases. It also explains how these phrases are put together to form cohesive solos. Many styles are covered – rock, blues, jazz, fusion, country, Latin, funk and more – and all of the concepts are backed up with musical examples. The companion CD contains 89 demos for listening, and most tracks feature full-band backing.

00695583 Book/CD Pack..$19.95

BLUES YOU CAN USE
INCLUDES TAB

by John Ganapes

A comprehensive source designed to help guitarists develop both lead and rhythm playing. Covers: Texas, Delta, R&B, early rock and roll, gospel, blues/rock and more. Includes: 21 complete solos • chord progressions and riffs • turnarounds • moveable scales and more. CD features leads and full band backing.

00695007 Book/CD Pack..$19.99

FRETBOARD MASTERY
INCLUDES TAB

by Troy Stetina

Untangle the mysterious regions of the guitar fretboard and unlock your potential. *Fretboard Mastery* familiarizes you with all the shapes you need to know by applying them in real musical examples, thereby reinforcing and reaffirming your newfound knowledge. The result is a much higher level of comprehension and retention.

00695331 Book/CD Pack..$19.95

FRETBOARD ROADMAPS – 2ND EDITION

ESSENTIAL GUITAR PATTERNS THAT ALL THE PROS KNOW AND USE

by Fred Sokolow

The updated edition of this bestseller features more songs, updated lessons, and a full audio CD! Learn to play lead and rhythm anywhere on the fretboard, in any key; play a variety of lead guitar styles; play chords and progressions anywhere on the fretboard; expand your chord vocabulary; and learn to think musically – the way the pros do.

00695941 Book/CD Pack..$14.95

GUITAR AEROBICS
INCLUDES TAB

A 52-WEEK, ONE-LICK-PER-DAY WORKOUT PROGRAM FOR DEVELOPING, IMPROVING & MAINTAINING GUITAR TECHNIQUE

by Troy Nelson

From the former editor of *Guitar One* magazine, here is a daily dose of vitamins to keep your chops fine tuned! Musical styles include rock, blues, jazz, metal, country, and funk. Techniques taught include alternate picking, arpeggios, sweep picking, string skipping, legato, string bending, and rhythm guitar. These exercises will increase speed, and improve dexterity and pick- and fret-hand accuracy. The accompanying CD includes all 365 workout licks plus play-along grooves in every style at eight different metronome settings.

00695946 Book/CD Pack..$19.99

GUITAR CLUES
INCLUDES TAB

OPERATION PENTATONIC

by Greg Koch

Join renowned guitar master Greg Koch as he clues you in to a wide variety of fun and valuable pentatonic scale applications. Whether you're new to improvising or have been doing it for a while, this book/CD pack will provide loads of delicious licks and tricks that you can use right away, from volume swells and chicken pickin' to intervallic and chordal ideas. The CD includes 65 demo and play-along tracks.

00695827 Book/CD Pack..$19.95

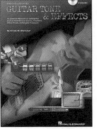

INTRODUCTION TO GUITAR TONE & EFFECTS

by David M. Brewster

This book/CD pack teaches the basics of guitar tones and effects, with audio examples on CD. Readers will learn about: overdrive, distortion and fuzz • using equalizers • modulation effects • reverb and delay • multi-effect processors • and more.

00695766 Book/CD Pack..$14.95

PICTURE CHORD ENCYCLOPEDIA

This comprehensive guitar chord resource for all playing styles and levels features five voicings of 44 chord qualities for all twelve keys – 2,640 chords in all! For each, there is a clearly illustrated chord frame, as well as *an actual photo* of the chord being played! Includes info on basic fingering principles, open chords and barre chords, partial chords and broken-set forms, and more.

00695224..$19.95

SCALE CHORD RELATIONSHIPS
INCLUDES TAB

by Michael Mueller & Jeff Schroedl

This book teaches players how to determine which scales to play with which chords, so guitarists will never have to fear chord changes again! This book/CD pack explains how to: recognize keys • analyze chord progressions • use the modes • play over nondiatonic harmony • use harmonic and melodic minor scales • use symmetrical scales such as chromatic, whole-tone and diminished scales • incorporate exotic scales such as Hungarian major and Gypsy minor • and much more!

00695563 Book/CD Pack..$14.95

SPEED MECHANICS FOR LEAD GUITAR
INCLUDES TAB

Take your playing to the stratosphere with the most advanced lead book by this proven heavy metal author. *Speed Mechanics* is the ultimate technique book for developing the kind of speed and precision in today's explosive playing styles. Learn the fastest ways to achieve speed and control, secrets to make your practice time really count, and how to open your ears and make your musical ideas more solid and tangible. Packed with over 200 vicious exercises including Troy's scorching version of "Flight of the Bumblebee." Music and examples demonstrated on CD. 89-minute audio.

00699323 Book/CD Pack..$19.95

TOTAL ROCK GUITAR
INCLUDES TAB

A COMPLETE GUIDE TO LEARNING ROCK GUITAR

by Troy Stetina

This unique and comprehensive source for learning rock guitar is designed to develop both lead and rhythm playing. It covers: getting a tone that rocks • open chords, power chords and barre chords • riffs, scales and licks • string bending, strumming, palm muting, harmonics and alternate picking • all rock styles • and much more. The examples are in standard notation with chord grids and tab, and the CD includes full-band backing for all 22 songs.

00695246 Book/CD Pack..$19.99

1011

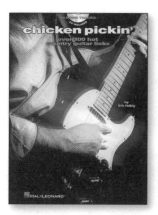
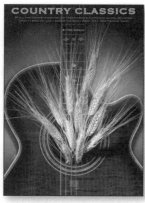

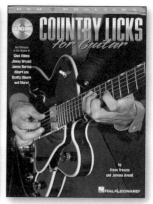

Guitar Instruction
Country Style!
from Hal Leonard

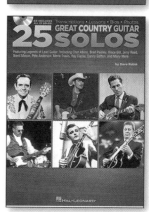

CHICKEN PICKIN' • *by Eric Halbig*

This book provides a "bird's-eye-view" of the techniques and licks common to playing hot, country lead guitar! Covers over 100 hot country guitar licks: open-string licks, double-stop licks, scales, string bending, repetitive sequences, and chromatic licks. CD includes 99 demonstration tracks with each lick performed at two tempos.

00695599 Book/CDPack...$16.95

COUNTRY CLASSICS FOR GUITAR • *arr. Fred Sokolow*

30 favorites arranged for solo guitar, including: Always on My Mind • Blue Eyes Crying in the Rain • Crazy • Folsom Prison Blues • If You've Got the Money (I've Got the Time) • Make the World Go Away • Rocky Top • Walking the Floor over You • Your Cheatin' Heart • and more.

00699246...$14.95

FRETBOARD ROADMAPS – COUNTRY GUITAR

The Essential Patterns That All the Pros Know and Use • by Fred Sokolow

This book/CD pack will teach you how to play lead and rhythm in the country style anywhere on the fretboard in any key. You'll play basic country progressions, boogie licks, steel licks, and other melodies and licks. You'll also learn a variety of lead guitar styles using moveable scale patterns, sliding scale patterns, chord-based licks, double-note licks, and more. The book features easy-to-follow diagrams and instructions for beginning, intermediate, and advanced players.

00695353 Book/CD Pack...$14.99

SONGBOOK
COUNTRY GUITAR BIBLE

Note-for-note transcriptions with tab for 35 country classics, all in one hefty collection! Includes: Ain't Goin' Down ('Til the Sun Comes Up) • Big Time • Blue Eyes Crying in the Rain • Boot Scootin' Boogie • Cannon Ball Rag • Friends in Low Places • I'm So Lonesome I Could Cry • Little Sister • My Baby Thinks He's a Train • T-R-O-U-B-L-E • Wildwood Flower • and more.

00690465 Guitar Recorded Versions $19.95

COUNTRY LICKS FOR GUITAR

by Steve Trovato and Jerome Arnold

This unique package examines the lead guitar licks of the masters of country guitar, such as Chet Atkins, Jimmy Bryant, James Burton, Albert Lee, Scotty Moore, and many others! The accompanying CD includes demonstrations of each lick at normal and slow speeds. The instruction covers single-string licks, pedal-steel licks, open-string licks, chord licks, rockabilly licks, funky country licks, tips on fingerings, phrasing, technique, theory, and application.

00695577 Book/CD Pack.............................. $17.99

COUNTRY SOLOS FOR GUITAR

by Steve Trovato

This unique book/CD pack lets guitarists examine the solo styles of axe masters such as Chet Atkins, James Burton, Ray Flacke, Albert Lee, Scotty Moore, Roy Nichols, Jerry Reed and others. It covers techniques including hot banjo rolls, funky double stops, pedal-steel licks, open-string licks and more, in standard notation and tab with phrase-by-phrase performance notes. The CD includes full demonstrations and rhythm-only tracks.

00695448 Book/CD Pack.............................. $17.95

RED-HOT COUNTRY GUITAR

by Michael Hawley

The complete guide to playing lead guitar in the styles of Pete Anderson, Danny Gatton, Albert Lee, Brent Mason, and more. Includes loads of red-hot licks, techniques, solos, theory and more.

00695831 Book/CD Pack..$17.95

25 GREAT COUNTRY GUITAR SOLOS

by Dave Rubin

Provides solo transcriptions in notes & tab, lessons on how to play them, guitarist bios, equipment notes, photos, history, and much more. The CD contains full-band demos of every solo in the book. Songs include: Country Boy • Foggy Mountain Special • Folsom Prison Blues • Hellecaster Theme • Hello Mary Lou • I've Got a Tiger by the Tail • The Only Daddy That Will Walk the Line • Please, Please Baby • Sugarfoot Rag • and more.

00699926 Book/CD Pack..$19.99

Visit Hal Leonard Online at www.halleonard.com
Prices, contents, and availability subject to change without notice.

HAL•LEONARD GUITAR PLAY-ALONG

INCLUDES TAB

This series will help you play your favorite songs quickly and easily. Just follow the tab and listen to the CD to hear how the guitar should sound, and then play along using the separate backing tracks. Mac or PC users can also slow down the tempo without changing pitch by using the CD in their computer. The melody and lyrics are included in the book so that you can sing or simply follow along.

1. ROCK
00699570.........................$16.99

2. ACOUSTIC
00699569.........................$16.95

3. HARD ROCK
00699573.........................$16.95

4. POP/ROCK
00699571.........................$16.99

5. MODERN ROCK
00699574.........................$16.99

6. '90s ROCK
00699572.........................$16.99

7. BLUES
00699575.........................$16.95

8. ROCK
00699585.........................$14.99

9. PUNK ROCK
00699576.........................$14.95

10. ACOUSTIC
00699586.........................$16.95

11. EARLY ROCK
0699579.........................$14.95

12. POP/ROCK
00699587.........................$14.95

13. FOLK ROCK
00699581.........................$15.99

14. BLUES ROCK
00699582.........................$16.95

15. R&B
00699583.........................$14.95

16. JAZZ
00699584.........................$15.95

17. COUNTRY
00699588.........................$15.95

18. ACOUSTIC ROCK
00699577.........................$15.95

19. SOUL
00699578.........................$14.99

20. ROCKABILLY
00699580.........................$14.95

21. YULETIDE
00699602.........................$14.95

22. CHRISTMAS
00699600.........................$15.95

23. SURF
00699635.........................$14.95

24. ERIC CLAPTON
00699649.........................$17.99

25. LENNON & McCARTNEY
00699642.........................$16.99

26. ELVIS PRESLEY
00699643.........................$14.95

27. DAVID LEE ROTH
00699645.........................$16.95

28. GREG KOCH
00699646.........................$14.95

29. BOB SEGER
00699647.........................$15.99

30. KISS
00699644.........................$16.99

31. CHRISTMAS HITS
00699652.........................$14.95

32. THE OFFSPRING
00699653.........................$14.95

33. ACOUSTIC CLASSICS
00699656.........................$16.95

34. CLASSIC ROCK
00699658.........................$16.95

35. HAIR METAL
00699660.........................$16.95

36. SOUTHERN ROCK
00699661.........................$16.95

37. ACOUSTIC METAL
00699662.........................$16.95

38. BLUES
00699663.........................$16.95

39. '80s METAL
00699664.........................$16.99

40. INCUBUS
00699668.........................$17.95

41. ERIC CLAPTON
00699669.........................$16.95

42. 2000s ROCK
00699670.........................$16.99

43. LYNYRD SKYNYRD
00699681.........................$17.95

44. JAZZ
00699689.........................$14.99

45. TV THEMES
00699718.........................$14.95

46. MAINSTREAM ROCK
00699722.........................$16.95

47. HENDRIX SMASH HITS
00699723.........................$19.95

48. AEROSMITH CLASSICS
00699724.........................$17.99

49. STEVIE RAY VAUGHAN
00699725.........................$17.99

51. ALTERNATIVE '90s
00699727.........................$14.99

52. FUNK
00699728.........................$14.95

53. DISCO
00699729.........................$14.99

54. HEAVY METAL
00699730.........................$14.95

55. POP METAL
00699731.........................$14.95

56. FOO FIGHTERS
00699749.........................$15.99

57. SYSTEM OF A DOWN
00699751.........................$14.95

58. BLINK-182
00699772.........................$14.95

60. 3 DOORS DOWN
00699774.........................$14.95

61. SLIPKNOT
00699775.........................$16.99

62. CHRISTMAS CAROLS
00699798.........................$12.95

63. CREEDENCE CLEARWATER REVIVAL
00699802.........................$16.99

64. OZZY OSBOURNE
00699803.........................$16.99

65. THE DOORS
00699806.........................$16.99

66. THE ROLLING STONES
00699807.........................$16.95

67. BLACK SABBATH
00699808.........................$16.99

68. PINK FLOYD – DARK SIDE OF THE MOON
00699809.........................$16.99

69. ACOUSTIC FAVORITES
00699810.........................$14.95

70. OZZY OSBOURNE
00699805.........................$16.99

71. CHRISTIAN ROCK
00699824.........................$14.95

72. ACOUSTIC '90s
00699827.........................$14.95

73. BLUESY ROCK
00699829.........................$16.99

74. PAUL BALOCHE
00699831.........................$14.95

75. TOM PETTY
00699882.........................$16.99

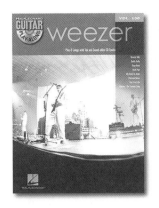  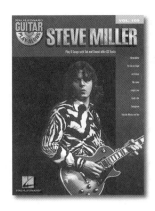  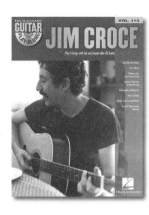

76. COUNTRY HITS
00699884.....................$14.95

77. BLUEGRASS
00699910.....................$14.99

78. NIRVANA
00700132.....................$16.99

79. NEIL YOUNG
00700133.....................$24.99

80. ACOUSTIC ANTHOLOGY
00700175.....................$19.95

81. ROCK ANTHOLOGY
00700176.....................$22.99

82. EASY ROCK SONGS
00700177.....................$12.99

83. THREE CHORD SONGS
00700178.....................$16.99

84. STEELY DAN
00700200.....................$16.99

85. THE POLICE
00700269.....................$16.99

86. BOSTON
00700465.....................$16.99

87. ACOUSTIC WOMEN
00700763.....................$14.99

88. GRUNGE
00700467.....................$16.99

90. CLASSICAL POP
00700469.....................$14.99

91. BLUES INSTRUMENTALS
00700505.....................$14.99

92. EARLY ROCK INSTRUMENTALS
00700506.....................$14.99

93. ROCK INSTRUMENTALS
00700507.....................$16.99

95. BLUES CLASSICS
00700509.....................$14.99

96. THIRD DAY
00700560.....................$14.95

97. ROCK BAND
00700703.....................$14.99

98. ROCK BAND
00700704.....................$14.95

99. ZZ TOP
00700762.....................$16.99

100. B.B. KING
00700466.....................$16.99

101. SONGS FOR BEGINNERS
00701917.....................$14.99

102. CLASSIC PUNK
00700769.....................$14.99

103. SWITCHFOOT
00700773.....................$16.99

104. DUANE ALLMAN
00700846.....................$16.99

106. WEEZER
00700958.....................$14.99

107. CREAM
00701069.....................$16.99

108. THE WHO
00701053.....................$16.99

109. STEVE MILLER
00701054.....................$14.99

111. JOHN MELLENCAMP
00701056.....................$14.99

112. QUEEN
00701052.....................$16.99

113. JIM CROCE
00701058.....................$15.99

114. BON JOVI
00701060.....................$14.99

115. JOHNNY CASH
00701070.....................$16.99

116. THE VENTURES
00701124.....................$14.99

118. ERIC JOHNSON
00701353.....................$14.99

119. AC/DC CLASSICS
00701356.....................$17.99

120. PROGRESSIVE ROCK
00701457.....................$14.99

121. U2
00701508.....................$16.99

123. LENNON & MCCARTNEY ACOUSTIC
00701614.....................$16.99

124. MODERN WORSHIP
00701629.....................$14.99

125. JEFF BECK
00701687.....................$16.99

126. BOB MARLEY
00701701.....................$16.99

127. 1970s ROCK
00701739.....................$14.99

128. 1960s ROCK
00701740.....................$14.99

129. MEGADETH
00701741.....................$16.99

131. 1990s ROCK
00701743.....................$14.99

132. COUNTRY ROCK
00701757.....................$15.99

133. TAYLOR SWIFT
00701894.....................$16.99

134. AVENGED SEVENFOLD
00701906.....................$16.99

136. GUITAR THEMES
00701922.....................$14.99

138. BLUEGRASS CLASSICS
00701967.....................$14.99

139. GARY MOORE
00702370.....................$16.99

140. MORE STEVIE RAY VAUGHAN
00702396.....................$17.99

141. ACOUSTIC HITS
00702401.....................$16.99

142. KINGS OF LEON
00702418.....................$16.99

144. DJANGO REINHARDT
00702531.....................$16.99

145. DEF LEPPARD
00702532.....................$16.99

147. SIMON & GARFUNKEL
14041591.....................$16.99

149. AC/DC HITS
14041593.....................$17.99

150. ZAKK WYLDE
02501717.....................$16.99

153. RED HOT CHILI PEPPERS
00702990.....................$19.99

157. FLEETWOOD MAC
00101382.....................$16.99

158. ULTIMATE CHRISTMAS
00101889.....................$14.99

161. THE EAGLES – ACOUSTIC
00102659.....................$16.99

162. THE EAGLES HITS
00102667.....................$17.99

166. MODERN BLUES
00700764.....................$16.99

7777 W. BLUEMOUND RD. P.O. BOX 13819 MILWAUKEE, WI 53213

For complete songlists, visit Hal Leonard online at
www.halleonard.com

Prices, contents, and availability subject to change without notice.

0113

RECORDED VERSIONS®
The Best Note-For-Note Transcriptions Available

ALL BOOKS INCLUDE TABLATURE

14037551 AC/DC – Backtracks $32.99	00701764 Guitar Tab White Pages – Play-Along $39.99	00690670 Queensryche – Very Best of $19.95
00692015 Aerosmith – Greatest Hits $22.95	00694854 Buddy Guy – Damn Right, I've Got the Blues ... $19.95	00690878 The Raconteurs – Broken Boy Soldiers $19.95
00690178 Alice in Chains – Acoustic $19.95	00690840 Ben Harper – Both Sides of the Gun $19.95	00694910 Rage Against the Machine $19.95
00694865 Alice in Chains – Dirt $19.95	00694798 George Harrison – Anthology $19.95	00690055 Red Hot Chili Peppers –
00690812 All American Rejects – Move Along $19.95	00690841 Scott Henderson – Blues Guitar Collection .. $19.95	Blood Sugar Sex Magik $19.95
00690958 Duane Allman Guitar Anthology $24.99	00692930 Jimi Hendrix – Are You Experienced? $24.95	00690584 Red Hot Chili Peppers – By the Way $19.95
00694932 Allman Brothers Band – Volume 1 .... $24.95	00692931 Jimi Hendrix – Axis: Bold As Love $22.95	00691166 Red Hot Chili Peppers – I'm with You $22.99
00694933 Allman Brothers Band – Volume 2 .... $24.95	00692932 Jimi Hendrix – Electric Ladyland $24.95	00690852 Red Hot Chili Peppers –Stadium Arcadium .. $24.95
00694934 Allman Brothers Band – Volume 3 .... $24.95	00690017 Jimi Hendrix – Live at Woodstock $24.95	00690511 Django Reinhardt – Definitive Collection $19.95
00690865 Atreyu – A Deathgrip on Yesterday $19.95	00690602 Jimi Hendrix – Smash Hits $24.99	00690779 Relient K – MMHMM $19.95
00690820 Audioslave $19.95	00691152 West Coast Seattle Boy:	00690631 Rolling Stones – Guitar Anthology $27.95
00690820 Avenged Sevenfold – City of Evil $24.95	The Jimi Hendrix Anthology $29.99	00694976 Rolling Stones – Some Girls $22.95
00691065 Avenged Sevenfold – Waking the Fallen $22.99	00690793 John Lee Hooker Anthology $24.99	00690264 The Rolling Stones – Tattoo You $19.95
00690503 Beach Boys – Very Best of $19.95	00690692 Billy Idol – Very Best of $19.95	00690685 David Lee Roth – Eat 'Em and Smile $19.95
00690489 Beatles – 1 .... $24.99	00690688 Incubus – A Crow Left of the Murder $19.95	00690942 David Lee Roth and the Songs of Van Halen . $19.95
00694832 Beatles – For Acoustic Guitar $22.99	00690544 Incubus – Morningview $19.95	00690031 Santana's Greatest Hits $19.95
00691014 Beatles Rock Band $34.99	00690790 Iron Maiden Anthology $24.99	00690566 Scorpions – Best of $22.95
00690110 Beatles – White Album (Book 1) $19.95	00690721 Jet – Get Born $19.95	00690604 Bob Seger – Guitar Collection $19.95
00691043 Jeff Beck – Wired $19.99	00690684 Jethro Tull – Aqualung $19.95	00690803 Kenny Wayne Shepherd Band – Best of $19.95
00692385 Chuck Berry $19.95	00690959 John5 – Requiem $22.95	00690968 Shinedown – The Sound of Madness $22.99
00690835 Billy Talent $19.95	00690814 John5 – Songs for Sanity $19.95	00690813 Slayer – Guitar Collection $19.95
00690901 Best of Black Sabbath $19.95	00690751 John5 – Vertigo $19.95	00690733 Slipknot – Vol. 3 (The Subliminal Verses) $22.99
00690831 blink-182 – Greatest Hits $19.95	00690845 Eric Johnson – Bloom $19.95	00120004 Steely Dan – Best of $24.95
00690913 Boston $19.95	00690846 Jack Johnson and Friends – Sing-A-Longs and	00694921 Steppenwolf – Best of $22.95
00690932 Boston – Don't Look Back $19.99	Lullabies for the Film Curious George $19.95	00690655 Mike Stern – Best of $19.95
00690491 David Bowie – Best of $19.95	00690271 Robert Johnson – New Transcriptions $24.95	00690877 Stone Sour – Come What(ever) May $19.95
00690873 Breaking Benjamin – Phobia $19.95	00699131 Janis Joplin – Best of $19.95	00690520 Styx Guitar Collection $19.95
00690451 Jeff Buckley – Collection $24.95	00690427 Judas Priest – Best of $22.99	00120081 Sublime $19.95
00690957 Bullet for My Valentine – Scream Aim Fire ... $22.99	00690975 Kings of Leon – Only by the Night $22.99	00120122 Sublime – 40oz. to Freedom $19.95
00691159 The Cars – Complete Greatest Hits $22.99	00694903 Kiss – Best of $24.95	00690929 Sum 41 – Underclass Hero $19.95
00691079 Best of Johnny Cash $22.99	00690355 Kiss – Destroyer $16.95	00690767 Switchfoot – The Beautiful Letdown $19.95
00691004 Chickenfoot $22.99	00690834 Lamb of God – Ashes of the Wake $19.95	00690993 Taylor Swift – Fearless $22.99
00690590 Eric Clapton – Anthology $29.95	00690875 Lamb of God – Sacrament $19.95	00690830 System of a Down – Hypnotize $19.95
00690415 Clapton Chronicles – Best of Eric Clapton $18.95	00690823 Ray LaMontagne – Trouble $19.95	00690531 System of a Down – Toxicity $19.95
00690936 Eric Clapton – Complete Clapton $29.99	00690679 John Lennon – Guitar Collection $19.95	00694824 James Taylor – Best of $16.95
00690074 Eric Clapton – The Cream of Clapton $24.95	00690781 Linkin Park – Hybrid Theory $22.95	00690871 Three Days Grace – One-X $19.95
00694869 Eric Clapton – Unplugged $22.95	00690743 Los Lonely Boys $19.95	00690683 Robin Trower – Bridge of Sighs $19.95
00690162 The Clash – Best of $19.95	00690720 Lostprophets – Start Something $19.95	00699191 U2 – Best of: 1980-1990 .... $19.95
00690828 Coheed & Cambria – Good Apollo I'm	00690955 Lynyrd Skynyrd – All-Time Greatest Hits $19.99	00690732 U2 – Best of: 1990-2000 .... $19.95
Burning Star, IV, Vol. 1: From Fear	00694954 Lynyrd Skynyrd – New Best of $19.95	00660137 Steve Vai – Passion & Warfare $24.95
Through the Eyes of Madness $19.95	00690754 Marilyn Manson – Lest We Forget $19.95	00690116 Stevie Ray Vaughan – Guitar Collection $24.95
00690593 Coldplay – A Rush of Blood to the Head $19.95	00694956 Bob Marley – Legend $19.95	00660058 Stevie Ray Vaughan –
00690962 Coldplay – Viva La Vida $19.95	00694945 Bob Marley – Songs of Freedom $24.95	Lightnin' Blues 1983-1987 .... $24.95
00690819 Creedence Clearwater Revival – Best of $22.95	00690657 Maroon5 – Songs about Jane $19.95	00694835 Stevie Ray Vaughan – The Sky Is Crying $22.95
00690648 The Very Best of Jim Croce $19.95	00120080 Don McLean – Songbook $19.95	00690015 Stevie Ray Vaughan – Texas Flood $19.95
00690613 Crosby, Stills & Nash – Best of $22.95	00694951 Megadeth – Rust in Peace $22.95	00690772 Velvet Revolver – Contraband $22.95
00690967 Death Cab for Cutie – Narrow Stairs $22.99	00691185 Megadeth – Th1rt3en $22.99	00690071 Weezer (The Blue Album) $19.95
00690289 Deep Purple – Best of $19.99	00690951 Megadeth – United Abominations $22.99	00690966 Weezer – (Red Album) $19.99
00690784 Def Leppard – Best of $19.95	00690505 John Mellencamp – Guitar Collection $19.95	00690447 The Who – Best of $24.95
00692240 Bo Diddley $19.99	00690646 Pat Metheny – One Quiet Night $19.95	00690916 The Best of Dwight Yoakam $19.95
00690347 The Doors – Anthology $22.95	00690558 Pat Metheny – Trio: 99>00 .... $19.95	00690905 Neil Young – Rust Never Sleeps $19.99
00690348 The Doors – Essential Guitar Collection $16.95	00690040 Steve Miller Band – Young Hearts $19.95	00690623 Frank Zappa – Over-Nite Sensation $22.99
00691186 Evanescence $22.99	00691070 Mumford & Sons – Sigh No More $22.99	00690589 ZZ Top Guitar Anthology $24.95
00690810 Fall Out Boy – From Under the Cork Tree $19.95	00694883 Nirvana – Nevermind $19.95	
00691181 Five Finger Death Punch –	00690026 Nirvana – Unplugged in New York $19.95	
American Capitalist $22.99	00690807 The Offspring – Greatest Hits $19.95	
00690664 Fleetwood Mac – Best of $19.95	00694847 Ozzy Osbourne – Best of $22.95	
00690870 Flyleaf $19.95	00690399 Ozzy Osbourne – Ozzman Cometh $22.99	
00690931 Foo Fighters – Echoes, Silence,	00690933 Best of Brad Paisley $22.95	
Patience & Grace $19.95	00690995 Brad Paisley – Play: The Guitar Album $24.99	
00690808 Foo Fighters – In Your Honor $19.95	00694855 Pearl Jam – Ten $22.99	
00691115 Foo Fighters – Wasting Light $22.99	00690439 A Perfect Circle – Mer De Noms $19.95	
00690805 Robben Ford – Best of $22.95	00690499 Tom Petty – Definitive Guitar Collection $19.95	
00694920 Free – Best of $19.95	00690428 Pink Floyd – Dark Side of the Moon $19.95	
00691050 Glee Guitar Collection $19.99	00690789 Poison – Best of $19.95	
00690943 The Goo Goo Dolls – Greatest Hits	00693864 The Police – Best of $19.95	
Volume 1: The Singles $22.95	00694975 Queen – Greatest Hits $24.95	

Prices and availability subject to change without notice.
Some products may not be available outside the U.S.A.

0812